WITHDRAWN

The Dissonant Legacy of *Modernismo*

LATIN AMERICAN LITERATURE AND CULTURE

General Editor
Roberto González Echevarría
R. Selden Rose Professor of Spanish and
Professor of Comparative Literature
Yale University

1. Manuel Bandeira, *This Earth, That Sky,* trans. Candace Slater

2. Nicolás Guillén, *The Daily Daily,* trans. Vera M. Kutzinski

3. Gwen Kirkpatrick, *The Dissonant Legacy of* Modernismo:
Lugones, Herrera y Reissig, and the Voices of Modern Spanish American Poetry

90-551

PQ
7082
.P7
K57
1989

The Dissonant Legacy
of *Modernismo*

Lugones, Herrera y Reissig,
and the Voices of Modern
Spanish American Poetry

GWEN KIRKPATRICK

UNIVERSITY OF CALIFORNIA PRESS
Berkeley   Los Angeles   London

Gramley Library
Salem College
Winston-Salem, NC 27108

University of California Press
Berkeley and Los Angeles, California

University of California Press, Ltd.
London, England

Copyright © 1989 by The Regents of the University of California

Library of Congress Cataloging-in-Publication Data

Kirkpatrick, Gwen.
  The dissonant legacy of modernismo : Lugones, Herrera y Reissig,
and the voices of modern Spanish American poetry / Gwen Kirkpatrick.
      p.   cm.—(Latin American literature and culture)
  Bibliography: p.
  Includes index.
  ISBN 0-520-06233-7 (alk. paper)
  1. Spanish American poetry—20th century—History and criticism.
2. Modernism (Literature)—Latin America.   3. Lugones, Leopoldo,
1874–1938—Criticism and interpretation.   4. Herrera y Reissig,
Julio, 1875–1910—Criticism and interpretation.   I. Title.
II. Series: Latin American literature and culture (Berkeley)
PQ7082.P7K57   1989
861—dc19   88-37129
                                                                  CIP

Printed in the United States of America

1   2   3   4   5   6   7   8   9

In memory of
Malinee Holmes Kirkpatrick

Contents

Acknowledgments

The writing of this book owes much to the advice and support of countless friends and colleagues. My studies on *modernismo* began at Princeton University. During that stage, and throughout the book's later phases, I am grateful to Sylvia Molloy, who has always been a thoughtful and generous reader. A turning point in the book's development was my opportunity to work with Roberto González Echevarría in two National Endowment for the Humanities Seminars at Yale University. The intellectual climate of these seminars fostered lively debate and feedback for my work, especially the chapters on Herrera y Reissig, López Velarde, and Vallejo. Among my colleagues at these seminars, Alicia Andreu stands out as a supportive friend and critic.

For the research on literary journalism, the family of Dr. Sergio Provenzano of Buenos Aires allowed me to consult materials in their extraordinary collection in Buenos Aires. In Montevideo, the staff of the Biblioteca Nacional shared my interest in the writings of Julio Herrera y Reissig and were helpful in every way possible. To the library's director, Enrique Fierro, and to Mireya Callejas, I am especially grateful.

During the book's final stages, I received assistance from Marta Morello-Frosch, who made valuable suggestions for the reorganization of the manuscript. Daniel Balderston, Emilie Bergmann, James E. Irby, Francine Masiello, and Eduardo Paz Leston gave careful readings and valuable advice. Other colleagues at Berkeley, especially Arthur Askins, Arnold Chapman, and José Durand, took the time to make important bibliographical suggestions.

The editorial help I received from graduate students at Berkeley was essential. Barbara De Marco was invaluable as a text editor, as was James Nicolopolus who, along with Steve Raulston and Ching-Ju Lee, helped in all aspects of manuscript preparation. Myrna García Calderón, Patricia Greene, and Steve Raulston showed real talent in their work as translators for the volume. Their interest and skill at the task are evident.

As all final versions are my own, all errors and infelicities of translation are my responsibility.

Fellowships from the National Endowment for the Humanities and the University of California Junior Faculty and Humanities Fellowships helped make my work possible. A travel grant from the Berkeley Center for Latin American Studies allowed me to consult libraries and archives in Argentina and Uruguay.

Introduction

The starting point of this book has been a study of the *modernista* poetry of Leopoldo Lugones within its historical and literary context. Literary criticism has found Lugones a literary figure of difficult classification, owing to the abundance and diversity of his work and, in addition, to the rapid shifts in his ideological and political stances. Yet the study of Lugones is made fascinating by the very reason of these changes and the contradictory nature of much of his work. The obvious asymmetries in his work give modern readers a clue to search for the fissures in the productions of *modernismo* as a total movement. They not only reveal the contradictions within the work of this Argentine writer but can lead us to see the less obvious similarities with writers of his epoch and subsequent generations. In the work of Lugones, one sees from the earliest writings of 1893 a push toward the breakup of models, including his inherited poetic tradition as well as social structures. The combination of unusual thematic elements with innovative technical procedures makes Lugones' work an especially fruitful field of study, while Lugones' drive toward authoritarianism and his reluctance to relinquish formal order in poetry are revealing elements for a study of the epoch's literature in transition. The topics of voyeurism, fetishism in language, and an analysis of the iconography of *modernista* poetry can serve as the basis for exploring the factors that make Lugones a true precursor of what might be called the dissonant trend in Spanish American poetry.

Lugones' poetry was met with enthusiastic acclaim by poets such as Rubén Darío, Amado Nervo, Ramón López Velarde, and even César Vallejo. More recently, Jorge Luis Borges has written of the paradoxes and importance of this literary father. Although Borges attacked Lugones in the 1920s, he later softened his early *ultraísta* criticism of Lugones' dogged adherence to rhyme. Borges stresses the Quevedian rather than Gongoran pattern of Lugones' poetry in order to highlight Lugones' abilities as craftsman, as a poet dedicated to the possibilities of the word as generator of new ideas. Studies by Borges and other poets will show Lugones' impact on the succeeding generation of poets.

Following a survey of Lugones' work, this book examines subtle subversion in *modernista* poetry and studies some of its followers. Julio Herrera y Reissig, along with other *modernista* and *postmodernista* poets questioned the very bases of the conventions of *modernismo*. This perspective is available to us by examining the works of these poets in the light of the works of more recent poets, such as Ramón López Velarde, César Vallejo, and Alfonsina Storni. As innovators within late *modernismo*, both Lugones and Herrea y Reissig insert moments of the colloquial or the ridiculous in *modernismo*'s stylized scenes and, even more importantly, carry the imitation of their models (such as Albert Samain and Jules Laforgue) to heights of frenzy. Although this tendency has often been viewed more as imperfect imitation than innovation, this study will attempt to show that such tendencies represent a resistance to or a subversion of the received European tradition.

The resistance to previous models is an especially important topic in illuminating the course of poetry in Spanish American literature after *modernismo*. It can offer a way to recast the notion of dependence in *modernismo*, as well as showing a more direct link between the works of *modernismo* and *vanguardismo*. In this regard, Lugones' appropriation of Laforgue's work is an important case in point. Although it is clear that Lugones borrowed heavily from Laforgue, the most radical experiments in the volume *Lunario sentimental* (1909) are found where the poetry owes least to Laforgue—when Lugones ventures into poetic frontiers unexplored up to this point in Spanish American poetry, especially in regard to his treatment of the urban middle class and the image of the modern woman, transformed from inert *femme fatale* to working-class citizen. Herrera y Reissig's poetry provides a similar example, for he borrowed from stylized Parnassian pastoral scenes and gave them the rustic contours of a provincial setting (a method also apparent in parts of *Los crepúsculos del jardín* [1905] by Lugones). In a sense both poets exaggerate and then naturalize the inherited conventions of European writing, and by doing so they change the very linguistic and ideological support base of its transmission.

Using the visual images of the map, the landscape painting, the decorated body, and the city itself as metaphors for the discussions of poetry, this book will show how *modernismo*'s overload of sensory paraphernalia creates the gaps that serve as openings for new productions in Spanish American poetry. The discussion of the transmission and transformation of sign systems, of parody, of subversion, and of "minus devices" (using Yuri Lotman's terms) will shape these discussions of visual images.[1] A combination of methods will allow us to see the ways thematic elements (such as eroticism and the urban and pastoral landscapes) are part of a mapped-out territory of poetic convention. The breaks of syntax, the eruption of the unintelligible, the "mysteriousness" of the much late *modernista* poetry prefigure the works of later *vanguardista* poets. Because external structures are dissolving (for example, the shifting and changing social-class alignments, a new role for the artist—writer, new economic structures due to industrialization), the structures of poetry (formal poetic meter, rhyme) also show rearrangement. Given these realignments, the position of the speaking subject in poetry must be shifting as well. We see the dispersal of the framing poetic voice, the fragmentation of landscape, and a heightened experimentation with conventions of rhyme, rhythm, and meter. Here the notions of voyeurism and fetishism in language aid us in establishing how these subversions in language are created. The breaks in logic and syntax in poetry resonate with the absence of former poetic patterns, making them even more haunting for the reader of today who can read with the tradition of modern poetry as well as the tradition of *modernismo*. The role of the reader must also be taken into account if we are to understand the changing evaluations of the impact of *modernista* poetry.

/ Any study of the historical context of *modernismo* must be attentive to the massive changes that took place in the late nineteenth century. A selection of statements by literary witnesses such as Rubén Darío, José Martí, Jaimes Freyre, Amado Nervo, as well as Lugones and Herrera y Reissig, shed light on their perception of their role as artists in a changing society. In addition, references to Baudelaire, Mallarmé, Walt Whitman, Edgar Allan Poe, and other foreign writers who were models for the *modernistas* serve as testimony to the rapidity of change in literary exchange.

The late nineteenth century witnessed the loss of the dream of the organic hierarchies of romanticism that had held sway even though romanticism itself stressed personal and turbulent self-expression. In essence, the oneiric tendencies of romanticism were difficult to maintain in a context of rapid modernization and relativization of values. The mythopoetic vision of the organic hierarchy reemerges in *modernista* poetry in only fragmented form, and here the return to the visual metaphors of the map, the landscape, the spatial contours of the city or of the interior space aid us in seeing this process of dislocation. In *modernismo* one sees the increasing cult of the object, especially in the reification of the female figure and in the fascination with the machine (even in a work influenced so profoundly by romanticism as *Las montañas del oro* by Lugones). Within the late nineteenth-century matrix, we see poets such as Lugones and Herrera reasserting, often with violence, certain elements of heirarchy in their poetry, only to deflate subtly within the poetry itself any claims to former totalities. With their seemingly blind ingenuousness faced with imported and local models, they open the space for a playfulness and experimentation in modern poetry which later poets have used to full advantage. They recast the vision of the city, the woman, and provincial landscapes through the eyes of a poetic self that makes few claims to structure. Later poets would use the fragments left by these late *modernistas* as the building blocks for a new diction (often an incoherent diction) that make Spanish American poetry of this century so distinct from its earlier models.

This book will attempt to show that an element of *modernismo* generated change in a way that has usually been credited to the more overtly political *mundonovista* inheritors of *modernismo* or to the *vanguardista* poets. While poets such as Lugones do not explicitly theorize on the Spanish American subject in their poetry (although Lugones does so abundantly in prose), the dislocations and questionings of the materials offered by the epoch combine to dissolve the very foundations of the assumptions of dependence in Spanish American *modernista* poetry.

1
THE TRADITION OF *MODERNISMO*

In *La expresión americana* José Lezama Lima speaks of "la tradición de las ausencias posibles"[1] ("the tradition of possible absences") as the great activator of artistic creativity in the New World. His general remarks on Spanish American art may serve as shaping images for a study of *modernismo*'s high energy and voracity of consumption and transformation: "[E]l americano no recibe una tradición verbal, sino la pone en activo, con desconfianza, con encantamiento, con atractiva puericia. Martí, Darío, y Vallejo, lanzan su acto naciente verbal, rodeado de ineficacia y de palabras muertas."[2] ("The American does not receive a verbal tradition, rather, he activates it, with mistrust, with enchantment, with attractive childishness. Martí, Darío, and Vallejo launch their nascent verbal act, surrounded by ineffectiveness and dead words.") The mixture of traditions that Lezama calls "ese protoplasma incorporativo," which distinguishes the assimilative capacity of great art, is present as well in the generating elements of *modernismo,* a movement that opened new spaces for change in South American literature. Roland Barthes distinguishes in *Writing Degree Zero* what he calls the "Hunger of the Word," which "initiates a discourse full of gaps and full of lights, filled with absences and overnourishing signs, without foresight or stability of intention, and thereby so opposed to the social function of language that merely to have recourse to a discontinuous speech is to open the door to all that stands above Nature."[3] Statements by both Barthes and Lezama Lima, two great observers and shapers of our contemporary way of studying literature in relation to its source, single out absences and gaps amidst overabundance as openings for new creation. *Modernismo*'s proliferation of styles and its abundance of poetic experiments constitute the rich matrix from which modern poetry has emerged.

Because *modernismo* does not highlight the social function of language, its contributions have been relegated often to the categories of verbal pyrotechnics and individual eccentricities. Such experiments have nevertheless been seeds of change for twentieth-century poetry. Why do contemporary readers dismiss *modernismo* as an ossified movement? Its impact would be easier to forget if its visions and rhythms were not still reverberating through a whole century of poetry celebrated for its novelties and distances from *modernismo*. Why is there so much suspicion of it as a movement? There seems to be a desire to collapse its multiplicity and subtleties into a single profile, despite the many fine studies on individual poets of the era. Inevitably, many discussions of *modernismo* are stereotypically describing a "rubenismo," the hackneyed copies of Rubén Darío's style, while forgetting the movement's audacity and its sweeping display of subject matter and styles.

By returning to a poet who fully participated in *modernismo*'s currents, but who at the same time maintained a skeptical questioning distance within his work, some fissures that vein the movement can come to light. Leopoldo Lugones exploded part of the masquerade of *modernismo* with *Lunario sentimental,* but only to the extent that he brought to the surface some of its latent questions. Suspicious, in the end, of a kind of urban modernism and of its dislocations, Lugones finally turned his back on change and sealed off the path toward the unknown with tight rhyme and patriotic melodies. This is surely not the direction foreseen by the *modernistas,* but Lugones' development gives us clues to a way certain ideologies speak through poetic form and poetic movements, and not only in their changing thematics. His voracious consumption of his epoch's poetic trends and his peculiar transformations of them are eloquent testimony of the constraints and possibilities of his cultural and social context.

Much of what seems tedious in *modernista* poetry for the modern reader is its overloading of rarefied objects, its jewel-studded interior spaces, the amethyst shafts of light that make vision difficult. We find it hard to move around these ornately furnished rooms and especially amidst the heavy-lidded goddesses who inhabit them. While modern taste prefers clean, spare lines, white walls, and open spaces, the *modernistas* work from a different set of culturally determined preferences. Just as they held a penchant for ornately decorated physical spaces, language itself had to be filled, decorated, and overburdened until it groaned under the excess of sensory paraphernalia. With rhyme, rhythm, and extended imagistic development, every inch of space was filled, inviting crowding, violence and, ultimately, parody. And this is precisely the process we see in several late *modernista* poets. Growing agitation, slicing through not only the images but the very contours of the poems themselves, carried *modernista* innovation to frenzies of linguistic activity.

Dealing with a set of culturally valued icons usually derived from a European, especially French, context, the Spanish American writer has often been seen in a position of dependence. The acceptance of codified images in *modernismo* (for example, the *femme fatale*, twilights, emphasis on luxury and sonority) usually implies acceptance of the whole cultural aura that surrounds these images.[4] Because these writers do not counter these images or icons with an opposing set (as Neruda attempted in *Alturas de Macchu Picchu*), nor make their questioning of these received images explicit, they are often seen as accepting all the implications of such patterns. One may look for a disruptive or questioning movement on other levels, however. A later poet, César Vallejo, offers a powerful example of a movement of disruption, of a dislocation of scenic elements, textual surface, and accustomed dialogue. Yet even in *modernista* poetry or prose that seems to have a fetishistic fascination with overloading itself with riches from a more highly ranked cultural order, a subversive movement is sometimes triggered by the overloading process, which calls attention to the overabundance within the closed circles of pleasure and excess by making stark contrast with the emptiness surrounding it.

In our desire to show temporal "progress" in poetic development, an anxiety to seek equations between social progression (or regression) and to see literature as its prophet or mirror, at times we exalt certain stages of poetry because of their explicit commentary on certain political or social movements. We judge them by their accessibility (direct communication between an assumed subject and object like poet and reader) and their innovations or revolutionary nature. It is interesting to note critical appraisals of *modernismo* and the polemics it has aroused. Our idea of *modernismo* often takes on the image of a closed space, an escapist, ivory-tower world or an old trunk full of faded costumes and photos. We see less often its disparity, its violence of language, its fetishistic insistence on the bodily form, and its legacy in more contemporary poetry. For instance, the female figure in *modernismo* is an object almost at one with the language, heavily decorated, distant and elusive, sometimes spied-on, while the veil of mystery surrounding her is like the web of musicality that encases the poetry. *Modernista* poetry is not uniform in its enclosure and encasement. Mocking irony, the intrusive presence of deflation by social issues and discordant sounds and voices, even in gentle pastoral scenes, cannot be reconciled within this setting.

What is most striking in the production of these poets is their violence, a violence turned inward against the grain of language and outward against the usual signs of fulfillment, plenitude, and richness. In general, this plentitude is seen as treasure of physicality, often as stolen treasure. These poets insist on showing the physicality of the referent, shoving it to the forefront, as well as accentuating the physical nature of the words themselves. Like resistant yet malleable bodies, words are to be used and taken apart. Severo Sarduy, in *Escrito sobre un cuerpo,* states:

> La casa es el lugar del Mismo, la ciudad el del Otro. Ambito de la búsqueda erótica; un cuerpo nos espera, pero el camino que conduce a él—nuestra *palabra*—es casi informulable en la codificación excesiva de la *lengua* urbana. Camino invadido, borrado en el momento mismo de su trazo, signo ciego en la repetición blanca, sin intersticios, de las calles.

> Crear neuvos índices, concebir superficies de orientación, marcas totalmente artificiales: esa es nuestra actitud frente a la ciudad, esa la explicación de *nuestro vértigo de señalización.*

> Sólo cuentan, pues, las percepciones visuales. Textos, luces, flechas, clavos, afiches, que surgen como presencias icónicas, autoritarias; fetiches: son nuestros índices naturales. Toda otra percepción—

auditiva, olfativa, etc.—desaparece en la ciudad de hoy, cuya única práctica es rápida, motorizada.⁵

(The home is the place of the Self, the city, [the place of] the Other. Arena of the erotic search; a body waits for us, but the road that leads to it—our *word*—is almost inexpressible in the excessive codification of city *language*. A road crowded, erased in the very act of its trace, blind sign on white repetition, without intervals, of the streets.

To create new indices, to conceive surfaces of orientation, completely artificial marks, this is our attitude in the face of the city, this is the explanation of *our frenzy of signposting*.

Only visual perceptions, then, are important. Texts, lights, arrows, keys, posters, that rise up like iconic, authoritative presences; fetishes: they are our natural indices. Every other perception: sight, sound, scent, etc.—disappears in the city of today, whose only method is rapid, motorized.)

Sarduy's remarks, here in the context of a comparison with the Renaissance city, may be set next to Jean Baudrillard's definition of the fetish.⁶ The fetish's power lies in the appeal of the fabricated, its artificial, "made" quality, which is related to its magical quality of enchantment. The attention is directed to the surface quality, to the construction process itself, not to the design as a whole. In other words, objects are emptied of their real (that is, tangible) information of representation, their physical density, and are presented in their signifying sense as signs, as emblems of the process of production. In this sense, their use is like that of objects in the baroque, not valuable for mimetic representation, but for their ability to be read as opposite signs, not straining to build bridges of relation between the objects of images themselves. In the same way *modernismo* is striking in its profusion of glittering sign–objects. Perhaps it is this almost fetishistic insistence of overloading signs which has closed it off to so many later readers.

Modernismo, today, is seen as a closed space, a silent theater in which rituals, gestures, and erotic ceremonies are carried out, with the body of language itself sharing this endless rehearsal of the rites of self-enclosure. Yet these scenes are dismantled time

and again by a distracting movement somewhere to the side, as
if we were to see behind the stage. This distracting or subversive
movement does not involve a confrontation of opposites. We
simply see the workings of the backdrop of the machinery. A
touch of decor is out of place—something prosaic wanders into
a rarefied setting, or the clanking of the rhyme becomes over-
bearing, drawing too much of our attention. Thus our gaze is
distracted by the distancing noise. These moments of hesita-
tion, withdrawal, or suspension serve as equivalents of elision in
a sentence, or, as described by Julia Kristeva, of an erasure of
the real object of the speaking subject, similar to the process of
desemanticization by obscene words or the fragmentation of
syntax by rhythm.[7]

With the passage of time we are given a new way to read
modernista poems. While working within patches of this *modern-
ista* discourse, later poets allow us to sense the absences, rather
than the accumulations, which make us feel that we are in new
territories. The received images that constitute our repertoire
for viewing the productions of *modernismo* allow us to see them
in a different light from their contemporaries. And it is pre-
cisely through the works of those poets who drew most heavily
from them that the movement in *modernismo* itself can be felt.
By *postmodernista* rejections, exaggerations, and parings-down
of *modernismo*'s stock images and procedures, we can trace the
shifting points of view that were already present in the construc-
tion of *modernismo*'s seemingly fixed scenes.

If we consider the procedures of *enclosure* or *binding* in *modern-
ista* poetry to be part of the exaltation of objects, of landscape
scenes, of the female figure, and of decorative form, then our
reading must also take into account our own fetishization of this
production. By freezing it in time, by surrounding it with rites of
previous and current criticism, *modernismo* becomes a useful ob-
ject, a museum piece or point of reference. Just as luxury can
point out poverty, or monstrosity normality, a limited view of
modernismo has restricted our sense of its power in our readings
of later poets. *Modernismo*'s enclosed scenes and clichés that turn
back on themselves, exalting their stereotypical nature, may rep-
resent a freezing of motion, but with another purpose than stasis

or regression. If order is a necessary precondition for transgression or for vice, these static landscapes and enclosed gardens, which seem to offer the reader a single, directed point of view, in effect are engineered for more possibilities. Their stillness contains a slight wayward movement or distracting gesture that destabilizes the entire backdrop. The metaphor of eroticism as one of the bases for inquiry is not merely a descriptive scheme. The body, as origin and object of desire, is constantly given to us, sometimes as a lavishly decorated spectacle, other times as a mutilated scrap heap. As one looks closer, this same insistence on dismantling the erotic image is reflected in the framing picture of these prized icons. Things will not stand still under the poetic gaze. Margins are always dissolving, and *fin de siglo* props are being undermined by the intrusion of off-key elements. As if engaged in a secret masked charade, Salomé laughs back. These poems are strategic, outflanking readers by beating them in the distancing game through means of more and more elaborate schemes and of towering lookout points of internal commentary.

The tear Lugones made in *modernismo*'s fabric of social and sexual dynamics is still being rewoven by contemporary poets. Lugones' intrusiveness created a lingering discordance, and no amount of dispassionate criticism can gloss over the uneasy spaces he created. Julio Herrera y Reissig, César Vallejo, Ramón López Velarde, Alfonsina Storni, to mention a few, are poets who have not let us forget this rupture.[8] Marked by violence, eroticism, and the disturbing entrance of urban elements in a textual space, these poets struggle with an ambivalence against allowing easily mappable patterns of perspective, beauty, and poetic structure to frame their poetry. The subversive shifts and overt disavowals they make of a veiled authoritative order are the weapons they use in dismantling hierarchical form, including a realignment of the speaking subject. They are not simply naive consumers of European influences. Each in his own way plots a path to lead the reader to question even the poetic forms that tradition supplies.

Lugones' dramatic confrontation with the upheavals of his times, with the disintegration of accustomed literary exchange (the pact between writer and complicit initiated reader) is ech-

Gramley Library
Salem College
Winston-Salem, NC 27108

oed more subtly by other writers. Unlike Rubén Darío who smiles at convention, with his flowing rhythms and often playful experiments with the brilliance of verse, Lugones rushes headlong into the crumbling hierarchies. Devouring several genres at once, lurching back and forth between extremes, Lugones dramatizes the conflict between *modernismo*'s formalism and the shift into the twentieth century's more private sense of poetic language. Still striving to preserve a mythic framework for poetry, which presupposes an underlying order or ultimate frame of reference, the dynamism of his work prefigures new rearrangements. Later poets find themselves with the task of reassembling fragments of symbolic structures, of a previous poetic heritage, now devalued as bearers of intention. Lugones' uneven experiments point the way for a revolution in poetic language.

THE HERITAGE OF *MODERNISMO*

In *Cuadrivio,* Octavio Paz states that works by two Spanish American *modernista* poets, Rubén Darío and Leopoldo Lugones, are the starting points of "all the experiences and experiments of modern poetry in the Spanish language."[9] Paz speaks of Lugones as a forerunner of *vanguardismo*:

> Todo lenguaje, sin excluir al de la libertad, termina por convertirse en una cárcel; y hay un punto en el que la velocidad se confunde con la inmovilidad. Los grandes poetas modernistas fueron los primeros en rebelarse y en su obra de madurez van más allá del lenguaje que ellos mismos habían creado. Preparan así, cada uno a su manera, la subversión de la vanguardia: Lugones es el antecedente inmediato de la nueva poesía mexicana (Ramón López Velarde) y argentina (Jorge Luis Borges); Juan Ramón Jiménez fue el maestro de la generación de Jorge Guillén y Federico García Lorca; Ramón del Valle-Inclán está presente en el teatro moderno y lo estará más cada día.[10]

> (All language, not excluding that of liberty, ends up becoming a prison, and there is a point at which velocity becomes confused with immobility. The great modernista poets were the first to rebel, and in their mature works they go beyond the language that they themselves have created. In this way they prepare, each one in his own

way, for the avantgarde subversion. Lugones is the immediate ante-
cedent of new Mexican [Ramón López Velarde] and Argentinian
[Jorge Luis Borges] poetry. Juan Ramón Jiménez was the master of
the generation of Jorge Guillén and Federico García Lorca; Ramón
del Valle-Inclán is present in the modern theatre, and will be more
present each day.)

Paz, in his now classic study of modern poetry, *Los hijos del limo*,
continues his distinction between the two great poets of *modern-
ismo*. Although Darío is the founder, it will be for others to
introduce a greater self-questioning, or ironic stance, into *mod-
ernista* poetry:

> La nota irónica, voluntariamente antipoética y por eso más intensa-
> mente poética, aparece precisamente en el momento de mediodía
> del modernismo (*Cantos de vida y esperanza*, 1905) y aparece casi
> siempre asociada a la imagen de la muerte. Pero no es Darío, sino
> Leopoldo Lugones, el que realmente inicia la segunda revolución
> modernista. Con Lugones penetra Laforgue en la poesía hispánica:
> el simbolismo en su momento antisimbolista.[11]

> (The ironic note, voluntarily antipoetic and therefore more in-
> tensely poetic, appears precisely in the noontime of *modernismo* [*Can-
> tos de vida y esperanza*, 1905] and appears almost always associated
> with the image of death. But it is not Darío, but Leopoldo Lugones
> who really initiates the second *modernista* revolution. With Lugones,
> Laforgue penetrates Hispanic poetry: symbolism in its antisym-
> bolist moment.)

Paz distinguishes two volumes of Lugones' poetry, *Los crepúscu-
los del jardín* (*The Twilights of the Garden*) and *Lunario sentimental*
as specific examples of "poesía con crítica de la poesía" ("poetry
with criticism of poetry"). Along with poetic techniques, Paz
also compares the natures of both poetic movements, *modern-
ismo* and *vanguardismo*, in their initial stages. Although both
movements were first tied to their European, especially French,
models, each movement turned later toward native or Ameri-
can sources.

> En su primer momento la vanguardia hispanoamericana dependió
> de la francesa, como antes los primeros modernistas habían seguido
> a los parnasianos y simbolistas. La rebelión contra el nuevo cosmopo-

litismo asumió otra vez la forma de un nativismo o americanismo. El primer libro de César Vallejo (*Los heraldos negros*, 1918) prolongaba la línea poética de Lugones.[12]

(In its first moment, the Spanish American vanguard depended on the French, just as before the first *modernistas* had followed the Parnassians and the Symbolists. The rebellion against the new cosmopolitanism assumed again the form of "nativism" or "Americanism."The first book of César Vallejo [*Los heraldos negros,* 1918] prolonged the poetic line of Lugones.)

How can it be that *modernismo,* a movement first celebrated (as well as attacked) for its audacity and claims to spiritual transformation, now is seen as a series of artifacts in a museum, relics of a deadened, almost asocial language?[13] How do *avant-garde* movements exhaust themselves, or gradually become accepted? The paradoxical nature of the claims of *modernismo*—its espousal of anarchic and egalitarian principles along with an aristocratic claim to power in language—are not so paradoxical as they seem. Although its poets often used the languages of both mysticism and politics, suppressing their inherent contradictions, their goals were generally directed toward a revolution of personal expression, seen in conflict with an authoritarian state of language itself.

Much of the attraction of the forbidden fruit of *modernismo* is lost to us now. As readers removed from the space of dangerous pleasure by the passage of time and the presence of new surprises, it is sometimes difficult to understand the uproar and scandal that moments of the poetic works of Leopoldo Lugones evoked. However, we can recreate some sense of understanding by following the traces of this poetry in works more accessible to us. The testimony of the impact of this writer on poets such as Julio Herrera y Reissig, Ramón López Velarde, Vicente Huidobro, César Vallejo, Jorge Luis Borges, Alfonsina Storni, Octavio Paz, and many others is found not only in their critical references to Lugones but in the works themselves, which reveal the mechanics of the process of perception and assimilation. Although the influence of Lugones (and of his contemporary Herrera y Reissig) is evident in these poets (and even in the sound plays of poets such as Mariano Brull and Luis Palés Matos), the icons they inherit are stripped of their message content and are endowed with intentionality of a different kind.[14] For example, the excesses of accumulation—the jewels, exotic coloration, the chinoiserie, a fleeting glimpse of the *femme fatale*—implied for the *modernistas* the luxury of accumulation in a tangible and palpable sense while also determining what was left out of the closed circle of *modernismo*. The elements of rarefaction, the flaunting of excess and riches, as well as a heavily loaded surface of verbal texture were in great part a reaction to what they saw as the poverty of their circumstantial reality.

If the *modernistas* remain unforgiven, it is neither for their luxury nor their abundance. The extravagance of style, the heaping up of exotic detail, is surely no sin. It is the self-containment or exclusiveness that offends. The poets of *modernismo* shut the door to their garden of delights. Invited in were only the initiates, those who knew the secret codes to decipher the mysterious rites of the poetic process. Like the preceding generation who flaunted their wealth by the ritual trip to Europe, thereby making more visible the poverty of those left behind, so the *modernistas,* rich only in knowledge, separated themselves from others by their European voyage of reading and reworking the treasures they brought back. In the same way they viewed what surrounded them as an impoverished state. This is the true insult of the excesses of *modernismo. Modernismo* seems to invite no antithesis within its confinement, and any conflicting movement is immobilized by being woven into the texture of the circle, redressed to appear in good company. The discordant element appears to be banished. Severo Sarduy described this same movement of excess and expulsion of dissonance in the Baroque:

El horror al vacío expulsa al sujeto de la superficie, de la *extensión multiplicativa,* para señalar en su lugar el código específico de una práctica simbólica. En el barroco, la poética es una Retórica: el lenguaje, código antónomo y tautológico, no admite en su densa red, *cargada,* la posibilidad de un *yo* generador, de un referente individ-

ual, centrado, que se exprese—el barroco funciona al vacío—que
oriente o detenga la crecida de signos.[15]

(The horror of the vacuum expels the subject from the surface of
the *multiplying extension,* to signal in its place the specific code of a
symbolic practice. In the Baroque, poetry is a Rhetoric: language,
the autonomous and tautological code, does not admit in its dense,
loaded net the possibility of a generating *I,* of an individual, cen-
tered frequent referent, who may express himself—the baroque
functions in a vacuum—who may orient or check the growth of
signs.)

The fixed scene cannot afford dissenting or distracting move-
ment within its confines, and the perspective of the viewer must
remain fixed also.

Modernismo then requires skilled readers,[16] those who can sift
through the layers of a codified image and take pleasure in its
ancestry, exclaiming over the discovery of the presence of Hugo
here and Verlaine there, as well as flowers from medieval paint-
ings as in the case of Rubén Darío. Even more pleasurable is the
recognition of a fragment from a text by D'Annunzio, signaling
perversity and rarefaction not permitted to the masses, whose
limitations (moral, social, or educational) prohibit them from
penetrating into the inner sanctum. Just as the paintings of Gus-
tave Moreau and the Pre-Raphaelites are made increasingly gro-
tesque by later exaggerations and transformations (one thinks of
the details in paintings by Klimt and the sadistic touches Munch
added to his erotic goddesses), so the excesses of the forbidden
fruit of *modernismo* are packed so closely together that they begin
to decompose. The spirit of play takes on its darker side. Just as
abundance creates poverty by contrast, so frivolity invites its lurk-
ing counterpart. Lost among the excesses of the textual surface,
the speaking or acting subject reasserts itself with a gesture that
draws our attention outside the static scene. The works of both
Lugones and Herrera y Reissig show the marks of this intrusive-
ness into the enclosure of preciosity and abundance.

In an article entitled "Acotación del árbol en la lírica," Jorge
Luis Borges offers an analogy between scenic and textual
spaces, using an image that suggests the curving, botanical de-
signs of the style of Art Nouveau with its "ramajes trabados."

Borges points out the traits that separate the works of *modernismo* from the tastes of later readers:

> Hasta aquí, empero, sólo se ha tratado del árbol como sujeto de descripción. En escritores ulteriores—en Armando Vasseur y paladinamente en Herrera y Reissig adquiere un don de ejemplaridad y los conceptos se entrelazan con un sentido semejante al de los ramajes trabados. El estilo mismo arborece y es hasta excesiva su fronda. A despecho de nuestra admiración ¿no es por ventura íntimamente ajena a nosotros, hombres de pampa y de derechas calles, esa hojarasca vehementísima que por *Los parques abandonados* campea?[17]

> (Up until now, however, the tree has only been treated as the subject of description. In later writers—in Armando Vasseur and openly in Herrera y Reissig—it acquires the gift of exemplar, and concepts intertwine like knitted branches. The style itself branches out and its foliage is even excessive. Despite our admiration, is not this vehement showiness which covers *Los parques abandonados* by chance intimately foreign to us, men of the pampa and straight paths?

In other writings of 1924, speaking during his *ultraísta* period, Borges gives clues to the subsequent rejection of the *modernista* movement by some of its more "modern" practitioners.[18] Like many critics of his generation, he speaks of a dependency factor,[19] a reliance on the exalted strands of symbolism and Parnassianism. Here he uses a graphic corporal analogy of wounding and scars:

> El error del poeta (y de los simbolistas que se lo aconsejaron) estuvo en creer que las palabras ya prestigiosas constituyen por sí el hecho lírico. Son un atajo y nada más. El tiempo las cancela y la que antes brillaba como una herida se oscurece taciturna como una cicatriz.[20]

> (The mistake of the poet [and of the symbolists who counseled him] was in believing that already prestigious words constitute the lyric act in themselves. They are a short cut and nothing more. Time cancels them, and what shone before like a wound darkens quietly like a scar.)

Even more clearly for the discussion of *modernismo* at hand, Borges continues by pointing up the static pictorial quality of much of Herrera y Reissig's verse, a reference that might equally well be applied to the staging of many *modernista* scenes:

A ese empeño visual juntó una terca voluntad de aislamiento, un prejuicio de personalizarse. Remozó las imágenes; vedó a sus labios la dicción de la belleza antigua; puso crujientes pesadeces de oro en el mundo. Buscó en el verso preeminencia pictórica; hizo del soneto una escena para la apasionada dialogación de las carnes.[21]

(This visual undertaking was joined to a stubborn desire for isolation, a prejudice against becoming personal. It polished up the images; it sealed its lips to the diction of ancient beauty; it put crushing weights of gold on the world. In verse it searched for pictorial preeminence, it made of the sonnet a scene for the passionate dialogue of the flesh.)

As it was then for Borges, it is the programmatic and derivative aspects of *modernismo* which still puzzle many readers. How could a movement that espoused the romantic principles of spiritual liberty, access to the sublime through synesthetic experiments of sound, color, and rhythm, be best known today for its formalism, for its sometimes grotesque exaggeration of the iconography of French Parnassian, symbolist, and decadent styles? The *modernistas* were seemingly shameless in the appropriation of the iconic symbols of all things exotic or distant. The very formalism of the verse form, enriched to saturation, distances the modern reader by its practiced theatricality.

Critics rarely treat the movement of *modernismo* for its intrinsic value. Its worth is measured instead by a series of resemblances—its differences from previous and subsequent changes in poetic practice. Yet *modernismo* is, quite distinctly, a movement, a self-identified and coherent esthetic program, despite its internal variations. Though the term *avant-garde* is applied to a later generation, the *modernista* quasi-militarist language and messianic claims for their work leave no doubt as to the movement's coherent purpose. Renato Poggioli discusses the militaristic and apocalyptic terminology adopted by avant-garde movements in *The Theory of the Avant-Garde:*

Avant-garde deformation, for all that the artists who practice it define it as antitraditional and anticonventional, also becomes a

tradition and a stylistic convention, as has often enough been real-
ized. . . . In this way, deformation fulfills not only a contrasting, but
also a balancing, function in the face of the surviving conventions,
academic and realistic, of traditional art. The deformation is deter-
mined by a stylistic drive, which inaugurates a new order as it
denies the ancient order.[22]

Modernismo has most often been seen as a movement of de-
pendence, as a group of poets who looked to Europe, especially
France, as a source of inspiration. Many have even seen this
movement as a trend based in imitation, as mere translation
from one literary culture into another. An examination of the
nature of information transmission from one culture to an-
other, however, as well as from one language to another, can
help in understanding the specific patterns of transmission of
poetic traditions. Given the developments in linguistics and se-
miology in recent decades, the study of a phenomenon such as
modernismo can find methods with which to examine this trans-
position of literary patterns from one culture to another, taking
into account extraliterary codes as parallel ways of enlarging
our perspectives. Even the simplest formulation as the dichot-
omy *langue* (*code, grammar, system*) as opposed to *parole* (*speech,
usage*) is especially relevant to a study of poetic transmission.
The use of these terms, along with other concepts, will provide
a basis for examining the poetic language of *modernismo* in its
transmission and transformations.

FOREIGN INFLUENCES

In *modernismo* we see the collision of several aesthetic codes at
once. The transmission from emitter to receptor is not direct,
however—the message does not necessarily remain intact in its
transmission. Receptive factors, such as comprehension of a
foreign language (accuracy of translation), completeness or in-
completeness of texts, cultural factors (audience, possibilities
for publication) are essential factors to consider in the reception
of the emitted message. In the case of artistic texts, the transmis-
sion is even more complex. Literature is not an isolable com-
modity. It shares various functions in a given epoch and cul-

ture. It is clear that differing opinions about *modernistas* are not rooted exclusively in the message content they bear nor even in the particular form (rhythm, meter, rhyme) that shapes content. Although the *modernistas* were first attacked for their audacity in breaking the traditional rules, within a decade they were scorned by *vanguardista* poets for their adherence to rigid form. Surely, cultural and artistic contexts alter not only the transmission of fixed message content but its recpetion as well. It is this reception (or reading) of texts in different contexts that produces "aberrant" texts or misreadings. These same variations of reception can be of profound importance for the generation of new texts.

A look at the pictorial qualities of *modernista* verse can clarify some puzzling issues. As Pierre Bourdieu suggests,[23] the way we design our living spaces reflects and determines our ways of ordering the metaphors by which we live. In the *modernistas'* eagerness to fill up space with the treasures of a more highly valued culture do they not also implant in these scenes a seed of doubt? At what point does gentle mocking of their borrowed wares become overt parody? Without falling into a simplistic criticism—singling out only "patriotic" elements in *modernismo* (such as those in the later poetry of Rubén Darío) and rejecting the rest, or assuming an aestheticized eulogy of the beautiful and spiritual nature of *modernista* poetry—we can read these *modernista* works without facile value judgments.

CRITICISM OF *MODERNISMO*

Any history of the evaluation of poetic *modernismo* in Spanish America would constitute in itself a history of social and esthetic values of this century.[24] As the contemporary Mexican poet and novelist José Emilio Pacheco has noted, however, the task of disentangling precursors, influences, and initiators has made many critics forget the works themselves and concentrate on previous critical evaluation. In the same manner, criticism with limited sociological vision "se ha limitado a darnos una visión acerca de lo que debió haber hecho el modernismo para redimir a nuestras sociedades, en vez de emplear los instrumentos de análisis a fin de explicarnos su carácter socialmente condicionado"[25] ("has limited itself to giving us a vision about what *modernismo* should have done to redeem our societies, instead of using the instruments of analysis to explain to us its socially conditioned character"). Although the modern critic does not expect consensus on the relative worth of a particular work nor even dare to prescribe definitive standards for what constitutes an exclusively "literary" work, *modernismo* is still strongly associated with "dependence." And although there is no total agreement on the role of "authorship" in the production of a literary text, *modernistas* are generally seen as slavish individual imitators of foreign, especially French, texts.

Criticism can reflect a society's ideas about itself, and much recent criticism reflects *modernismo*'s own self-questioning. With the nineteenth century's emphasis on the idea of romantic "genius," of the specially selected transmitter of spiritual energy or revelations, the classical division of public and private languages breaks down. And to a large degree, the stability of genre is shaken. The late nineteenth century refuses even more the notion of writer as public spokesperson, either as legitimizer or adversary–critic of society. (One has only to think of the role of poet–statesman in early nineteenth-century Spanish America to see the contrast with the generation of *modernistas*.) The emphasis on interiority and personal expression even fragments the idea of the author or the book concept. The individual writer is seen on personal terms, and the concept of a coherent work gives way to fragmentary expression. As personal consciousness rather than social or ethical norms becomes increasingly the organizing principle, the individual style itself acquires new functions. If the frame of reference is personal consciousness and individuality, then style must allow for personal idiosyncrasy, even invention or destruction of genre. The highly self-conscious stylistics of *modernista* poetry (most notably that of Rubén Darío), with its highly personal thematics and expressiveness, have led many critics to focus heavily on biographical data rather than on external circumstances or more generalized literary influences.

Perhaps the most common criticism of *modernismo* is the attack on its lack of social commitment, with a few notable exceptions such as José Martí. If we read these works of *modernismo* as clues to a changing cultural consciousness, and not only as singular productions of individual talents, then our analysis must grow more complex. Except for the clearly defined stance of those who take the adversary role to a certain power group (as is the case in protest literature), even national literatures receive ongoing evaluations and reassimilations. A case in point is the recent revival of the figure of Rubén Darío as "patriot poet" of Nicaragua. Darío's case shows history's turns between rejection and canonization. From viewing Darío as the poet of the ivory tower to the newer category as poet–patriot is only one example of the flux of literary criticism. In this vein, a general tendency in Spanish American criticism has been to lump together all *modernista* writers under the label "rubenista" and to assume that the enclosure of the rich poetic forms of *modernismo* were prisons from which more recent poets have needed to liberate themselves. Although countless studies have pointed out the many styles, sources, and individual patterns of *modernista* poets, the survival of a facile critical grouping is difficult to overcome.

THE PROFESSIONAL WRITER

In "What Is an Author?" Michel Foucault finds an introduction to the historical analysis of discourse in the study of "transgressive discourses."[26] In his study of the evolution of the concepts of ownership and codification of discourses, he states:

> Texts, books, and discourses really begin to have authors (other than mythical, "sacralized" and "sacralizing" (figures) to the extent that authors became subject to punishment, that is, to the extent that discourses could be transgressive. (148)

Foucault also calls for a study of the author function and its modification:

> Perhaps it is time to study discourses not only in terms of their expressive value or formal transformations, but according to their modes of existence. The modes of circulation, valorization, attribution, and appropriation of discourses vary with each culture and are modified within each. The manner in which they are articulated according to social relationships can be more readily understood, I

believe, in the activity of the author-function and its modifications, than in the themes or concepts that discourses set in motion. . . . In short, it is a matter of depriving the subject (or its substitute) of its role as originator, and of analyzing the subject as a variable and complex function of discourse. (158)

The movement of *modernismo,* which is usually chronologically delineated between the years 1888 and 1910, has been credited with revitalizing the Spanish poetic idiom by means of three major contributions: (1) innovations in meter, rhyme, and syntax; (2) an expansion of subject matter; and (3) a change in the perception of the poetic function. *Modernismo* has most often been examined in its derivative aspects, that is, its debt to the French Parnassians and symbolists, and to the Americans Edgar Allan Poe and Walt Whitman. This type of criticism centers on the rebellious aspects of the movement, its attempt to break away from the models and archetypes of Spain and the colonial heritage. Variously called *torremarfilismo, cosmopolitismo,* or *decadentismo,* the movement of *modernismo* has been criticized as an aberrant faction of escapist writers who would not accept their immediate environment nor reflect it in their poetry. Less attention has been focused on the reasons for the conscious attempt to join another order of writers, however, an order more far-reaching than their present one.

The innovations of *modernismo* are based on the *modernistas'* widening awareness of their dependence, both economic and cultural, on traditional and European models and their decision to fill the cultural vacuum resulting from this dependence. Their innovations arose from a necessity of invention. Having become aware of the smaller sphere of action accorded to the writer, they sought to reclaim the lost importance and to develop a different role for the poet.[27] The heavily loaded surfaces of *modernista* poetry, its amazing variety of revived and new poetic forms, the cult of the exotic and of the self, were all ways of filling a void. In the same manner, their rebellious attitude manifested itself in a willful transgression of the public norm and its tastes. Their rebellion united them in a common purpose, with an emphasis on virtuosity and individual expression. An important element in defining the goals of the *modernistas* is the examination of the reasons for their choices and for their conscious attempt to join another order of writers. A look at their social and economic position can clarify the reasons for their decisions.

During the last part of the nineteenth century the major cities in Spanish America, especially Buenos Aires and Mexico City, were assimilating European movements at an accelerated pace. The transmission was manifold and simultaneous, and the proliferation of new ideas and styles—in the sciences, in the arts, and in literature—constantly thrust a choice upon the intellectuals. In part, the adoption of a style inaccessible to a large public was a reaction against the narrow range of roles assigned to the writer. With the diversification of society, due in large part to massive European immigration and growing industrialization,[28] there was no longer an absolute identification between the ruling classes and the intellectual.

New immigration, varying degrees of industrialization, and labor-oriented social movements changed the maps of Spanish American cities in the early twentieth century.[29] Just as workers' movements disrupted previous patterns of political privilege, so frantic rhythms wrenched poets from pastoral contemplation and reveries of palatial interiors. As the poet was thrust into the marketplace (for example, journalism and adoption of new "marketing" techniques), so poetry would follow its poets into turbulent urban spaces.

At the same time that *modernismo* as a poetic movement is flowering, poets and intellectuals are calling for an upheaval of old traditions. Manuel González Prada, a *modernista* poet better known for his role as essayist and political activist in late nineteenth-century Peru, reflects the dominant stamp of the organic metaphor in his analysis of Peru's need for revitalization. In his "Discurso en el Politeama" of 1888 he calls for the overthrow of the old order:

En esta obra de reconstitución y venganza no contemos con los hombres del pasado: los troncos añosos y carcomidos produjeron ya sus flores de aroma deletero y sus frutas de sabor amargo. ¡Que vengan árboles nuevos a dar flores nuevas y frutas nuevas! ¡Los viejos a la tumba, los jóvenes a la obra![30]

(In this work of reconstitution and vengeance we cannot count on the men of the past: the aged and decayed stumps have already produced their evil-smelling flowers and their bitter-tasting fruits. We want new trees to give new flowers and fruit! Old ones to the tomb, young ones to the task!)

Modernismo's emphasis on the ideal of an intellectual, and not necessarily an economic, aristocracy was part of a persistent search to create a new role for artists in a society whose hierarchies were being dissolved.[31] The role of the intellectual was being questioned, for the intellectual or writer no longer acted as he did previously as a spokesman for the reigning social order. Nor was the status of writer now usually linked to an explicit social function or political activity, although the life of the poet and leader José Martí presents a striking exception. As professional roles became more specialized, the role of the intellectual was also being reduced. No longer a sideline activity in addition to other professional ones, writing was becoming a specialized occupation, although a financially precarious one.

Literary and social critics such as Walter Benjamin and Michel Foucault have provided cogent explanations for the elevation of art to a religious discipline in the latter half of the nineteenth century.[32] They stress the historical situation as determining the particular stance of the artist. With the advent of photography and other means of reproduction, literature seemed to be losing its hold on the quasi-mystical role assigned to the artist. The rising demands of egalitarian social movements also threatened to displace the artist's rank. A cult of writing was aroused to restore confidence in literature as a separate reality, rather than as a range of styles, interchangeable and therefore dispensable. Poets were to be interpreters of a medium that offered mystical insights. Attention to the techniques of such a discipline was therefore of the highest importance.

Several studies in Spanish America have been especially influential in their examination of the changes in the writer's status and the impact of these changes of poetic practice. Angel Rama's *Rubén Darío y el modernismo*, Noé Jitrik's *Contradicciones del modernismo* and *Producción literaria y producción social*, and

Françoise Perus' *Literatura y sociedad en América Latina* have opened the way for a specific discussion of *modernismo* within its system of social productions.[33] Octavio Paz' *Los hijos del limo* and *Cuadrivio,* which include extensive discussions of *modernismo* within a Spanish American and Western poetic tradition, focus on constants and contrasts with Western poetic tradition.[34]

Among the critics who have interpreted the nature of this artistic as well as social phenomenon, some have concentrated more on the socioeconomic aspect of its web, while others have sought its secrets in the rich texture of surging aesthetic theories and practices current in Europe at the time. The analyses of Rama and Paz point up the two complementary aspects. In his classic text on Rubén Darío, Rama establishes first the socioeconomic outlines of Darío's artistic context, with special attention to the market values that determined Darío's formation:

> Hay aquí una comprobación primaria, tan general, que fue un lugar común de las dos últimas décadas del siglo: la deserción de los poetas es consecuencia de la nueva época maquinista, más exactamente, del sistema de relación económica que imponía, la que además, transforma a los poetas en servidores de las necesidades económicas imperativas.[35]

> (There is here a primary proof, so general, that it was a commonplace of the last two decades of the century: the desertion of the poets is a consequence of the new machine age, more precisely, of the economic system which it imposed, which, in addition, transformed the poets into servants of imperative economic necessities.)

Rama's chapter, "Los poetas modernistas en el mercado económico" (49–80), clarifies the position of journalism in the formation of the new aesthetic, distinguishing also the different possibilities of the newspaper or journal according to public access (for example, literacy, affluence) in Spanish American countries of varying industrial development.

Yet even to speak of markets, machines, and modernization in terms of the artist hardly brings forth the image of the hurried businessman–writer. As Rama points out, "Por el momento, el 'mercado' literario no existía; los libros no tenían compradores y, por lo mismo, tampoco había editores"[36] (For the moment, the literary 'market' didn't exist; there were no buyers for books, and by the same token, neither were there editors").

As Roberto J. Payró makes clear in a statement of 1894, periodicals were not accustomed to the idea of paying their national contributors for literary works. He sees the efforts of certain periodicals as being heroic ones in the "campaña" to create a national literature:

> El mercado de libros está en plena paralización, lo que como es natural—viene a reflejarse en el movimiento literario, escasísimo, que ha tenido que refugiarse casi exclusivamente en la prensa. *La Revista Nacional* ha sido el primer periódico que en Buenos Aires haya pagado su colaboración, demostrando así que era hora de que las producciones del ingenio comenzaran a estimarse en lo que valen, para facilitar el advenimiento de los escritores de profesión, únicos que podrán dotarnos de una literatura propia.[37]

> (The book market is completely paralyzed, which naturally is reflected in literary activity, extremely scarce, which has had to take refuge almost exclusively in the press. *La Revista Nacional* has been the first periodical in Buenos Aires that has paid its contributors, thus demonstrating that it was time for productions of genius to be valued for what they were worth, to facilitate the advent of professional writers, the only ones who can give us our own literature.)

Rubén Darío also offers testimony to the difficult situation of the writer in Latin America when he speaks of the martyred condition of the writer and of the limited audience and chances for publication apart from periodicals. Darío, however, embraces journalism itself as a writing apprenticeship. Striking is his description of the magical practice involved in pushing out the daily passages, as if the heightened speed of market rhythm increased the flow of creative power. He not only explains the economic necessity of working with periodicals but praises it as a new source of inspiration. Writing about commonplace events provides practice for less mundane efforts:

> Tú sabes de la lucha del hombre de letras, en todos lugares atroz y martirizadora, pero en ninguna parte como en estas sociedades de la América Latina, donde el alma aún anda a tientas y la especulación del intelecto casi no tiene cabida. Has tenido un buen campo de experiencia y ése es el diario. ¡El diario! Yo le oigo maltratar y sé

que le pintan como la tumba de los poetas. Pues si el trabajo
continuado sobre asuntos diversos no nos hace ágiles y flexibles en
el pensar y en el decir, ¿qué nos hará entonces?[38]

(You know about the struggle of the man of letters, everywhere
atrocious or martyred, but nowhere as in these societies of Latin
America, where even the soul feels its way about, and intellectual
speculation has almost no place. You have had a good field for
experience, and that is the daily newspaper. I have heard it ma-
ligned and depicted as the tomb of the poets. Well, if continued
work on different topics doesn't make us agile and flexible in
thought and in speech, what then will?

Despite the vision of Darío as romantic dreamer caught in
the cogs of the modern machine, perhaps he is the poet who
best shifted to catch its changing, quickening rhythm. It is clear,
despite his attachment to the ideals of the superiority of beauty,
that the changing sounds and rhythms entered his perception.
Unlike many *modernista* poets, who chose an ironic, mocking
stance toward modernity, Darío in effect used its power as coun-
terforce, as measure against his own flowing rhythms.[39]
    The dependence on Europe by the financial and social elite
had also led to a devaluing of local productions of all kinds. In
the case of literary production and outlets for publication, the
lack of faith in local writers resulted in little financial support
for their efforts. In Argentina, for example, publishers cited
the scarcity of national literary works of quality and the absence
of a large reading public as reasons for promoting mostly for-
eign works. Paul Groussac, when introducing the influential
journal *La Biblioteca* in 1896, describes the attitude he wished to
counter with the creation of his new publication:

Se nos ha dicho, por una parte, que no hallaríamos en la Argentina
la suma de colaboración bastante a llenar mensualmente las páginas
de una gran revista, faltando a la par entre nosotros la preparación
y el vagar indispensables; se agrega por la otra, que serán tanto más
escasos los lectores de este linaje de producciones, cuanto más se
alejen de la improvisación diaria y noticiosa.[40]

(It has been said to us, on the one hand, that we will not find in
Argentina the necessary amount of contributions to fill monthly
the pages of a great journal, lacking among ourselves the necessary

leisure and preparation; it is added, on the other hand, that read-
ers of this kind of production will be ever scarcer, the farther we
move from daily and newsworthy improvisation.)

The devaluing of local writers and of the public in general was
heightened by the financial crisis of the last decade of the nine-
teenth century. Publishers found it more convenient and less
costly to copy foreign works for which they did not have to pay
royalties, and they were assured of a readership by the already
established fame of major European writers:

> Entre una obra extranjera que nada cuesta y cuyo éxito está
> asegurado con la popularidad del autor, y una obra nacional, por la
> que hay que ahorrar unos cuantos centenares de pesos, corriendo
> el azar que sea mal recibida por el público, la elección no es
> dudosa. . . . Como si hubiera formado empeño en ser constantes
> tributarios de Europa, nos mantenemos exclusivamente do lo que
> aquélla produce en artes, ciencia, industria y literatura. ¿Qué más?
> Hasta las obras que sirven de texto en las escuelas elementales,
> colegios nacionales y aún en las mismas Facultades, son, en mayor
> parte, extranjeras.[41]

> (Between a foreign work that costs nothing and whose success is
> assured by the popularity of the author, and a national work, for
> which one must set aside several hundred pesos, running the risk
> that it will be badly received by the public, the choice is clear. . . . As
> if we had made a pact to be constant tributaries of Europe, we
> maintain ourselves exclusively on what it produces in the arts, sci-
> ence, industry and literature. What's more, even the texts in ele-
> mentary schools, high schools and even in the University are, for
> the most part, foreign ones.)

In Argentina the literary and social elite that immediately
preceded Lugones and his generation was losing its sense of
homogeneity and its all-encompassing directive role in the estab-
lishment of political and social values. This was due to the re-
alignment of social and economic forces and to the increasing
complexity of Argentine society. The Generations of 1837 and
1880 had seen their role as a political as well as an artistic one,
and their task as the stabilizing and maintaining of the authority
of their social class. The majority had defined their role as

writers as a sideline activity to complement their roles as states-
men and defenders of their society. This is the environment to
which the *modernista* grouping (including Darío and Lugones)
reacted, an environment that they sought to invade and helped
to dismantle.

José Juan Tablada, in a retrospective view, describes the con-
sciousness of rebellion in matters of taste and the *modernistas'*
attitude toward themselves as a displaced aristocracy:

> El radicalismo de la religión del arte exigía el sincero desprecio
> hacia el burgués y el burgués era todo aquel que no pensaba como
> nosotros en asuntos estéticos, pues los sociales y económicos nos
> parecían muy secundarios. Era todo una dislocación de categorías
> que llegaba en su grotesca ingenuidad hasta hacernos creer que la
> sociedad ideal sería una integrada por poetas más o menos baude-
> larianos o en salmuera de ajenjo como Verlaine o doctorados en el
> claro oscuro satánico del acuarelista Rops o escenógrafos de misas
> negras como Huysmans.[42]

> (Radicalism of the religion of art required a sincere disdain for the
> bourgeoisie, and the bourgeois was anyone who did not think as we
> did on aesthetic issues, since social and economic issues were secon-
> dary to us. It was a complete dislocation of categories which, in its
> grotesque ingenuousness, led us to the point of believing that the
> ideal society would be composed of poets more or less Baude-
> lairian, or pickled in absinth like Verlaine, or trained in the satanic
> chiaroscuro of the watercolorist Rops or in the theatre of black
> masses like Huysmans.)

The style of excess that Tablada stresses took the form of a
rebellion in taste and personal behavior, which often led to an
unconscious parody of the very codes the *modernistas* sought to
follow. Slavish copying was an attempt to approximate as closely
as possible the European mode, and much of Lugones' produc-
tion strikes this note time after time.

The *modernistas'* cult of the exotic and of the self is in part a
reaction to what they saw as their poverty. By striking a blow
at the neo-realists among other writers, they were also object-
ing to diversification and compartmentalization. Their empha-
sis on virtuosity arose from the necessity of inventing a place
for themselves.[43]

THE ORGANIC METAPHOR AND THE IDEA OF PROGRESS

Octavio Paz evaluates the movement's negations as a positive search for universals and for modernity:

> Se ha dicho que el modernismo fue una evasión de la realidad americana. Más cierto sería decir que fue una fuga de la actualidad local—que era, a sus ojos un anacronismo—en busca de una actualidad universal, la única y verdadera actualidad.[44]

> (It has been said that *modernismo* was an evasion of the American reality. It would be truer to say that it was a flight from the local present reality—which was, in their eyes, an anachronism—in search of a universal reality, the only true reality.)

The search for universality was indeed a prime motive, with a keen desire for participation in a cosmopolitan world of modernity as much as for timeless universals. The goal of progress, so strong in nineteenth-century thought, was an important motivating factor, although it is a concept difficult to reconcile with a spiritual ideal of timeless unity, or with a cult of art. The idea of progress for the *modernistas* was not merely an abstract concept. Increased contact with other nations, growing industrialization, and new immigration from Europe brought an expanded network of communication. José Martí, the earliest poet of *modernismo* and a participant in both political and aesthetic battles, wrote of the changing nature of expression and the rapidity of its exchange:

> Ahora los árboles de la selva no tienen más hojas que lenguas las ciudades; las ideas se maduran en la playa en que se enseñan, y andando mano a mano, y de pie en pie. El hablar no es pecado, sino gala; el oír no es herejía, sino gusto y hábito y moda. Se tienen el oído puesto a todo; los pensamientos no bien germinan, ya están cargados de flores y de frutos, y saltando en el papel, y entrándose, como polvo sutil, por todas las mentes; los ferrocarriles echan abajo la selva, los diarios la selva humana. Penetra el sol por las hendiduras de los árboles viejos. Todo es expansión, comunicación, florescencia, contagio, esparcimiento. El periódico desflora las ideas grandiosas. Las ideas no hacen familia en la mente, como antes, ni larga vida. Nacen a caballo, montadas en relámpago, con alas. No

crecen en una menta sola, sino por el comercio de todas. No tardan
en beneficiar, después de salida trabajosa, a número escaso de lec-
tores; sino que, apenas nacidas, benefician.[45]

(Now the trees of the forest have no more leaves than the cities
have tongues; ideas mature on the beach where they are learned
and, going hand in hand, and step by step. Speaking is not a sin,
but a glory. Listening is not heresy, but taste and habit and custom.
Everyone's ears are always open; thoughts barely germinate before
they are loaded with flowers and fruits, and jumping onto the
paper; they enter everyone's mind like fine powder; the railroads
tear down the forest; the newspapers, the human forest. The sun
penetrates the fissures of the old trees. Everything is expansion,
communication, flowering, contagion, dispersement. The periodi-
cal deflowers grandiose ideas. Ideas don't create a family in the
mind, as before, nor long life. They are born on horseback,
mounted on lightning, with wings. They don't grow in a single
mind but through the commerce of all minds. They don't delay in
benefiting, after a difficult emergence, a small number of readers;
rather, as soon as they are born, they show benefit.)

Martí favors the analogy with nature to show the changes
brought about by the influx of new ideas and their rapid com-
munication: "El hablar no es pecado, sino gala; el oír no es
herejía, sino gusto y hábito y moda." The purpose of communi-
cation for Martí is not necessarily didactic, nor does it aspire to
permanent meaning.

José Martí illustrates, with a metaphor drawn from nature, the
quickening pace of the modern world and the resulting rapidity
of communication. Like leaves falling from a tree, ideas are dis-
persed and lost even as they are born. It is notable that Martí
would choose as the referent in his analogy the tree, which would
seem to better fit with a romantic ideal of organic unity and with
rootedness than with fluidity and dispersion. Yet such an anal-
ogy illustrates some of the paradoxical spirit of *cosmopolitismo*
embraced by the poets of the moment. Although exalting a com-
mon language of beauty and universal rhythms, at the same time
this mixed analogy rejects the rootedness of a national past pro-
file and the boundaries imposed by strong national identity.
Spiritual universalism and a mystical aestheticism combine con-

trast with a cosmopolitanism, of varied strains, to produce an aesthetic difficult to define.

In 1899, about midpoint in *modernismo*, José Enrique Rodó gives his evaluation of Rubén Darío, a statement later edited and used by Darío as a prologue.[46] He notes that Darío's apparent "anti-americanismo involuntario" ("involuntary anti-Americanism") arises in part from his "adversión a las ideas y las instituciones circundantes" ("dislike for the surrounding ideas and institutions") (83). He singles Darío out from other American poets, giving two images, one from the world of man-made treasures and the other from nature:

> Joya, es esa, de estufa; vegetación extraña y mimosa que mal podía obtenerse de la explosión venal de savia salvaje en que han desbordado hasta ahora la juvenil vitalidad del pensamiento americano; algunas veces encauzada en toscos y robustos troncos que duraran como las formas brutales, pero dominadores de nuestra Naturaleza y otras muchas veces difusa en gárrula, lianas, cuyos despojos enriquecen el suelo de tierra vegetal, útil a las florescencias del futuro. (73–84)

> (It is a hothouse flower, a strange and pampered vegetation that could scarcely arise from the venal explosion of wild sap which the youthful vitality of American thought has poured out until now, sometimes channeled into coarse and robust trunks that endure like brutal forms, but dominators of our Nature; and more often diffused in babbling, tropical vines, whose remains enrich the ground with vegetal earth, useful for future flowerings.)

Rodó and Martí both employ the tree metaphor to reinforce the idea of growth and systemic change in art itself. Rodó's tree is useful because of the rich subsoil that will grow from its fallen leaves. The image, in both the forms of Martí and Rodó, attempts to reconcile apparently wayward growth within a system of organic growth and change. It is balance and harmony for which Nature strives, allowing for the occasional orchid, ruby or diamond, swan or pheasant. Interestingly enough, women also are included by Rodó in this beauty, as if they too could be rare birds, populating the "crónicas de Gyps y cuentos de Mendes" (93).

As they reject the referential emphasis on language and turn away from "realism" and civic poetry, the *modernista* poets idealize poetry as a striving toward beauty and the ideal. The cult of the exotic, the emphasis on sonority, the enrichment of poetic meter, the delight in verbal play for its own sake, helped create for the *modernistas* a self-containment for poetry, setting it off from the everyday, communicative functions of language.[47]

By attributing conscious moral decisions to each artistic gesture of its practitioners, critics have either condemned, defended, or condoned the *modernista* production with its context of "modernization." Yet there is another way out of this dilemma. If we analyze modernity and *modernismo* not as separate and parallel systems, but as exchange systems, we may examine how such new systems of production are entwined with new systems of representation. In the midst of the shifting systems of representation and the fascination with the new products of science and industry, the *modernistas* encountered a perplexing situation. Exposed, by means of greater communication to the images of modernity, nevertheless, it is clearly apparent that the Spanish American did not share fully in the production of such novelties. Roberto González Echevarría gives us the kernel of this uneasy dilemma:

> Si Hispanoamérica es nueva por autonomasia, ¿cómo puede fundarse una modernidad sin historia, sin la densidad de pasado y evolución requerida para la 'ruptura'? El carácter más sobresaliente de la modernidad en Hispanoamérica es la conciencia que ésta tiene de su falsedad. Si la modernidad, según Octavio Paz, es sinónimo de crítica y se identifica con el cambio, la modernidad en Hispanoamérica se caracteriza más por su fragilidad, de la cual tiene conocimiento.[48]

> (If Spanish America is new by autonomy, how can modernity be founded without history, without the density of the past and the evolution required for the "breakthrough"? The most striking characteristic of modernity in Spanish America is its awareness of its falseness. If modernity, according to Octavio Paz, is synonymous with criticism and is identified with change, then modernity in Spanish America is characterized more by its fragility, of which it is aware.)

González Echevarría also notes the proliferation of sign–objects in *modernismo:*

> El lenguaje modernista es moderno porque es un lenguaje que destaca su desconexión crítica del mundo de las cosas, e insiste en esa desconexión poniendo de manifiesto no ya los mecanismos de su propia producción, sino sobre todo el carácter de producto que el mismo tiene (de ahí la abundancia de lugares comunes en la poesía modernista). Las cosas proliferan, pero precisamente porque aparecen no en una red de relaciones que reflejan la realidad, sino en un código inmediato, poético, que las conjuga. La hipóstasis temática de este fenómeno se encuentra en la escandalosa artificialidad del ambiente creado por el modernismo. Todo artificio es producto, no naturaleza; producto, no proceso. (159)

> (*Modernista* language is modern because it is a language which highlights its lack of critical connection to the world of things, and insists upon this lack of connection, no longer making manifest the mechanisms of its own production, but above all its character of product [and thus the abundance of commonplaces in *modernista* poetry]. Things proliferate, but precisely because they appear not in a net of relations which reflect reality, but in an immediate, poetic code which joins them together. The thematic hypostasis of this phenomenon is found in the scandalous artificiality of setting created by *modernismo*. Every artifice is production, not nature; product, not process.)

Modernity, then, enters as a reflection of the industrial world's fabricated nature. *Modernista* art reflects a fascination with the possibility of the endless reproduction of an image.[49] Machine power is certainly one of *modernismo*'s later topics, although references to it are often shrouded in another kind of language.[50] However, the fascination with a new technological order took many stances, often ambivalent ones. Given concrete historical circumstances, it must be noted that such references to new technologies were often part of stylistics rather than a reflection of local realities, since the industrialization and modernization of Spanish America was by no means consistent in different countries.[51] Saúl Yurkiévich in *Celebración del modernismo* has taken an innovative approach to this topic in *modernista* and *postmodernista* poetry, noting even the emergence of the

modern tourist in late *modernismo* as an extension of its fascina-
tion with *cosmopolitismo* and the rapidly increasing possibilities of
travel.[52]

Aníbal González in "La escritura modernista y la filología"
examines *modernismo*'s spirit of critical inquiry along with its cos-
mopolitanism and relationship to philology in the nineteenth
century. As examples, he offers the works of José Martí and
Rubén Darío to illustrate the highly self-conscious nature of *mod-
ernismo*'s productions. Far from being innocent consumers of a
European series of productions (valued more highly because of
their origin), these poets, sharing in the critical tradition of philol-
ogy and science, offered up their own literary productions as an
affirmation of this "Yo organizador" that sought to integrate,
within a new aestheticism, the multiple strains of both mythic
and scientific inheritance. Striving toward an eclecticism of sev-
eral foreign cultures and literary movements, they also reor-
dered scientific information. The critical stance of the *modernistas*
was more encompassing than is generally believed. They sought
to refound literature in its vital connection with the natural
world and to discover its secret basic harmonies, its underlying
organic structure. According to González, literature attempts to
hide its mimesis of this scientificism, substituting the idea of the
studio for the laboratory and the interior private space for the
study.[53] Although the fascination with new technologies is mani-
fested by a new level of technical perfection and by the use of
images from the industrial world, poetry seeks to disguise its
presence with a veil of mysticism.

LITERARY MAGAZINES

From all over Spanish America writers circulated ideas and
formed a network of exchange by means of the many literary
magazines founded during this period, in addition to those that
combined political statement as well. The two most important
centers of publications were Mexico City and Buenos Aires.
Among the most important magazines were the *Revista Azul* and
Revista Moderna of Mexico, and *Revista de América* of Buenos
Aires.[54] Rubén Darío, who along with Jaimes Freyre founded

the short-lived *Revista de América*, best exemplifies the lifelong commitment to the principles of art espoused by *modernismo*.

Selections from *Revista de América* illustrate the direction which the *modernistas* postulated for their production. "Nuestros propósitos" ("Our Purposes"), the opening statement of 1894, expressed a striving toward a pure form of art combined with more utilitarian goals.[55] Though these ideals seem to be contradictory, they represent the special amalgam that *modernismo* formed from its European sources. Despite their insistence on being the enemies of utilitarianism and other manifestations of positivist thought, the manifesto clearly shows a dialectic between the ideals of an art striving toward pure form and an awareness of the role of the artist in society. Although the aim expressed is that of a quasi-religious striving toward ideal perfection in art, the terminology has a utilitarian and combative import: "ser el vínculo" ("to be the link"), "combatir" ("combat"), "levantar la bandera" ("raise the flag"), "visible esfuerzo" ("visible effort"). This crusade, despite its direction toward realms of art and regions or dream, retains a sense of place, time, and political motivation.

Although stressing the merits of innovation to revive poetic traditions deadened by lifeless imitation, the possibilities of the "Nuevo Mundo" are inextricably linked with a past, though partly buried, tradition. According to most of the *modernista* generation, the responsibility to develop or mine these treasures is in the hands of the intellectual aristocracy, the group formed within a strong poetic tradition. Instead of a break, this change in poetic process is to involve a new focus. Significantly, the direction of the crusading impulse is inward-turning, to better recover elements from a distant past, as well as the outward turning to exotic realms of legend and history.

The notions of mission and combat—the holy crusade—are constants in the poetic manifestoes of the *modernistas*. They view their role not as visionaries who have chosen isolation but as prophets who have been forcefully removed from certain spheres by their enemies, the forces of utilitarianism and bourgeois conservatism. Darío speaks of the need in America for spiritual and artistic concerns to combat these forces:

En nuestras repúblicas latinas, el viento de la mediocridad sopla
sobre el alma criolla. Nuestras sociedades recién formadas no se
cuidan del alma; el Arte no puede tener vida en donde la Religión
va perdiendo terreno, y en donde el Lucro y la Politíca hinchan
cada día más sus enormes vientres.[56]

(In our Latin republics, the wind of mediocrity blows over the
Creole spirit. Our recently formed societies don't take care of the
spirit; Art cannot have life where Religion is losing ground, and
where Profit and Politics swell up their enormous bellies more ev-
ery day.)

THE PROBLEMATIC HERITAGE OF EUROPEAN
ROMANTICISM AND SYMBOLISM

Despite *modernismo*'s connections with the legacy of romanti-
cism, a closer look shows a refusal of many of romanticism's
values. This legacy is more in the spirit of the monstrosity of
Victor Hugo, in the suspended time of Baudelaire, than in
Wordsworth's or Coleridge's attempts to mingle mind and na-
ture. It singles out oddity, distorts organic form, and exalts
discontinuity.

The spatial dimensions of *modernista* scenes give an idea of
the rearrangement of values that romanticism linked with or-
ganic form. The mountain and the abyss are more likely to
appear in miniature form (perhaps enclosed in a Parnassian
literary landscape painting with their scale reduced to manage-
able terms). Single figures draw the focus, rather than pan-
oramic scenes.[57] As scenic description highlights the fragment,
it moves away from organic unities.

A distinguishing feature of *modernista* aesthetics is the inclu-
sion of all the arts in theories of artistic creation. The creative
function can express itself through music, the plastic arts, and
literature, especially poetry. Creative power is bestowed on cer-
tain individuals as a mysterious gift, enabling them to perceive
the series of concordances between nature, humanity, and divin-
ity. From this concept arises the belief in the natural aristocracy
of the artist. The *modernista* concept of the artist as one who is
divinely inspired and who possesses the gift of perceiving the
interrelationship of nature and spirit, has its roots in romanti-

cism.[58] Though the *modernistas* responded directly to many doctrines of the symbolists, they were responding at the same time to the influence of the romantics. Many of the social doctrines of romanticism, received quite differently in Spanish America at an earlier stage, were partially incorporated along with later doctrines.[59]

The doctrines of romanticism were a primary factor in the later development of the concepts of the poet and poetic function, and the work of Victor Hugo was central to this development. René Wellek stresses the powerful influence of Hugo in European romanticism:

> In Hugo, then, all the romantic convictions and themes are summarized: organic, evolving nature, the view of poetry as prophecy, the view that symbol and myth are the instruments of poetry. In Hugo the reconciliation of opposites, the stress on the grotesque and evil ultimately absorbed in the harmony of the universe, is particularly clear even in his early aesthetic theories, as in the preface to *Cromwell* . . . the romantic view of nature, the great scale of nature, and the final perfection, man.[60]

Victor Hugo's work, so important for later poets, has a long history in Latin America.[61] Yet Hugo's influence is not as often recognized in *modernista* poetics. Among the *modernistas*, Salvador Díaz Mirón is most often mentioned as his main disciple. Because of the impact of his work on the leaders and poets of the nineteenth century (such as Echeverría and, later, Víctor Andrade and Sarmiento), his work was transmitted through a long literary heritage in Spanish America. The call for liberty, the allegory of nature, and the role of the poet as prophet[62] had a special meaning in the years of the formation of national entities. As will be shown in the discussion of Lugones' early work, Hugo's ideas on the function of poetry left an important and unmistakable stamp on Lugones, as well as on other *modernista* poets.

Romantic writings on the controlling principles of poetic creation and interest in the symbolic power of mythology showed a tendency to create an allegory of the spirit by means of natural and mythological symbols. In romanticism, a secular theology of language joined with concepts of human creativity and genius. The artist was to be not only artisan but a force for human-

ity as well. The particular turns of these doctrines in different
historical contexts have been explored in the European context.
Both René Wellek and Julia Kristeva have examined the differ-
ent results in Germany and France of the romantic adherence
to the doctrines of organic unity and Genius. Wellek compares
the German movement to its French counterpart and notes that
romanticism in Germany was far more pervasive than in other
countries, affecting all human endeavors: "Romanticism was
more completely victorious in Germany than elsewhere for very
obvious historical reasons. German romanticism, more so than
English and French, was the movement of an intelligentsia
which had loosened its class ties and hence was particularly apt
to create a literature remote from ordinary reality and social
concerns."[63] Julia Kristeva also points to the importance of the
realignment of social structures in the development of romanti-
cism and symbolism. She points to the social base of romanti-
cism and its heritage in the work of later poets such as Lautréa-
mont and Mallarmé, noting the contradictions involved in their
adoption of models. Of particular importance is the redefini-
tion of the position of the individual subject with regard to
language, sexuality, and the group:

> Ainsi, les sympathies symbolistes et celles de Mallarmé vont aller
> de la droite libérale à l'anarchisme, uniquement dans la mesure où
> ces mouvements politiques exigent des recompositions et des rup-
> tures de la chaîne des institutions bourgeoises, et par la même
> supposent—ou laissent supposer—une levée et une dialectisation
> des inhibitions concernant le sujet dans son rapport à la langue, à
> la sexualité, au groupe.

> Cette situation de l'Etat bourgeois détermine *en dernière instance*
> l'aspect libertaire, anti-étatique et anti-nationaliste de l'avant-garde
> française depuis cette époque, quelles que soient les variations de
> ses positions politiques concrètes à travers les partis et les mouve-
> ments constitués, des libéraux aux anarchistes. Mallarmé assume
> cette situation, et s'il est amene à glorifier l'élitisme et à fétichiser
> parfois l' "oeuvre" d'art, ces phénomènes sont les formes histor-
> iques que prend la nécessité d'une phase thétique pour la disposi-
> tion du procès en texte, mais ne deviennent jamais une idéologie
> oppressive, étatique ou nationaliste. Lautréamont . . . positivité par
> un appel au classicisme et au rationalisme . . . ne devient jamais une
> apologie de l'autorité.[64]

(Thus, symbolist sympathies and those of Mallarmé move from the liberal right to anarchism, only to the extent to which these political movements require reconstitution and breaking the chain of bourgeois institutions, and by the same token imply a breaking up and a dialectic of the inhibitions regarding the subject in its relation to language, sexuality, and the group.

This situation of the bourgeois State determined *in the last instance* the libertarian, anti-state and anti-nationalist aspect of the French avant-garde since that period, whatever the variations of its concrete political positions across the established parties and movements, from the liberals to the anarchists. Mallarmé assumed this situation, and if he was led to exalt elitism and sometimes the fetishize the work of art, these phenomena are the historic forms which the necessity of a thetic phase takes for the disposition of the textual process, but which never become an oppressive ideology, statist or nationalist. Lautréamont ... positivized by an appeal to classicism and to rationalism ... never became an apologist for authority.)

Kristeva's remarks are particularly relevant for a discussion of the exaltation of art itself in *modernista* practices. If one accepts her explanation of the fetishization of art as a reordering of the hierarchies of discourse patterns, larger meanings associated with the exaltation of art and the preference for aristocratic models emerge:

Le modèle aristocratique, féodal, pour autant qu'il est fondé sur une hiérarchie et préservé ainsi des enclos pour les expériences diversifiées des sujets, séduit Mallarmé, en l'apparentant ainsi à Renan.... La hiérarchie est donc nécessaire pour maintenir le conflit (la contradiction): seul producteur d'un sujet libre qui 'tient debout.'[65]

(The aristocratic, feudal model, inasmuch as it is founded on a hierarchy and is preserved thus for the different experiences of the subjects, seduced Mallarmé, linking him thus to Renan.... Hierarchy is then necessary in order to maintain the conflict [the contradiction: the sole producer of a free subject who "stands upright").

In the same way, the adoption of often conflicting symbolic systems of natural and mythological imagery creates contradictory impressions on reading *modernista* texts. Yet within romantic and *modernista* doctrines, such contradictions are to be resolved through the particular visionary power of the poet. By controlling language, poets might return to the source of thought by creating increasingly complex metaphors. The transmission of the metaphors would have a shaping force on a reading public's personal systems of analogy. With their special gifts, such poets were to transmit radically different ways of perception.

The romantic analogy of progress and light, favored by many of the *modernistas,* was rejected by others. The spirit of the decadents—largely transmitted by the writings of J. K. Huysmans, Gabriele D'Annunzio, Oscar Wilde, the paintings of Gustave Moreau, and the engravings of Félicien Rops (especially the illustrations of Baudelaire's poetry)—appealed to many as the reverse side of the coin of technological progress and rationalism. The exotic underworlds of the spirit, usually tinged with satanism, threatening eroticism, and the macabre, presented an alternative to the didactic or sentimental type of poetry offered by the *modernistas'* Spanish and Spanish American predecessors. By turning to another realm of the spirit, the *modernistas* avowed their transgression of public standards of morality, asserting at the same time the primacy of interiority over outwardly established canons of conduct and taste. For some, like Jaimes Freyre, this was a return to a distant past of mythology or medieval legend; for others, as in the early work of Rubén Darío, it was first an evocation of the eighteenth-century landscape and court scene in the style of paintings by Watteau. For others, such as José Asunción Silva and Julián del Casal, Baudelaire's dream landscape and Edgar Allan Poe's unearthly visions represented the new frontier. Baudelaire's exaltation of the dandy and the cult of self found many followers, for example Julio Herrera y Reissig, while for Amado Nervo, religious symbols provided access to a mystical realm. Some poets, such as José Juan Tablada, favored the iconography of the Orient. The *modernistas* generally renounced the goal of material progress and turned away from explicit nature references to a stylized allegorical realm.

Music and color received high priority in the synesthetic experiments of the *modernistas*. Combining the symbolist theories of language and music with the Parnassian concern for form, they sought to obtain the perfect mingling of form and content. The symbolist and Parnassian iconographies of color, especially those found in the work of Leconte de Lisle and Théophile Gautier and later in the work of Paul Verlaine, are present throughout much of *modernista* verse. The poetry of Rubén Darío best represents this attention to perfection of form and synesthetic experimentation. The subtle shadings of color, the focus on symmetry, and the attention to details of objects replace the significance of the objects themselves, and much more attention is given to nonnatural imagery. Objects and scenes described are chosen from a special range of scenes that are weighted with codes of meaning. Natural phenomena such as sunsets, lakes, and reflections on ancient monuments are stylized according to established procedures. Gautier's Parnassian precept of "Sculpte, lime, cisèle" ("Sculpt, polish, chisel") found followers in poets such as Rubén Darío, Gutiérrez Nájera, Julián del Casal, Leopoldo Lugones, Julio Herrera y Reissig, and others. This precept led away from the extended poem to shorter sketches, like those of Verlaine's landscapes.

THE LANGUAGE OF *MODERNISMO*

Seeing the preceding generation's interest in the past as a conservative tendency, it is not surprising that the *modernistas* would turn away from those models, since their social values were not aligned with those of the previous controlling classes. Many critics of the period saw the inclination toward Europe as a betrayal of an indigenous line of evolution, a series of copying, rather than of original inventions. For example, Paul Groussac, in his review of *Los raros* by Rubén Darío, criticized the reverence for French writers. He saw such admiration as another step in a long line of cultural dependency:

> ¿Qué podría valer su brusca inoculación a la literatura española que no ha sufrido las diez evoluciones anteriores a la francesa, y vive todavía poco menos que de imitaciones y reflejos, ya propios, ya extraños?. . . El arte americano será original—o no será.[66]

(What value could there be in its brusque injection into Spanish
literature, which has not [yet] suffered the ten evolutions previous
to the French one, and still lives on little more than imitations and
reflections, sometimes its own, sometimes foreign?. . . American
art will be original—or it won't exist at all.)

In *modernista* theory and practice, newly revived poetic theo-
ries are tempered by local realities. There are not two clear
stages of *modernismo,* one being an idealistic, escapist stage, and
the other a sudden awareness of the potentialities of the Ameri-
can idiom. For the *modernistas,* the preoccupation with formal
beauty involves a notion of the projection of these ideal forms
onto the structure of society by means of language.

Attention to innovative form is the one characteristic of *mod-
ernismo* that is clearly distinguishable in its main practitioners.
Whether based on symbolist precepts of synesthetic correspon-
dence or on a desire for experimental surprise and innovation,
formal dexterity constitutes an indispensable characteristic of
modernismo.

José Lezama Lima speaks of the importance of formal defini-
tion in any epoch:

> Y la adquisición de una forma o de un reino, está situada dentro del
> absoluto de la libertad. Sólo se relatan los sucesos de los reyes, se
> dice en la Biblia, es decir, los que han alcanzado una forma, la
> unidad, el reino. La forma alcanzada es el símbolo de la permanen-
> cia de la ciudad. Su soporte, su esclarecimiento, su compostura.[67]

> (And the acquisition of a form or of a kingdom is situated inside the
> absolute of liberty. Only the events of kings are related, the Bible
> says; that is, those who have achieved a form, a unity, the kingdom.
> Form achieved is the symbol of the permanence of the city. Its base,
> its merit, its dignity.)

Attention to form, above all, innovative form, and the impor-
tance assigned to the nature of poetic language are the two
concerns that occupy central place in *modernista* poetics.[68] These
concerns overshadow thematic changes, and poetry becomes its
own reason for existence. Like other aspects of the movement,
the changes in poetic theory arise from an expanded percep-

tion of contemporary issues and a revival of former values. *Modernismo* differs most strikingly from its literary predecesors in its view of language itself. A constant in the poetics outlined by its exponents is the insistence on the specific nature of poetic language as opposed to language of everyday use. The reading public is perceived as humanity in general, as a brotherhood, and the poet as its redemptive voice.

The romantics had stressed the primacy of imagination in poetry, and other artists seized on this concept of the power of sensory freedom as a way to knowledge. Rimbaud and Lautréamont are prime examples. Rimbaud's figure of poet–seer is based on conscious dislocation of sensory perception: "[L]e poète se fait voyant par un long, immense et raisonné dérèglement de tous les sens" ("The poet becomes a seer through a long, immense and methodical disordering of all the senses"). Gustave Moreau, whose symbolist paintings offers a rich fund of iconography for *modernista* poets (especially for Julián del Casal),[69] perhaps as powerful an influence as that of the symbolists, adhered to the rule of imagination rather than reason. The improbable figures and visions presented by the painters of the latter half of the nineteenth century are linked to some of the same sources that poets drew from, and have their origins in much of romantic art. The Swedenborgian vision that inspired William Blake in the latter half of the eighteenth century also influenced many others.

In contrast to the civic, outwardly directed messages found in Spanish and Spanish American romanticism, *modernismo*, in its rediscovery of the romantics and the discovery of the symbolists, focused on human interiority, which is seen to be physiologically and spiritually connected to an outer reality. In discussing the poets of *modernismo* Amado Nervo emphasizes the special nature of the poet and the role of introspection in learning to see the interrelationship of outward things:

> Pero los sentidos de la especie, singularmente los sentidos del poeta, que es el ser representativo, por excelencia, de la humanidad, se han ido afinando y hemos empezado a ver "hacia dentro." Hemos comprendido que las montañas, el mar, los astros no son más que grandes aglomeraciones de materia o grandes

equilibrios de fuerza. . . . Que, por último, todas las cosas tienen
una fisonomía especial, un alma, una vida poderosísima; que es
necesario, en el sistema del espíritu, pegar el oído al vasto pecho
de la tierra para escuchar los cien mil latidos de sus cien mil
corazones; y que seguir cantando al mar, a la montaña, al cielo,
así, en bruto, sin contemplar sus tenues e infinitas estructuras
maravillosas, sus variadísimas modalidades, la innumeridad de sus
matices y el milagroso enredo de sus afinidades secretas, es ofen-
der al cielo, al mar y a la montaña.[70]

(But the species' senses, singularly the poet's senses—who is the
representative being, par excellence, of humanity—have been re-
fined and we have begun to look "within." We have come to
understand that the mountains, the sea, the stars are nothing
more than great agglomerations of material or great equilibriums
of force. . . . That, ultimately, all things have a special physiog-
nomy, a soul, a very powerful life; that it is necessary, in the
system of the spirit, to place one's ear to the vast breast of the
earth to listen to the hundred thousand heartbeats of its hundred
thousand hearts; and that to continue singing to the sea, to the
mountain, to the sky in that way, in a rough manner, without
contemplating their tenuous and infinite marvelous structures,
their extremely varied modes of being, their innumerable shades
and the miraculous intertwining of their secret affinities, is to
offend the sky, the sea and the mountain.)

Poetry is to be estranged from all other forms of writing, by
virtue of not being used as a measure of exchange. The poet, by
using as his material the world's form of exchange, enters into a
problematic and paradoxical relationship to it. The poet deals
with worldly materials but seeks to transcend them. On a cer-
tain level, this refusal to use words for their practical exchange
value, or communicative usage, deprives the poet of an active
participatory function in external reality.

Edgar Allan Poe is often quoted by the *modernista* poets in
support of their poetic ideals. He stresses the nonreferential
aspects of language, comparing poetry to music rather than to
other denotative systems:

It is in Music, perhaps, that the soul most nearly attains the great end
for which, when inspired by the Poetic Sentiment, it struggles—the

creation of supernal beauty. . . . I would define, in brief, the poetry of words as the Rhythmical Creation of Beauty. Its sole arbiter is Taste. With the intellect or with the Conscience it has only collateral relations. Unless incidentally it has no concern whatever either with Duty or with Truth.[71]

Not only was Poe's poetry influential, but his theories of poetry were in wide circulation. Defined by Poe, poetry owes no acknowledgment to the outside world for its aims; as in romantic definitions, the role of the poet is bestowed by carpicious destiny. Unlike some romantic ideals, however, for Poe the poet's responsibility does not extend outward toward a greater public.[72] By its self-reflexive nature, it presumes no larger sphere of influence than its own self-contained world.

Baudelaire, whose work almost all the *modernistas* adapted and admired, emphasized the higher powers that are an attribute of the poet:

Il y a dans le mot, dans le *verbe*, quelque chose de *sacré* qui nous défend d'en faire un jeu de hasard. Manier savamment une langue, c'est pratiquer une espèce de sorcellerie évocatoire.[73]

(In the word, in the *Word*, there is something *sacred* that prevents making it into a game of chance. To handle a language wisely is to practice a type of evocative sorcery.)

Poetry is a sacred rite. Deriving from an inner source, its practice and message are not to be judged by utilitarian standards. The theory of pure poetry, the idea of transforming external signs or objects into a new pattern to conform with a wholly new internal reality, has Mallarmé as its foremost exponent:

Narer, enseigner, même décrire, cela va et encore qu'à chacun suffirait peut-être pour échanger la pensée humaine, de prendre ou de mettre dans la main d'autrui en silence une pièce de monnaie, l'emploie élémentaire du discours dessert l'universel *reportage* dont, la littérature exceptée, participe tout entre les genres d'écrits contemporains. . . . Au contraire d'une fonction de numéraire facile et représentatif, comme le traite d'abord la foule, le dire, avant tout, rêve et chant, retrouve chez le Poète, par nécessité constitutive d'un art consacré aux fictions, sa virtualite.[74]

(To narrate, point out, even to describe is fine, and for exchanging human thought, perhaps it would be sufficient for each one to take or put a coin silently in the hand of another. The elemental use of discourse communicates the universal reportage in which all genres of contemporary writings, with the exception of literature, participate. . . . In contrast with an easy and representative numeric structure, as the masses treat it in the first place, speech, above all dream and song, recovers in the poet its virtuality, by the necessity of an art dedicated to fictions.)

For Darío the word is not a means of expressing set ideals but is enmeshed in an underlying world consciousness, like music, which is nonreferential and only acquires referential or signifying power by an externally imposed scheme of values. Poetry is linked to problems of life and death: "El don de arte es un don superior que permite entrar en lo desconocido de antes y en lo ignorado de después, en el ambiente de ensueño o de la meditación"[75] ("The gift of art is a superior gift that allows entrance into what is unknown previously and afterward, into the atmosphere of dream or meditation"). The art of poetry, of evocation, is a gift, a superior gift bestowed by grace, not by a set of circumstances or an application to cultivation of forms:

En el principio está la palabra como única representación. No simplemente como signo, puesto que no hay antes nada que representar. En el principio está la palabra como manifestación de la unidad infinita, pero ya conteniéndola. *Et verbum erat Deus.*

La palabra no es en sí más que un signo, o una combinación de signos; mas la contiene todo por su virtud demiúrgica.[76]

(In the beginning is the word as sole representation. Not simply as a sign, since there is nothing beforehand to represent. In the beginning is the word as manifestation of infinite unity, yet already containing it. *El verbum erat Deus.*

The word in itself is nothing more than a sign, or a combination of signs; yet it contains everything due to its demiurgic virtue.)

Darío's unending search for the perfect form to express the enigmatic fusion of spirit and matter often contrasts with the practices of other *modernistas*. Poets such as Lugones and Herrera y Reissig strenuously point to the failing mechanics of their works and lead the reader to question the steadfastness of its spiritual cornerstones. They break with a world view profoundly influenced by romanticism and its artistic legacy. While Darío laments the discordant elements that disturb the harmonic universe, other poets seize upon them and generate a new poetics, a process that parallels early twentieth-century music's fascination with dissonance and atonality.

Lugones too points out the superior, sacred nature of language and its powers of symbolic expression. But it is its use–value that determines its sacred or profane powers, not its inherent qualities: "Sagrada prenda es la lengua. . . . Pero es al mismo tiempo infame instrumento que degüella y envenena, cuando el alma que la mueve ha descendido hasta la rabia contra el ideal"[77] ("Language is a sacred gift. . . . But it is at the same time a vile instrument that beheads and poisons, when the spirit that moves it has descended into rage against the ideal"). For Lugones, language being an instrument, its use can be cultivated. A richly expressive language can be acquired not only by natural gifts but by incessant study. Verbal equivalents for all emotions may be found with proper application:

> Hay que poseer, ante todo, una lengua rica, superlativamente rica, hasta el extremo de que ninguna emoción se quede sin su expresión real y verdadera. Una lengua rica, y sobre todo, una lengua propia. (*PL* [1897] in "Negro y oro")

> (One must possess, above all, a rich language, superlatively rich, to such an extreme that no emotion remains without its real and true expression. A rich language, and above all, one's own language.)

This emphasis on the necessary richness of poetic language, the belief in the possibility of extracting the exact expression to express any given emotion, best characterizes the nature of Lugones' poetry. It is also the quality in this verse that has attracted the attention of his most fervent admirers and critics. By directing attention to language as a technical instrument, Lugones initiates a dissonant trend in modern Spanish American poetry.

2
LUGONES: POETRY, IDEOLOGY, HISTORY

The literary productions and public activities of Leopoldo Lugones are vast in scope. He wrote eleven volumes of poetry, and his work in prose—novels, histories, biographies, short stories, journalistic prose, translations, and philological studies—is even more diverse. In addition to his writing career, he was a public school official and librarian. In politics he was active as a socialist in his youth, but he later moved from the left to fascism, defending an authoritarian state based on militarism culminating in his now infamous speech, "La hora de la espada."

An overview of the poetic works of Lugones produces amazement in many readers at such producitivity, virtuosity, and technical skill. At the same time there arises a certain distrust for the craftsman who could house so many different types of creation beneath one roof. Lugones' eager acceptance of other literary models, his frequent borrowings or copyings from other writers, and their displacement in different contexts combines to make his work seem willfully contrived. In addition, the sometimes grudging acclaim accorded Lugones results not only from his multiple literary poses but also from his rapidly changing ideological stances. The diversity of the poetry of Lugones raises the question of the proper critical viewpoint. Is there a unifying personality behind the creative process, or is his work merely a succession of very skilled copyings and reworkings of the material offered to Lugones by his epoch? These questions have been posed ceaselessly by his critics since the first publication of his works. Yet perhaps this is the wrong approach, that is, the concept of a single unifying presence of author throughout. These texts instead may be analyzed as the productions of a creative mind in convergence with the cultural and literary codes of his day. Different codes are combined, transgressed, and transformed by a series of acceptances and rejections. The work of Lugones is best studied within the context of his epoch, by noting the reception of his work and the network of mutual influences. For a writer such as Lugones, who delights in the mysterious aspects of poetry and who wholeheartedly accepts the daimonic powers attributed to its execution, the principles and practices of the code of *modernismo* are a garden of delights. Avidly striving to extend to its limits each convention he adopts, he manipulates *modernismo*'s varieties of symbols into a series of experiments within a hothouse atmosphere. In his crossing of different strains of poetic inheritance, Lugones creates strange hybrids. Like the self-generating process of growth, Lugones' productions point back on themselves, reflecting not only their origins but their differences from their models. Among the new productions are creations of exceptional concision and beauty, as well as mutations that seem grotesque by their heightening of certain features, such as rhyme, to the exclusion of others.

In choosing model texts from different contexts and re-arranging them within other contextual system, *modernista* poets did not adopt the total array of meanings associated with a particular sign. In the move from one language to another, from one culture to another, and from an immediate literary text to another, many associations clustered around a particular image or ideogram are lost or rearranged, and new ones emerge. For example, certain groups of images in Lugones' early work function as automatic signs, signaling a previously established thematic function. These signs operate not only within his particular aesthetic system but relate as well to the conventions of a total cultural system. In tracing the sign system of Lugones to previous and coexisting ones, as well as tracing the pattern of perception and rearrangement of these sign systems, it must be remembered that certain signs may be emptied of their original content and forced to function as different signals in a different context. It is the pattern of rearrangement and displacement of previously coded signs (and not the continuous presence of the signs themselves) that reveals constants.[1] For example, the same codes of eroticism and physical beauty were used by many *modernista* poets, yet their presence in Lugones' poetry is frequently used for different purposes, as is the presence of natural or technological imagery. The presence of certain codes of imagery is not necessarily the mark of an organically evolving individual system. Always eager to create an impact with his writings, Lugones sought out culturally approved models, particularly foreign ones, on which to pattern his own productions. Exaggeration and elaboration of given patterns are his favored methods for achieving novelty, and he often seems to unwittingly destroy his own foundation by ranging too far from his starting point. Rather than overt self-expression, one finds in Lugones' poetry a type of ritualized expression. Speaking from the vantage point of first one platform, then another, the succession of stances creates an aura of impersonality.

CRITICAL ATTITUDES TOWARD LUGONES

Lugones' writings have provoked a body of criticism that is astounding in the extremes of its passionate acclaim or derision. Appraisals of his work reflect the contradictory impulses that led to his disconcerting mixture of all the models available to him. Impersonality, virtuosity, and farce are the characteristics most often attributed to Lugones' work. Although his work has undeniably influenced many other writers, his readers have often labeled him as a gigantic misdirected talent. Roberto F. Giusti's review of *Lunario sentimental* in 1909 shows a negative reaction to the effort to achieve constant novelty: "¿Cuál es la personalidad literaria de Lugones? Difícil es contestarlo por la simple razón que no [la] tiene"[2] ("What is Lugones' literary personality? It is a difficult question to answer due to the simple fact that he lacks one"). Giusti speaks disparagingly of the heterogeneity of the work, singling out a trait that links Lugones to an important aspect of the *modernista* movement: "Será la suya una continuada labor de mosaísta, empeñado en pavimentar sus estrofas con sólo expresiones absolutamente novedosas, nunca usadas"[3] ("His will be the continuous labor of a mosaicist, bent on paving his stanzas with only absolutely novel, never-used expressions"). Other contemporaries praised the virtuosity, power, and encyclopedic knowledge of Lugones' verse, but they also pointed out the multitude of apparent models and the flaunting of erudition. In 1910, Amado Nervo reappraised *Las montañas del oro*, defending it for its force, despite the volume's obvious derivative nature:

> No hay alma de artista que no sea dinástica, y a cada uno podemos encontrarle su genealogía; las influencias son mutuas, se compenetran, se enredan, se ligan. Estamos todos influídos por todos; pero, aún así, vamos amasando cada uno nuestra personalidad. Y la de Lugones es poderosa, la más poderosa de nuestra América. ¿A qué incurrir en la petulancia infantil de analizar sus lecturas? El lo ha leído todo, las ajenas influencias, las varias reminiscencias, las leves e íntimas sugestiones de sabios, de poetas, de artistas, se entrechocan en su espíritu con las propias y múltiples ideas.[4]

> (There is not an artist whose soul is not dynastic, and for each one we can trace a genealogy; influences are mutual, they are shared, intertwined, joined together. Although we are influenced by one another, we continue to develop our own personality. Lugones' personality is powerful, the most powerful in our America. Why concur in the childish petulance of analyzing his readings? He has read it all; the outside influences, the variety of reminiscences, the trivial and intimate suggestions of sages, poets, and artists clash in his soul with his own and diverse ideas.)

Rubén Darío is equally extravagant in his praise for the early work of Lugones. Like Nervo, he considers Lugones' work as evidence of a new spirit in the young generation of Spanish America. The bonds of a mutually supportive fraternity of artists are as evident as his critical viewpoint when he records his first impressions of Lugones in 1896:

> Es uno de los *modernos*, es uno de los "Joven América". El y Ricardo Jaimes Freyre son los dos más fuertes talentos que siguen los pabellones nuevos en el continente. Mi pobre y glorioso hermano Julián del Casal hubiera amado mucho a este hermano menor que se levanta en la exuberancia de sus ardores valientes y masculinos, obsedido por una locura de ideal. Sigue los pabellones por ser su temperamento de artista puro, su espíritu violento vibrante, su vocación manifiesta e invencible para padecer bajo el poder de los Pilatos de la mediocridad.[5]

(He is one of the "moderns", he is part of "Young America". He and Ricardo Jaimes Freyre are the two most forceful talents to follow the new banners of the continent. My dear and glorious brother Julián del Casal would have greatly loved his younger brother, who, obsessed by the madness of an ideal, arises with the exuberance of his brave and masculine zeal. He follows the banners due to his temperament of a pure artist, his violent and vibrant spirit, his evident and invincible vocation to suffer under the power of some Pilate of mediocrity.)

Both Nervo and Darío stress Lugones' spirit, artistry, and power as a creator, and Darío takes note of the vibrant and violent aspects of his spirit. Many writers, however, have not seen these same traits united in Lugones' poetry. Ezequiel Martínez Estrada uses the criterion of sincerity when he comments on Lugones' use of language as a logical instrument:

> Lugones ha sido siempre así; ha negado en su obra, subconscientemente, los impulsos secretos y dominantes de su alma. Le vemos variar, contradecirse, pero jamás le vemos expresarse con absoluta sinceridad.[6]

> (Lugones has always been that way, denying unconsciously in his work the dominant and secret impulses of his soul. We see him change and contradict himself, but we never see him express himself with absolute sincerity.)

The fact that different generations see Lugones so differently has, obviously, much to do with his political activity and his polemics with other writers. Yet the different criteria applied are also reflections of a differing perception of the poetic function and a changing attitude toward the notion of individuality and the necessity of its expression in poetry.

For contemporaries of Lugones, his verbal excesses create an impact lost to later readers. Ramón López Velarde, intrigued by what he calls Lugones' "lujuria de creador" ("lustfulness of the creator"), praises the theatricality of Lugones' presentations, describing the characters as "insólitos, reacios, esotéricos, híspidos"[7] ("startling, stubborn, esoteric, bristling"). Comparing Lugones' capriciousness to that of Góngora, he finds that, "El sistema poético hase convertido en sistema crítico. . . . Lo evidente y lo explícito se hacen oír con un ceceo cada vez más insufrible, y recordamos a Wilde siempre que un caballero nos reseña en letras de molde, espisodios suyos, 'con el escrúpulo de los iliteratos' " ("The poetic system has become a critical system . . . the evident and the explicit is heard with a Castilian accent that is increasingly insufferable, and we think of Wilde when a gentelman reviews, in block letters, his own stories 'with the scrupulous care of the ignorant' "). Praising what later readers have found oppressive and hackneyed, Lugones' "morbidez de estilo" ("mobidity of style"), López Velarde inspects the technique of narrowing focus which produces the voyeuristic position of the reader in *Los crepúsculos:*

> Lujuria que vale lo que un propósito a la vez minucioso e integral, como el que hay en el remanque de una falda que permite ver un pie encubierto por la lenidad de una media, y bajo la media una vena serpeando rítmica en una ladera del empeine.[8]

> (Lust that is like a design at once detailed and integral in its purpose, like that in the fold of a skirt that lets one see a foot lightly covered by a stocking and through the stocking a rhythmic, serpentine vein on the instep.)

The parceling out of detail, the fragmentation of total schemes, and the attention of gesture produce a heightening and not a deflation of pleasure for López Velarde:

> Guiños, parpadeos, esguinces, mohines . . . el gesto gradual y total de nuestra compañera recodada en las tinieblas, es para nosotros palmario como una estatua a mediodía, y permanente, como su faz. Nuestra emoción es como una linterna sorda que horada la cúbica negrura de los aposentos, a deshora. Instante novelesco, de novela centrípeta.[9]

> (Winks, fluttering, eyelashes, twistings, postures . . . the gradual and total gesture of our female companion turning in the shadows is for us as evident as a statue at midday, and permanent, like its face. Our emotion is like a dark lantern that pierces, untimely, the cubic blackness of rooms. A novelesque instant, from a centripetal novel.)

What López Velarde singles out here, the "gesto gradual" ("the gradual gesture"), which produced revelations "a deshora" ("untimely"), is a condensation process that will be speeded up in *Lunario sentimental*. There the development of gesture will be telescoped, the winks distorted to grimaces, and theatricality extended to farce and buffoonery. Viewed within the conventions of its epoch, however, these possible extensions of a style are more suggested than explicit in *Los crepúsculos del jardín*. Perspectives given from the reading of later codes, such as *ultraísmo* or surrealism, show the extent of the foreshortening process in sonnets from *Los crepúsculos del jardín* such as those included in "Los doce gozos." Later poems such as "Mi prima Agueda" by López Velarde illustrate the poetic possibilities of prosaic elements in many of the sonnets of Lugones' volume, especially "Emoción aldeana."[10]

LUGONES AND ARGENTINA

In the poetic tradition of Argentina, Lugones has been no less polemical a figure. As Carlos Altamirano and Beatriz Sarlo note in their study "Vanguardia y criollismo: La aventura de 'Martín Fierro' ": "En Lugones se aprende a escribir: los argentinos tienen que escribir como Lugones o contra él. Y ambas opciones forman una estructura" ("From Lugones one learns to write: the Argentines must write like Lugones or write against him. And both options form a structure"). In the *vanguardia* of the 1920s: "Lugones reaparece como obsesión: es a su retórica a la que hay que retorcerle el cuello, el enemigo, así como Macedonio Fernández, otro gran viejo, es el maestro" ("Lugones reappears like an obsession. It is his rhetoric that must have its neck wrung, the enemy, just like Macedonio Fernández, another great man, is the master"). For the *vanguardistas*, Lugones' work served as a symbol of a more traditional aesthetic: "Lugones, como figura en negativo, siguió siendo parte del sistema literario de la vanguardia"[11] ("Lugones, as a figure of negative force, remained a part of the literary system of the avant-garde").

A survey of the critical attitudes toward Lugones mirrors almost all the ideological and esthetic debates in Argentina throughout the century. Alfonsina Storni sums up the general attitude of her generation in discussing Lugones shortly after his death in 1938.[12] She acknowledges Lugones' power as a writer, yet shifts from a discussion of "el más alto Lugones" ("the most lofty Lugones") to his "mugido de toro"[13] (his "bull's bellow"). Recognizing him as a rejected master of a generation of poets, parenthetically she lists the lesser attributes of which he also was undisputed master:

> Rima tecnizante; mesura de la confidencia, búsqueda insistida del buen idioma; afincamiento en el tema nacional; lirismo amatorio de ordenación sacramental; influencias y apetencias eclécticas; todo esto muy argentino y en algunos puntos nada hispanoamericano.[14]

> (Technical rhyme, restraint in his use of secrecy, insistent search for good language, adscription to the national theme, amatory lyricism of a sacramental order, eclectic influences and desires: all of this very Argentine in character and in some aspects not at all Spanish-American.)

Lugones' adherence to rhyme and his insistence on certain types of versification was the basis of the *ultraístas'* rejection of much of his poetry. Although they admired the ironic and iconoclastic tone of the *Lunario* and its inventiveness, they rejected what they saw as a narrow-minded attention to form and not to spirit. Criticizing the obvious copyings from Laforgue, they derided Lugones' self-conscious defense of the introduction of these images and forms into Spanish as useful innovation. They labeled him as a master of style but a poet lacking in inspiration. Poets such as Leopoldo Marechal saw Lugones' adherence to rhyme and to clear formal definitions of poetry as evidence of the mind and spirit of a cataloguer of rhetorical tricks. In 1925 in *Martín Fierro* Marechal states:

> Lugones es un frío arquitecto de la palabra; construye albergues inhabitables para la emoción y sus versos tienen el olor malsano de las casas vacías. El ha dicho alguna vez que 'la rima es el descanso de la poesía'; yo agrego que no sólo es el descanso sino el sueño y que en sus consonantes la poesía se ha dormido para siempre.[15]

> (Lugones is a cold architect of the word; he constructs uninhabitable shelters for the emotions, and his verses have the unhealthy odor of empty houses. He once said that "rhyme is poetry's repose"; may I add that it is not only its repose but also its sleep and that poetry has fallen asleep forever in his rhymings.)

Lugones retains rhyme as poetry's last vestige of formalism, and often it dominates his poetry, drawing attention to the mechanics of his verse. Rhyme's presence in the *Lunario sentimental* illustrates the volume's importance as a bridge between earlier poetry in Spanish and the work of the *vanguardistas*, who sought to strip poetry of its formal aspects. It illustrates the "strenuous work of traditional art forms when they work toward effects which later are effortlessly obtained by the new ones."[16] The attempt to achieve simultaneity, to go against the time logic of language and to achieve the effects found later in practices such as surrealism, were only partially achieved by Lugones in the *Lunario sentimental*. The traces of formalism that defined a former type of poetry remain as a reminder of Lugones' directing principles in art. Moving in *Lunario sentimental* toward a poetry whose subject matter defies previous notions of idealism and beauty, Lugones retains the marks of tradition for its form. Other poets, less intent on retaining for poetry its elevated nature, were able to develop fully some of the techniques of the *Lunario sentimental*.

BORGES AND LUGONES

Jorge Luis Borges attributes the inclination to parody or caricature in Lugones' poetry to an overloading process. In commenting on *Los crepúsculos del jardín* he states:

> Cada adjetivo y cada verbo tiene que ser inesperado. Esto lo lleva a ser barroco, y es bien sabido que lo barroco engendra su propia parodia.[17]

> (Each adjective and each verb must be unexpected. This leads him to be baroque, and it is well known that the baroque creates its own parody.)

In an earlier article, the criticism is more explicit. Lugones' verse is a "sistema premeditado de epítetos balbucientes y adjetivos tahures"[18] (a "premeditated system of babbling epithets and gambling adjectives"). Borges' statement from "Palabrería para versos," although not in reference to Lugones' work, describes the future of the poetic practice of the *Lunario sentimental:* "El mundo aparencial es un tropel de percepciones barajadas. . . . Le lengua es edificadora de realidades"[19] ("The apparent world is a jumble of shuffled perceptions. . . . Language is the builder of realities"). The aim of the *ultraístas* was to shock the reader out of accustomed sets of perception by joining two distant categories, leaving the gap to be closed by the reader. This reconciliation was to be followed by a reordering of other categories, thus creating new ways of viewing the world. The *Lunario*'s element of surprise, its devaluation and reevalution of previous poetic hierarchies, constituted its appeal for the new group of poets. What they refused in the *Lunario,* however, was its insistence on rhyme, an element they found unnecessary, just as they saw the definition of poetry as music as unnecessary. Poetry did not have to fit into any formal patterns. It was to be an end in itself.

After *Lunario sentimental* Lugones will cling to rhyme as the last remnant of an earlier order and will turn his back on the territories into which he has ventured. These new territories—a mocking eroticism, vignettes of urban life, casual juxtaposition of unrelated categories—will be left to begin again the "titánica epopeya" (the "epic of titanic proportions"). This time its path will be more closely circumscribed, and the glories of a more parochial world will be extolled. As Lugones draws back again to achieve panoramic balance, the colloquial phrases and prosaic moments will be integrated into an encompassing view of the "patria" or "homeland." Leaving the urban scene and its open door to cosmopolitan adventure, Lugones will insist on the unification of perspectives within this local scene. He will draw together disparate elements under the composition of a grand portrait. The harmonies will be justified by their approximation to song, this time of a more local cadence.

Once an iconoclastic innovator, Lugones will become a rhymer. His poetic journey, at once the most rapid and widely ranging of any *modernista* poet, will end back at the doorstep, praising the "latinidad" (the "Latinity") of a cultural order now undergoing radical upheaval. Avid experimentation becomes dogmatic adherence to rigid aesthetic principles in his later works, a tendency hinted at in his early prose. Lugones' new paths met more success in prose than in poetry. His poetic work now begins to be received as a rigid form, serving only as an opposing force rather than as an inspiration. Despite his rejection by younger poets, however, he is nonetheless seen as the master craftsman, the perfect stylist. Some of the comments recorded in a survey by the magazine *Nosotros* in 1923 illustrate his position as an influence, even a negative one.[20] In this survey young poets were asked to discuss their literary ideals and formative influences. Time and again Lugones is mentioned as an important influence, but is also constantly disparaged as a failed talent: "Lugones es un lamentable ejemplo de claudicación y malabarismo" ("Lugones is a lamentable example of a juggler who bungles his act"). Others speak of his "dudoso gusto" ("questionable taste") and mention that, "Lugones, como poeta, no tiene personalidad, a pesar de su gran talento" ("Lugones, as a poet, lacks personality, in spite of his great talent"). Julio Noé, in his review of *El payador,* says of Lugones, "parece un eximio 'dilettante' cuya fuerza intelectual no salva los errores de sus asombrosas improvisaciones"[21] ("he resembles a distinguished 'dilettante' whose intellectual strength cannot overcome the errors of his astonishing improvisations"). Lugones, in an effort to make his poetry resistant to a cursory reading, falls prey to a self-generating parody. In faithful adherence to his models, he overloads his productions, always walking a tightrope between the truly striking and the jangling contortions of sound and imagery systems.

Jorge Luis Borges, once one of Lugones' sternest critics and more recently one of his defenders, never fails even in his most favorable statements to point out obliquely Lugones' failings. Borges has explained his debts to Lugones, his admiration for him, and even his dislike for him in diverse writings. What seems to interest Borges most about Lugones is his personality and its reflection, or suppression, in his writings, as in the statement: "El defecto de Lugones es la falta de intimidad, por eso Lugones es inferior a Darío"[22] ("The problem with Lugones is his lack of intimacy; that is why he is inferior to Darío"). Like Martínez Estrada he also comments on Lugones' use of successive styles and its distancing effect:

Lugones está, por decirlo así, un poco lejos de su obra; ésta no es casi nunca la inmediata voz de su intimidad sino un objeto elaborado por él. En lugar de la inocente expresión tenemos un sistema de habilidades, un juego de destrezas retóricas. Raras veces un sentimiento fue el punto de partida de su labor; tenía la costumbre de imponerse temas ocasionales y resolverlos mediante recursos técnicos.[23]

(Lugones, one could say, is somewhat distanced from his work; this is rarely the immediate voice of intimacy but an object elaborated by him. Instead of innocent expression we find a system of clever resources, a game of rhetorical skill. Rarely has a feeling been the point of departure for his work; he had the habit of imposing upon himself incidental themes and working them out through technical means.)

Having followed a path similar to Lugones' up to a certain point—working within highly acclaimed distant models and theorizing about literature as a world of its own which provides directing force for other systems—Borges also exaggerated his own mannered style until it could no longer be controlled without a willed acceptance of its limitations. Recognizing, unlike Lugones, that any literary system is but a manipulation of a certain set of devices, he concentrates on available energies and thus is able to move into new territories. An ironic stance allows Borges to begin again when the recognition comes that no more originality is to be found in the same source. When Lugones reaches this point, at the time of *Lunario sentimental,* the ironic self-knowledge of the poet as trickster and manipulator stops the process of renewals. He turns back to accustomed territory and familiar ground, clinging to rhyme and to elaborately worked metaphors. Rather than leaving the earlier frameworks in shambles and going on to work through ambiguity about the poet's function, Lugones returns to recognizable, comfortable harmonies.

In the collection of Borges' statements about Lugones, what begins to emerge is an ironic self-portrait of Borges himself. Borges comments on Lugones' successive use of masks along with his alienation. For Borges, the fact that these poses or styles were sequential and not simultaneous points out Lugones' denial of himself as a creator. Lugones' attempts to aestheticize and, at the same time, to caricature his own experience, avoid the demand for moral sincerity. Borges also repeatedly stresses Lugones' insistence on the use of language as a **logical** instrument (in the same manner he stresses the use of logic in his essay "Quevedo" from *Otras inquisiciones*). In his statements on Lugones, Borges makes analogies between Lugones and himself as well as with his entire generation. It is as if Borges presented Lugones as a prefiguration of himself, for both undergo a continual extinction and invention of new personalities in their roles as writers. For example, he states, "Lugones fue más que un espejo de los libros que iba leyendo"[24] ("Lugones was more than a mirror of the books he reads"). Lugones, like Borges, was concerned with his standing as a poet in the eyes of future generations, and even the choice of prose or poetry for the two was not always clear.

Borges has accorded to Lugones a rather dubious distinction in the light of the century's reevaluations of poetry. In 1941, with a softened and ironic posture toward Lugones, he diminishes the work of other poets of his *ultraísta* phase. After Almafuerte:

> Lo sigue el múltiple Lugones, cuya obra prefigura casi todo el proceso ulterior, desde las inconexas metáforas del ultraísmo (que durante quince años se consagró a reconstruir los borradores del *Lunario sentimental*) hasta las límpidas y complejas estrofas de nuestro mejor poeta contemporáneo, Ezequiel Martínez Estrada. No es imposible que los críticos de un porvenir remoto juzguen que todos los poetas actuales son facetas o hipóstasis de Lugones.[25]

> (Then comes the multiple Lugones, whose work prefigures almost all the subsequent process, from the disjointed metaphors of Ultraism [which for fifteen years was dedicated to reconstructing the drafts of *Lunario sentimental*] to the limpid and complex strophes of our best contemporary poet, Ezequiel Martínez Estrada. It may not be impossible to think that critics of some remote future may judge today's poets as facets or hypostases of Lugones.)

Such a stance is in striking contrast to his earlier vehement criticism of Lugones, as in his introductory comments to an anthology of 1929, where he proclaims the end of "rubenismo."

Announcing early on, "se gastó rubenismo ¡al fin, gracias a Dios!" ("Thank God that Rubendarismo is finally over!") Borges continues from what is as much a sociological as a poetic perspective:

> . . . el rubenismo fue nuestra añoranza de Europa. Fue un suelto lazo de nostalgia tirado hacia las torres, fue un largo adiós y regó el aire del Atlántico, fue un sentirnos extraños, y descontentizados y finos.[26]

> (. . . Rubendarismo was our homesickness for Europe. It was a loose ribbon of nostalgia, thrown to the towers; it was a long good-bye, and it watered the Atlantic winds; it was a way for us to feel foreign, unhappy, and refined).

LUGONES' DISSONANT LEGACY

Few writers of his epoch were as vehement as Lugones in espousing the civilizing aims of art. His rigid adherence to poetry's most obvious mark of form, that of rhyme, set him up for a whole generation's parodies of his work. What is less obvious beneath so many of his exalted pronouncements, as in the preface to *Lunario sentimental,* is his steady undercutting of his own preachings. Willful twistings of rhyme, meter, and grotesque exaggerations of form in general mark much of his verse. In this sense, Lugones' work is one of the most dynamic productions of *modernismo.* Although to many modern readers its overloading makes it inaccessible, if not unpleasant, some of his closer contemporaries saw his work through eyes trained otherwise. For Ramón López Velarde, Lugones' "lujuria de creador" (his "lustfulness of the creator") was on a par with that of Góngora.[27]

Lugones' depiction of provincial scenes and freckled beauties in *Los crepúsculos del jardín* and the *Lunario* did not seem trite by the standards of the beginning of the century. It was like an opening of new territory, one which took its standards not from the museums of Europe, but from the everyday scenery. Although far from the *mundonovista* current, and also unlike Manuel Gutiérrez Nájera's lighthearted verses to a more coquettish *femme fatale,* Lugones' new types of images often appear in settings not designed for them. They threaten to redirect our

attention away from the formal patterns he so carefully chisels
out, mixing dawn's more rustic aspects with exotic twilights. At
times the rhyme and the images appear to be going in opposite
directions. "Tul" ("Tulle") reappears as an old rhyme to pair
with "azul" ("blue"), so many times that it begins to jangle.
Azure skies give way to disturbingly frenzied fireworks specta-
cles, and even its viewers are discordant elements. They are just
the lower middle class out for a treat, not the usual audiences of
fine artistic productions.

The urban element in Lugones' poetry is an exceedingly rich
vein that later poets mined with greater clarity. Lugones wrote
on the eve of great changes in his society. An order to which he
eagerly was attaching himself found its foundations crumbling.
While early on the provincial is used in his poetry as a fresh and
often subtle contrast to scenes of purple passion, it later be-
comes a refuge of tradition, of the unchanging, a tribute to a
more "natural" order than the dissolving and tumultuous re-
arranging of heirarchies in Buenos Aires. In *Lunario sentimental,*
as well as in parts of *Los crepúsculos del jardín,* images of the city,
if not disturbing in themselves, upset the balance of the poems
in a sometimes elusive way.

LUGONES: FORGING A POETIC IDEOLOGY

Within *modernismo* the problem of "originality" presents fascinat-
ing perspectives. Lugones, in particular, with his self-avowed
"modelings" on already consecrated writers (Dante, Hugo,
Whitman, to name three of his early heroes) is often so star-
tlingly obvious in his antecedents (or literary fathers)[28] that the
question of literary propriety comes into play. Remembering
Rubén Darío's statement on imitation and originality, in his
preface to *Prosas Profanas,* we can see that notions of originality,
copying, parody, and even plagiarism are not exclusive terms in
modernismo.[29]

In search for a coherent system of symbolic systems or ideolo-
gies which would explain the changing nature of Lugones' writ-
ings, many critics have looked at his personal and public life as
parallel activities that could explain the diversity of his writ-
ings.[30] Undoubtedly, Lugones' changing social and personal posi-

tion, in relation to his growing stature as an approved national writer, must have tempered his early iconoclastic behavior and political attitudes. Many see the return to poetic orthodoxy in the period after 1910 as a sign of his growing identification with the ruling class. In examining Lugones' poetry in reference to other writings in circulation at the time, it is clear, however, that Lugones always selected frameworks from highly prized models. There is no abrupt break from the revolutionary stance expounded in early journalistic writings and poetry, to the aggressive mockery in *Lunario sentimental,* and to the later publications such as *Los horas doradas.* As will be shown later, certain themes and poetic treatments (as well as ideological stances) recur with great regularity.

Lugones was conscious of his models and their social and symbolic importance, as is evident in his method of grouping poems in collections. None of the three volumes to be examined here, *Las montañas del oro, Los crepúsculos del jardín,* and *Lunario sentimental,* was grouped in the chronological order in which it was written.[31] If there is one clear differentiating element in the production and arrangements of these poems, it is that Lugones was aware of the function of different poetic styles and their relation to literary convention. His view of the poetic function, different from that of other *modernistas,* provides the link among different types of poetry. Highly conscious of the literary models in circulation, and of their relative importance, Lugones did not aim so much for originality of concept as for an artful reworking of given patterns. With an emphasis on poetry not as an alternate reality but as a pattern of perception transmittable to a public at large, the technical aspects of writing acquired even greater importance. Since the stated intention was to affect a readership and to redirect its aims, the importance of personal experience as reflected in poetry was also to be diminished. Poetry's function was not to mirror interiority but to present a transpersonal vision.

The different stages in Lugones' view of the function of poetry, as seen in his expository prose and in the poetry itself, may be termed an "evolution" in the sense that the changes in the theory and practice of poetry show a process of adaptation to model texts in circulation. The process of evolution, a concept

Lugones often applied to the course of humanity in general and to poetry in particular, provided for him a rationalization of the ongoing process of assimilation and change, even though the changes might not seem to fit within a coherent personal viewpoint. Eclecticism, one of the traits of *modernista* poetry in general, was carried to extremes by Lugones. The necessity of continuity was not valid for him, except in the larger sense of the function of literature. To view Lugones' poetic system as a strictly individual one, cutting it off from its historical context, would rob it of wider implications. Just as Darío's and Martínez Estrada's judgments about Lugones and about a particular type of intentionality in poetry can be traced to the matrix of their personal and cultural contexts, the background of Lugones' system of aesthetics is related to a larger pattern. Lugones did not produce his texts in a vacuum nor, on the other hand, can one establish a series of one-to-one correspondences between his work and that of his predecessors. These correspondences do, however, refer back to a pattern he will often subvert.

The models of Lugones' early systems of imagery and their ideological associations are clearly apparent, partly because of similarity and partly because Lugones copiously cited his models, paying homage to his literary ancestors and, perhaps, attempting to elevate his own works by association with already canonized writers. The identification of the many influences on his thought and poetry has already been accomplished. Yet the listing of these influences or models leads to little understanding of Lugones' production itself. The pattern of reception and assimilation of these influences is the key to understanding the synthesis that he created from many sources. One may, for example, look at the impact of Victor Hugo and Nietzsche on Lugones' system of aesthetics and political ideals. Although those writers are widely separated chronologically and philosophically, Lugones studies them simultaneously, assimilating their ideas into a new amalgam, resolving their contradiction for his own purposes.

Selections from Lugones' early prose writings help identify his methods in approaching his models. The writings to be examined present his appraisals of different texts no matter what their nature. A passage from an article of 1899 succinctly expresses his approach to poetry during his early career. Its description of the poetic function is a constant in Lugones' work. Skeptical, polemic, and attentive to the techniques of his craft, Lugones assigned to poetry a demystifying, didactic intent. Like many religious writers of previous ages, he saw his vocation to be the task of revealing hidden truths by the process of disillusionment (*desengaño*). Urging his readers to sweep aside apparent realities and distractions, his zealous tone foreshadows the process of deconstruction that he will apply to his models:

> Dos bondades le debo á Dios en mi corta vida literaria: haberme dado el olfato de lo ridículo y haberme hecho leer á tiempo libros de don Francisco de Quevedo. Lo uno me convirtió en polemista, lo otro me enseñó á hablar con razón y con pensamiento. Aprendí á chupar bien mi hueso, según el consejo de Rabelais, á carpir mis originales, á mondar mis frases. . . . El badulaque doblado de combatiente que hay en todo poeta de quince años, desapareció por suerte á los primeros latigazos. Quedaron el admirador de la belleza y el constructor, ásperos, si se quiere, por consecuencia de semejante régimen, pero entusiastas. Comprendí, entonces, que América exigía una amarga misión: la misión de justicia, y decidí ser en la medida de mis fuerzas, ante todo y sobre todo, el hombre que dice la verdad. Principié por mí. Ahí está mi obra, que es, principalmente, una perpetua rectificación. . . . Yo les dije sencillamente que América nada hacía para sacudir su virginal ignorancia; que vivíamos de imitación y de idolatría boba, pescando en un balde como el pequeño Simón de la fábula; que nuestras borrascas literarias no eran más que microfónicas sarracinas entre cucarachas de diccionario y cínifes de bohemia; y que todas estas cosas habíanse de remediar, solamente cuando el arte dejara de ser pretexto y fuera causa, cuando el aplauso de definiera por el mérito y no por el interés mutuo de los figurantes. (*PL,* 111)

(Two gifts I owe to God in my short literary life: having given me a sense of the ridiculous and having me read early on the works of Francisco de Quevedo. The first made me a polemicist and the second taught me to speak with reason and thought. I learned to gnaw my bone well, following Rabelais' advice, as well as to weed my originals and prune my sentences. . . . The fighting sly rougue within every fifteen-year-old poet fortunately disappeared after the first few lashes. The admirer of beauty and the builder remained, toughened, if you like, due to the treatment received but nonetheless enthusiastic. I understood, then, that America demanded a bitter mission: a mission of justice, and I decided to be, within the means of my power, above and beyond all, the man who speaks the truth. I began with myself. There you have my work, which is, mainly, a perpetual rectification. . . . I stated that America did nothing to rid itself of its virginal ignorance; that we lived off imitation and foolish idolatry, fishing in a small boat like Simon of the Biblical fable; that our literary storms were nothing more than microphonic sarracins amongst dictionary cockroaches and Bohemian mosquitos, and that all these problems would be resolved only when art stopped being a pretext and became a cause, when applause could be measured by merit and not by mutual interests.)

The passage is striking, for it shows that Lugones, at so early an age (twenty-five years old), is already outlining the characteristics of his work which will become increasingly apparent. The zealous and polemic tone, the disdain for his contemporaries, and biting sarcasm grow even sharper in later years.

Only by referring to the ideas espoused by Lugones, that is, his belief in the efficacy of the written word to remake the thought processes of the public, in the natural aristocracy of the artist, in language as thought incarnate, and in literature as a system parallel to music, can Lugones' efforts be clearly understood. His ideas can best be viewed from the perspective of his cultural heritage and his response to it. The standards that inform his work are common to his epoch, although few embraced certain of these principles so wholeheartedly. For Lugones, the literary work was the postulation of a future society. In his system aesthetics is a discipline absorbed by dogma and metaphysics. Literature in this sense can be viewed as a branch of moral argument. Lugones' selection of his models reflects his theories of literature's purpose. His range of choices resembles that of other *modernistas*, but the structure of his ideology determined a degree of acceptance of current literary theories and models different from other *modernistas*. The rapid leaps in style and content of his writings serve to give substance to what he saw as a devalued reality, to seize outside elements and incorporate them into his work and his own culture.

From the final flourish of romanticism in "Los mundos" to the fragmentation of metrical and metaphorical patterns in *Lunario sentimental,* Lugones' poetry shows a simultaneous adaptation of previous texts within a new context, a practice that is the very essence of *modernista* writing. In Lugones' first three volumes of poetry, as well as in the journalistic prose and poems published in periodicals, almost all the elements of *modernista* writing can be found. Because no single style is consistently privileged, the array of styles has been described as confusing and artificial. Certain patterns of order can be found in these early works, however, not only by noting certain hierarchies but also by examining patterns of recurring displacement, such as the different stances of the unifying narrative voice, growing use of metonymy, and lessening attention to continuity of theme and treatment within a single volume.

What draws most attention to Lugones' poetry is the constancy of attention to form and the sometimes too obvious process of manipulation to comply with formal demands. The impossibility of achieving total restraint, the fall into bathos, pedantry, and hackneyed repetition, are the marks of such attempts. Swinging from highs to lows, Lugones as poet can be described as the "mosaísta eterno" that Roberto F. Giusti labeled him. The discrepancy between different levels of success and the variety of expression have led many readers to remark on the "impersonality" of his work. Yet it is this very quality that calls attention to his place within a rapidly changing literary environment and his efforts to experiment and to create new systems. The challenge in studying Lugones' work is to trace the constants in adaptation, to note the changes in perspective by which he transformed his sources, and to uncover a perceptual framework that would allow for the inclusion of many different adaptations of models. As one moves from the massiveness of scale and expressions in *Las montañas del oro,* to the magnifying-glass perspective in *Los crepúsculos del jardín,* to the overthrow of metaphorical patterns in *Lunario sentimental,* some practices remain constant, while many change. The aim of the next discussion will be to trace the perceptual framework that informs the poetry and to relate Lugones' stated aesthetic creed to his actual work.

LUGONES AS JOURNALIST: POLITICS AND ART

During the earliest period of Lugones' career—from his first published writings in 1893 in *El Pensamiento Libre* (*Free Thought*; a socialist periodical he cofounded in Córdoba with Nicolás González Luján), to his contributions to periodicals in Buenos Aires from 1893 to 1897 (*El Tiempo, La Vanguardia, La Libertad*), to the founding of the short-lived periodical *La Montaña* (cofounded with José Ingenieros in 1897)—the tenuous professional situation of Lugones, his eagerness for acceptance, and his immediate receptivity to changes within his environment, explain the rapid alternation of styles and contents. In this period, while struggling to gain a foothold in the literary circles of Buenos Aires, Lugones sought to integrate himself into the major movements of the day. Both the inconsistencies and the contradictions expressed in his work during this period reveal a constant experimentation with different models. The often strident tone and prolific production are indicators of an insistent desire to be heard, to make his voice not just one in the multitude. It is evident from his early writings on politics, literature, art, and society that Lugones accepted the notion of an intellectual and artistic elite, created by the gift of "Genius," and considered his own development to be a fulfillment of the destiny already imposed upon him. In this aspect, more than in any other, Lugones shows his close ties to romanticism. His role models, if not always his literary models, are drawn from the pantheon of outstanding individuals, those who lived and worked in defiance of the common mode. In his work the constant search for novelty of thought and expression is a reflection of this attempt at self-definition, seen in terms of differentiation from the multitudes. As paradoxical as it may seem, Lugones combined these views with an avowal of socialist principles. The romantic view of the poet as prophet and rebel provides the organizing principle for the vision of the writer within the emergence of a different kind of social organization.

The early journalistic writings of Leopoldo Lugones, published between 1893 and 1898, provide a valuable source of information about his early literary developments. They constitute, in effect, a theory of his poetry during the *modernista* epoch, since at this time he did not systematically compile his theories of literature in a coherent manner, as he would do extensively in following years. Critics, with few exceptions, have searched for a code of aesthetics in his later, more coherently developed treatises on art (especially in *Las limaduras de Hephaestos*, *Piedras liminares* [1910], *Prometeo* [1910], and *El payador* [1916]) and have applied a much changed poetics to his earlier works.[32] Very little attention has been given to the journalistic commentaries written in the same years as the publication of many poems that would later be included in *Las montañas del oro* (1897), *Los crepúsculos del jardín* (1905), and *Lunario sentimental* (1909).[33] Constants and variations in thematics and techniques in the three volumes of poetry are first suggested in articles about widely differing subjects. These writings reveal not only Lugones' appraisals of the epoch's literature but also show his reaction to immediate historical circumstances that were very closely linked to his literary opinions. They provide striking parallels with his early poetry in tone, vocabulary, and ideological frame of reference.

"GENIUS" AND THE AMERICAN CONTEXT

From the very beginning of his writing career, Lugones gives evidence of his belief in the superiority of the true artist (the "Genius") over the mass of the populace and of his adherence to a high degree of formalism in art. His early writings foreshadow the traits that would change him from one of *modernismo*'s most daring innovators to a rigid stylist who adhered increasingly to his particular definition of classic art.[34] Like many *modernista* writers, Lugones also shared in the veneration of France, often showing an unquestioning acceptance of whatever he understood to be currently fashionable. His attitude was in part a reaction against the parochialism of his upbringing. By defending an alien culture, he could strike a blow at the constraints of his own.

Lugones discounts the American setting as being too primitive to allow for the development of a complex and refined expression. An 1896 review of *Primitivo,* a novel by the Uruguayan Carlos Reyles, gives Lugones an opportunity to comment on the situation of writers in Latin America; in it, he underscores his disdain for the Spanish American context:

> A fe que pocas veces se ha oído en América una profesión de arte así, puesto que nuestro irrespetuoso republicanismo ha inducido siempre á los escritores por esa mansa ruta que conduce finalmente á la estrecha teoría nacionalista en que aún estamos debatiéndonos.
>
> Salga de ella valientemente el escritor uruguayo, escriba para sus *semejantes,* dejando de lado la tradicional plebeyería de esta candorosa América latina, recién salida de las rudimentarias coreografías á son de tam-tam (en materia artística, quiero decir), sin tomar por plebeyerías las grandes voces de la plebe, porque él, como otros pocos, debe saber que, por ejemplo, las águilas son la plebe de las cumbres. (*PL* [1896], 53)
>
> (Rarely have I heard in America such an avowal of art, since our disrespectful republicanism has always induced writers to follow that meek route which ultimately brings us to the rigid nationalist theory that we are still debating today.
>
> Let the Uruguayan writer bravely leave behind this [nationalist theme]; he should write for his equals; he should leave aside the traditional plebeianism of this ingenuous Latin America, which only recently left behind its rudimentary choreography to the beat of gongs [I refer to artistic matters]; he should not mistake the great voice of the people for vulgarities, because he, like few others, should know that, for example, the eagles are the plebeians of the heights.)

In this case the *semejantes* are "los espíritus delicados" ("the delicate spirits") whose senses are refined to the extent that they can appreciate an art of subtlety, as opposed to the gaucho hero of Reyles' novels who, lacking the refinement of the senses, cannot effectively serve as the subject of a psychological novel. As Lugones comments in the same review, "Los celos de nuestros bárbaros no son el resultado de una pasión sino de un instinto. Nada de cerebral en ellos. Todo simple resultado de una efusión cardiaca más ó ménos profunda" (*PL* [1896], 53): ("The jealousy of our barbarians is the result of instinct, not passion. There is nothing cerebral about them. Everything is the simple consequence of a somewhat deep, cardiac effusion"). Obviously here Lugones is far from his later romanticization of the national folk hero that will emerge later in *La guerra gaucho* and in *El Payador*.

Lugones was very eclectic in his borrowings, and the simultaneous reception of many elements of Victor Hugo's work, along with thematic and visual elements from writers such as Huysmans, Flaubert, and D'Annunzio, gives a strange, uneven quality to much of his early work. The presentation of the underworld of the spirit along with its redemptive possibilities (as outlined by Hugo in *Les Contemplations*) is combined by Lugones with satanism, eroticism, and a fetishistic insistence on the physical. Unlike its presentation in his later poetry, as in the first two cycles of *Las montañas del oro* or parts of *Los crepúsculos del jardín,* the emphasis on physicality in the earliest poetry and prose journalism is usually contained within harsh criticism of bourgeois morality and a denial of anti-idealist tendencies, as in the article "Porcus-Rex" of 1896:

> El amor físico, como la gula, como todos los apetitos que aguijonean la carne, son productos del vientre. Y el vientre es el órgano superior en las decadencias. El oro, el capital sus servidores.
>
> Entonces se produce este extraño fenómeno: hay una inmensa, una espantosa necesidad de carne viciada: una verdadera necrofagia, se apodera de los degenerados. (*PL* [1896], 42)
>
> (Physical love, like gluttony, like all the other appetites that spur on the flesh, are products of the belly. And the belly is the superior organ of decadence. Gold, capital, its servants.
>
> Then a strange phenomenon occurs: there is an immense, a dreadful need for corrupt flesh: a real case of necrophagy seizes the degenerates.)

Although an antithetical framework of transcendent meaning usually overshadows such passages throughout the earliest writings, Lugones finds ample opportunity to make analogies with elements taken from the darker world of sensations. The defiant tone of these comparisons is often based on an antagonistic

stance toward his audience. A possible self-censorship is pro-
jected outward to an unworthy audience.

SOCIALIST ART

In his literary criticism, historical investigations, and political
journalism, Lugones took the stance of a self-appointed apostle
of civilization who sought not the role of alienated poet–
intellectual, but that of crusader.

For Lugones, radicalism led by the intellectual elite is inevita-
ble, and he acted on this belief by promoting it in his writings as
well as actively organizing socialist groups in Córdoba and Bue-
nos Aires for almost a decade. Almost all of the periodicals for
which he wrote at this time were involved in promoting social-
ism, and he also devoted many public lectures to this theme at
meetings primarily of workers' organizations.[35] It is true, as
many critics of Lugones have stated, that his politics were of an
"aestheticized socialism," but the political activism of the work-
ers' neighborhoods and trips through the provinces proselytiz-
ing for socialism and for the organization of strikes can hardly
be interpreted as a purely intellectual commitment. Lugones,
however, also acted out his intellectual commitment to the no-
tion that self-realization is the best way of serving the group,
with all the inherent dangers of solipsism implied in this belief.
The latter belief created the pathway that led him later to em-
brace tyrannical fascism as an ideal for directing society.

In his earliest political writings of 1893, Lugones not only
promoted the socialist and anarchist theories he inherited from
French and English socialists, but he also combined them with
the ideas of Darwin and Nietzsche. While advocating equality
for all mankind, Lugones also accepted the idea of the "elect,"
those who are blessed with the genius to direct the masses.
Great artists (a general term for "Genius") are seen to be proph-
ets or *videntes* who can predict and direct the future.

In the years immediately following, socialist writings were
more explicitly linked with specific issues. Book reviews, public
addresses, and a series of caricatures of contemporary politi-
cians served as the forum for expounding his ideas on society.
Lugones' descriptions of *el Pueblo,* the People, are worth re-

counting because they are typical of the constellation of terms that always surrounds *el Pueblo* in his early poetry as well as in these articles. References are made to "el León–Pueblo" ("the Lion–People"), "el Pueblo, eterno mártir" ("the People, eternal martyr"), "el Pueblo, inmenso colaborador del infinito, con la cabeza centelleante de ira" ("the People, immense collaborator with the infinite, its head gleaming with rage"). The voice of *el Pueblo* is like the voice of the sea: "El mar es la imprecación eterna del universo contra el límite. Es amargo tal vez porque es esclavo" ("The sea is the eternal curse of the universe against the limit. Perhaps it is bitter because it is enslaved"). The scale of gigantism describing the people undoubtedly owes much to romanticism and to the political slogans of the epoch, but it is also an indication of Lugones' favored analogical framework, a cosmological scheme. Lugones' early defense of *el Pueblo* is a far cry from his later pronouncements, as in the prologue to *El Payador* of 1916 where he returns to a rural tradition as the source of the true voice of the people, distinguishing this sector from "La plebe ultramarina" ("the foreign rabble"), the threatening urban populace of the "ralea mayoritaria" ("the majority breed") created by "las lujurias del sufragio universal" ("the lust of universal suffrage"), the same crowd who, "a semejanza de los mendigos ingratos, nos armaba escándalo en el zaguán, desató contra mí al instante sus cómplices mulatos y sus sectarios mestizos"[36] ("resembling ungrateful beggars, were making a scene in the vestibule, instantly unleashing against me their mulato accomplices and mestizo sectarians"). Even earlier, in *Lunario sentimental,* Lugones shows his aversion to the proletariat and his racism in poems such as "Fuegos artificiales" and "Luna ciudadana."

The redemptive socialism that Lugones promotes is directed toward renewing and rejuvenating a spirit of adventure. He professes astonishment that socialism has not taken greater hold among the youth of Argentina. Yet his definition of socialism must be examined, for the last decade of the century of Argentina saw an enormous immigration of foreign, primarily Italian, workers who brought with them the socialist and anarchist principles of workers' rights and strikes. In 1889, fifty-three percent of the population of Buenos Aires was composed of foreign immigrants, many of whom were actively engaged in workers' movements.[37] In 1897 Lugones addresses himself to another audience, the intellectual youth of the country, and his case for socialism is not so much a revolutionary one but an appeal for a return to the democratic principles of the founding of the nation:

> Causa, por ejemplo, verdadero asombro, el que la juventud, la juventud intelectual del país argentino no sea más socialista de lo que es. Tradiciones no le faltan. Los hombres del 25 de mayo, los campeones de la epopeya revolucionaria con todos sus candores y sus inocencias heróicas; los amigos de Echeverría, aquellos precursores del "Dogma Socialista", cuyas siluetas ha recortado Groussac en un pergamino histórico no arrancado por cierto de las circumvoluciones de un peritóneo bovino; los mismos centauros del caudillaje, con sus anchas carótidas y sus tendones salvajes—¡esos sí que eran jóvenes y no engordaban con la salsa de sus laureles! ¿Por qué no toma ejemplo de ellos la juventud contemporánea? (*PL* [1897], 65)

> (It truly amazes me, for example, that [our] youth, the intellectual youth of Argentina, is not more socialist that it is. It [socialism] is part of our tradition. The men of the 25th of May, the champions of the revolutionary epic, with all their heroic candor and innocence; Echeverría's friends, those precursors of the "Dogma Socialista", whose portraits Groussac has traced upon historic parchment which, by the way, was not taken from a bovine's periteneum; those very same centaurs of caudillo leadership, with their wide carotids and wild tendons—this generation was definitely young and did not fatten itself on the sauce of its laurels! Why doesn't the contemporary generation follow their example?)

This appeal to historical precedents is in part founded on the unity of rhetoric of the writings of these early heroes and that of Lugones' contemporary socialists. Lugones' rhetoric is a legacy of the social nature of romanticism to which he was a late heir. As early as 1837, Echeverría had adopted the romantic formula for the program of the Asociación de Mayo. Among the founding principles were the familiar ones of liberty, fraternity, equality, and progress. In the writings of Sarmiento, another great culture hero of Lugones, the aims of art and politics are also united with those of utilitarian reform. A passage from Sarmiento's writings illustrates the basic similarity between the rhetoric of both writers and the abstractness of the terminology.

> Hemos sido siempre i seremos eternamente socialistas, es decir, haciendo concurrir el arte, la ciencia, la política, o lo que es lo mismo, los sentimientos del corazón, las luces de la inteligencia i la actividad de la acción, al establecimiento de un gobierno democrático fundado en bases sólidas, en el triunfo de la libertad i de todas las doctrinas liberales, en la realización, en fin, de los santos fines de nuestra revolución.[38]

> (We have always been and forever will be socialists, that is to say, aligning Art, Science and Politics, or their equivalents, the sentiments of the heart, the brightness of reason and the activity of action, with the establishment of a democratic government founded upon a solid base, in the sacred objectives of our revolution.)

Yet despite the unity of abstract concepts expressed by both these writers, there is a marked difference that lies in Lugones' addition of a series of cosmological analogies to his political writings. For Lugones, writing is valued not so much as a means of direct communication—as in Roland Barthes' definition of political writing: "writing . . . meant to unite at a single stroke the reality of the acts and the ideality of the ends"—but in the sense of literature, not meant to be purely representational nor to promote direct communication.[39] The same rhetorical figures based on jolting contrast of abstract concepts and physical description, used to comment on contemporary politicians, recently published literary works, art, and architecture, are carried directly over into poetry. Just as Lugones expresses social liberation in terms of the clash of the forces of nature, he transforms the struggle of writing itself into a metaphor for individual and social struggle. The discovery of an appropriate idiom of expression therefore could resolve the antithetical clashes in society.

While exalting the aims of art for the redemption of society, Lugones sees society at the same time as incapable of understanding its own redemption. A paradoxical art ostensibly directed toward humanitarian aims but which can only be understood by a select few, produces alternations between glorification of a mythicized "pueblo" and a turn toward distant, foreign models. The dichotomy "Civilización–Barbarie" ("Civilization–Barbarism") expounded by Sarmiento is transformed into another opposition. The "barbarian" of the cities—in Lugones' view, the animalistic mass of mediocrity—replaces the "barbarian" of the interior. Yet the same rhetoric is present, and a confusion of concepts arises because Lugones uses the same labels while the referents are shifting.

In almost every reference to socialism and to the condition of the masses Lugones includes at least one mention of "Genius," linked with the role of artist, prophet, visionary, or historical figure. The superior man may work in any field of endeavor, but his destiny is to foresee and direct the future. On the occasion of the visit of the Duke of Savoy to Buenos Aires in 1894, Lugones expounded his theories of the necessity of aristocracy in an article ("Saludo") that was to cause great division among the socialist groups with which he worked. Here he anticipates a twentieth-century historical interpretation of Argentina's earlier political consolidation, as he exalts both Sarmiento *and* Rosas:

> En este país, Señor, han existido dos genios: Domingo Faustino Sarmiento y Juan Manuel de Rosas. Del segundo os dirán que fue un bárbaro tirano. Yo sólo puedo aseguraros que se parecía mucho á aquel rey don Pedro, llamado por unos el *Cruel* y por otros el *Justiciero. (PL* [1896], 36)

> (In this country, Sir, there have been but two geniuses: Domingo Faustino Sarmiento and Juan Manuel de Rosas. People will tell you that the latter was a barbaric tyrant. I can only assure you that he resembled King Peter, known to some as *the Cruel* and to others as *the Just.*)

Combining the notion of the romantic Genius and Nietzschean Superman, Lugones selects models from an idealized past to serve as prototypes for leaders of the future.

For Lugones the emotional return to his country's own past, as well as to a classical past, took a different direction from that of many other *modernista* poets. The solipsistic principle would take a turn with him toward tyrannical fascism, as well as toward introspective throught. In the same year as the publication of *Las montañas del oro*, Lugones expresses a solipsistic ideal in connection with the liberty of the artist:

> El artista, como la Naturaleza, no conoce el pudor. . . . El Hombre verdaderamente libre tiene que ser violentamente libre. Por otra parte, el concepto idealista no deja lugar a dudas. Si el mundo no es más que una objetivación exteriorizada de mi *yo*, claro está que poseo el derecho absoluto de transformarlo a mi manera. . . . Sólo tengo, pues, una moral mía, totalmente diversa de los demás. La lógica está dentro de mí mismo y soy el único que puede cambiarla. De ahí la negación del pudor social.[40]

> (The artist, like Nature, does not know modesty. . . . The truly free Man must be violently free. On the other hand, the idealist concept leaves no room for doubt. If the world is nothing more than an exteriorized objectivization of my Self, it is assumed that I possess the absolute right to transform it as I see fit. . . . Therefore, I have only one morality, mine, completely different from others. The logic is within me and I am the *only one* who can change it; henceforth the negation of social modesty.

The ideal of absolute individual liberty frees the artist from the constraints of customs that prevent the expression of individuality: "Y los hombres tienden, por lo general, con irresistible impulso a esas anulaciones del *yo*" ("And men, in general, tend with irresistible impulse to these cancellations of the Self"). The true artist is exempt from the laws of society by having discovered a higher principle within himself.[41]

In Lugones' discussion of art, the concept of liberty or freedom, exhibited as beauty, is nearly always present. The notion of liberty and its manifestation in the individual, in society, and in art is a motif in all his early works. Lugones uses the concept of freedom as an interpretative device rather than as a philosophical essence or ideal, a tool for creating analogies rather than as an explict goal. As Frederic Jameson states:

> This formal character of the concept of freedom is precisely what lends itself to the work of political hermeneutics. It encourages analogy: assimilating the material prisons to the psychic ones, it serves as a means of unifying all these separate levels of existence, functioning, indeed, as a kind of transformational equation whereby the

data characteristic of one may be converted into the terms of another.[42]

Thus Lugones uses social concepts to show the power of metaphor in explaining and directing society, and literature itself is seen as one stage in directing thought and society.

LITERARY CRITICISM AND THE TWO AMERICAS

The same apocalyptic, cosmological imagery that unifies the political writings and the early poetry is present in the literary criticism. In the article "Lenguas públicas" of 1897, Lugones responds to harsh criticism of his own work and gives an extended comparison of the language of calumny:

> Hay ciertas bocas en las cuales reina una perpetua noche. Bocas llenas de hongos, como los sótanos. Hay otras, más repugnantes aún, que parecen tumbas con un cadáver parlante adentro. Esas pequeñas cavernas son espantosas porque están llenas de alma. No es raro ver surgir por ellas la espuma de las mareas interiores, la espuma verde o roja del apóstrofe o de la envidia. Así como la boca suele ser un tabernáculo, puedo también resultar un antro. (*PL* [1897], 68)

> (In some mouths there reigns a perpetual night. Mouths full of fungus, like cellars. There are others even more revolting; they resemble tombs occupied by a talking cadaver. Those small caverns are dreadful because they are full of spirits. It is not surprising to see the foam spurt up through them from the tides within, the green or red foam of apostrophe or of envy. And so, just as the mouth may be a tabernacle, it also can prove to be a cesspool.)

Like an "espada de dos filos" (a "double-edged sword") language can cut two ways, sacred and profane. And for Lugones, both edges must be used. If one item is mentioned, its opposite must be brought in as contrast, to clarify by shock. In his systems of imagery there is a fascination with the underside of the visible surface. In this same article "Lenguas públicas" ("Public Languages") he attributes sacred and demonic powers to language itself and attacks and discredits certain rhetorical modes. He continues by saying that nature possesses a harmony of sounds, even in violence. It is the human tongue that is adept at spoilage:

> Le falta esta ingeniosa infancia del odio humano: la perífrasis. Ella es la pata felina de la retórica, el ala cómplice del vampiro que hace brisa sobre su víctima para chuparla mejor, la saliva azucarada sobre los colmillos de la calumnia. (*PL* [1897], 68)

> (It lacks that clever infancy of human hatred: circumlocution. It is the feline paw of rhetoric, the conniving wing of the vampire that stirs up a breeze around its victim so as to suck it better, the sweetened saliva on the fangs of slander.)

He sees literature as the expression not just of the individual, but of the collectivity that produces the individual. And the circumstance present in Spanish America for him is one of youthfulness, with close ties to an almost primeval past, more suited for heroic action than for contemplation.

Lugones' judgments on the relative merits of Spanish American and North American literature are interesting in part because of the contrasts he makes with other writers of the epoch. Like Rodó, Lugones criticizes the materialism of the north, but he is also dissatisfied with more local literary productions. He mixes political attack with disparaging remarks about what he sees as the primitiveness of Spanish American literature. In both cases, Lugones takes the position of the removed and superior observer.

In an article of 1898 concerning the release of the second edition of Julián Martel's *La Bolsa,* he stresses the idea that American literature is still in an early formative period:

> Atravesamos aun el período de la lírica y de la leyenda, la floración espontánea, podría decirse, de las literaturas nacientes. Oímos muy de cerca todavía los rumores de la selva vírgen para escapar á su impresión poderosa. No tenemos la costumbre de meditar. (*PL* [1898], 75)

> (We are still passing through a period of lyricism and legend, the spontaneous blossoming, it could be said, of nascent literatures. We

still hear the sounds of the virgin jungle too closely to escape its powerful impression. We lack the habit of meditation.)

Appropriateness of literary genre will be the product of historical circumstances, a theory combining the romantics' belief that literature is an expression of the innate structure of society with the positivist theory of the shaping forces of environment.

In the same year (1898) Lugones examines "the other America"—"El Tío Sam [Uncle Sam], Jonathan, Calibán." In comparing the two cultures of America (in the article "4 de julio" ["Fourth of July"]), he sees their characters as factors in the differing natures of their literatures. Although he criticizes the furious rush of the United States toward industrialization—"El martillo domina con excesivo despotismo" ("The hammer dominates with excessive despotism")—for Lugones, its literature's gigantic vitality contrasts with what he views as the paleness of Spanish American writings:

> No obstante, aquella fealdad de adolescente robusto contrasta radicalmente con nuestra flacura de niños encanijados. Lo del norte es denso, pesado, brutal. Lo del sur, fofo simplemente. Podríamos responder con nuestra profusa literatura, con nuestros afeites poéticos más próximos al tatuaje que a la pintura. Desde la "Oda a la agricultura de la zona tórrida" hay mucho que trillar seguramente. (*PL* [1898], 77)

> (Nevertheless, that robust, adolescent ugliness contrasts sharply with our puny, childlike thinness. What comes out of the North is dense, heavy, and brutal. What comes from the South is simply flaccid. We could respond with our own literatures, with our lyrical powders and oils, closer to tatoos than to Art. Since the "Ode to the Agriculture in the Torrid Zone," surely there is a lot to thresh out.)

This concept of North American literature undoubtedly owes much to Lugones' readings of Whitman, whom he includes in *Las montañas del oro* as one of the four great writers the world has known. Whitman as a poet "casi desconocido en este país" ("almost unknown in this country") is the embodiment of the heroism of the new world, uniting vital expression and prophecy in verses unhindered by constraining, outworn forms.

Concentrating on the fusion of the creative personality with environment, Lugones mixes literary criticism with sociological judgments, launching an attack upon North American expansionism as well as a defense of his own culture. Even writers who seem to defy the cultural molds that produced them can be explained within this critical context. Edgar Allan Poe, seen often as the "víctima del monstruo gigante entre cuyos tobillos tuvo la desgracia de nacer" ("victim of the monstrous giant between those ankles he had the misfortune of being born") is no exception. Poe's work expresses a defense against that same invading, expansive American spirit that informs Whitman's work. Like Darío, whose early "Salutación al águila" praises the vitality of the United States, Lugones admires its force but anticipates its increasing dominance in Latin America and sounds a warning note. The "arrogante cóndor andino" (the "arrogant Andean condor") must not send unqualified praise to the "águila capitolina" (the "Capitoline eagle"). Yet, as Lugones reminds us in "4 de julio," reality tempers more explicit criticism: "Además, cuando el cañón tiene la palabra, todo discurso resulta vano, todo juicio perturbado o prematuro" (*PL* [1898], 77) ("Furthermore, when the cannon speaks, all discussion is in vain, all judgment is disturbed or premature").

In his role as literary critic, Lugones saw his function to be the passionate defender of new writers who, by their originality and dedication to innovation in literature, were comrades in battle "contra las viejas formas" ("against the old forms"). His reviews of works by writers such as Ricardo Gutiérrez, Leopoldo Díaz, Rubén Darío, Federico Gamboa, and Julián Martel are especially significant in their discussion of poetic language.

According to Lugones the necessity of cultivating new techniques in poetry is not only for the purposes of individual expression, for it is its use-value that determines its sacred or profane powers, not the inherent qualities of language itself. By 1897, at the time of a review of a volume of poetry, *Negro y oro* by the Mexican Francisco de Olaguíbel, Lugones is aware of the possibilities of automatization of the practices of *modernismo* and the dangers of its becoming an ossified form susceptible to parody. Olaguíbel still possesses a trace of "modernismo oficial" ("official *modernismo*") with "insistencias verbales sobre palabras completamente anodinas, sobre adjetivos gastados por el uso,

como cantos rodados, hasta los últimos extremos de la denuda-
ción" (*PL* [1897], 68) ("insistence on completely anodine words,
on adjectives worn out with use, like smoothed pebbles, to the
extreme limit of being stripped"). Constant invention and nov-
elty, achieved only through incessant study, are necessary to
discover an individual poetic idiom.

CONCLUSION

These early writings show the first stages in Lugones' aesthetic
code and his attempts at systematization, revealed by the use of
an explicit analogical system to deal with many topics. He at-
tempted to create an all-encompassing ideological, symbolic
frame of reference that would incorporate art, politics, and
personal justification within one pattern. He emphasized the
principle of organic unity, which was much later converted into
a rigid code of aesthetics, as in the *Estudios helénicos*. Some recur-
ring topics that illustrate this attempt at systematization are the
principle of organic unity, the role of art in society and, allied
with the last, the concept of "Genius," especially in regard to the
natural aristocracy of the artist. Lugones' continuing return to
these concepts, despite his adoption of techniques and themes
that are in direct contradiction to them, demonstrates his adher-
ence to some type of formal structure. The oscillation between
extremes and the presence of violent backlashes in his later
poetry arise from the same insistence on contradiction that is
present in his earliest work. The presence of the grotesque, the
deflation of transcendent schemes, and elements of deliberate
disruption in his early journalistic writings grow more pro-
nounced in his later works. In time, Lugones will turn away
from his early, ambivalent loyalties to socialism and will em-
brace a different concept of the "patria," or homeland, in which
the writer must stand in a superior, didactic role. As these early
writings illustrate, such changes were not abrupt ones but were
developing during the earliest stages of his writing career.

3

LUGONES AS *MODERNISTA* POET

Lugones' earliest published poetry (poems not collected in separate volumes) reflects many of the same contradictory impulses that appear in the early journalism. Although the structuring metaphor of organic form, the role of evolution, and the notion of "Genius" and sacred role of the poet–artist are abundantly present, their expression is increasingly disrupted by violent images often accompanied by the theme of eroticism or the upheaval of the carnival. Jarring notes of modernity strain the classical series of dualities. Alternating grandiloquent allegorical statement with intimate introspection, these poems are like a rough outline of what is to come later in the carefully selected volumes. In one of his earliest published poems, "Los mundos" ("The Worlds") (1893), the poet–prophet, with marks of an almost adolescent zeal, stands at the summit of an ordered universe and thunders out to the multitudes, a pose that anticipates a recurring element of *Las montañas del oro.* At the same time Lugones is experimenting in other poems with patterns much like those of *Los crepúsculos del jardín* and *Lunario sentimental,* in which the Romantic frame of reference is shattered or absent, and the ordering, defining poetic persona disappears from the scene.

If the early poetry merely suggests these variations, *Las montañas del oro* (1898) celebrates the clash of poetic impulses. The recurrent allegorical framework struggles to enclose the often incongruous juxtapositions. If some sections were not bound together by the volume as a whole, their hybrid appearance would seem to be a parody of the fanciful and often bizarre mixtures *modernismo* created with its inherited and new symbols.

85

Poetry of accumulation, *Las montañas del oro* possesses as well the mark of originality. Uniform in its collection of excesses, it is daring in its expansion of boundaries. Although the origins of many of the individual themes and poetic devices are recognizably borrowed ones, the curious and sometimes monstrous mixture Lugones creates breaks earlier constraints. *Las montañas del oro*'s particular traits—its overt exaggeration, monumental excesses, overloading, willful twistings of form and content, and elements of grotesque humor—will be intensified in different functions in later collections.

The poem "Los mundos," first published in *Pensamiento Libre* in 1893, is important because it prefigures the first and last cycles of *Las montañas del oro* and sets forth in rudimentary fashion the early framework of Lugones' allegorical system. Although often ponderous in its progression and redundant in its vocabulary, it is worthy of analysis for its presentation of the light–darkness dichotomy, the roles of Genius and Poet, and the idealized "Pueblo," topics already seen in the early journalism. Derivative though this poem may be, it shows a highly developed control of imagery systems. It is, in short, a highly unified description of exterior structures of fecundity and flowering, with cosmological elements linked to a grid of assigned meanings.[1] These elements, though trite even by the standards of that age, are never consciously used for ironic or parodic effects. The presentations give panoramic, unified perspectives. However, the poem's redundance and excesses do indeed produce distorted visions. The energy of excess, constrained here, will be extended and used for different effects in *Las montañas del oro*. There the shifting of perspectives and resulting distortion will be incorporated into a thematic plan.

Although the poet's stance on the mountain summit will be repeated in the first and third cycles of *Las montañas del oro,* the role of Hugo's visionary prophet will be reduced in later works. The dissonance and fragmentation briefly glimpsed in the rhyme schemes and natural imagery of some of the early poems will begin to enter on its own terms, especially in the first and third cycles of *Las montañas del oro*. There, metonymical displacement of the natural iconography gives a macabre, fetishistic tone to the interior cycles. The elemental forces of nature, first presented in association with a noble organizing voice, are tinged with sinister qualities, as is seen in the treatment of the wind. History's advances, the poet's role, religion, and nature itself enter in disturbing contexts by the introduction of eroticism.

THE RECEPTION OF *LAS MONTAÑAS DEL ORO*

Lugones' first published volume of poetry, *Las montañas del oro,* was received with fervent acclaim by contemporaries such as Amado Nervo, Rubén Darío, and José Juan Tablada. Later readers express more conflicting views. For Octavio Paz, *Las montañas del oro* represents one of *modernismo*'s most important characteristics, "la conciencia del ser dividido y la aspiración hacia la unidad"[2] ("the consciousness of a divided being and the aspiration of unity"). He sees the volume as the completion and fulfillment of the true spirit of romanticism previously absent in most Spanish American poetry. Another contemporary critic, Noé Jitrik, has judged Lugones' poetry of *modernismo* in a different light: it is "huguiano y desmesurado . . . sin llegar al simbolismo ni a ninguna otra derivación más autónoma del romanticismo. Su modernismo es la versión para jóvenes"[3] ("Hugoesque and excessive . . . far from reaching Symbolism or any more autonomous derivation of Romanticism. His *modernismo* is the version for the young"). Jitrik finds that Lugones' search for meaning in the past led him to "la ortodoxia romántica más sólida e incuestionable, la variación dentro de la regla, la legalidad sumisa y concordante"[4] ("the most solid and unquestionable romantic orthodoxy, the variation within the norm, a submissive and concordant legality"). He finds, furthermore, that Lugones' unquestioning adherence to already acclaimed models and reluctance to give words a life of their own make it only poetry of accumulation, "acumulación de temas, ciertemente, pero también de los éxitos obtenidos con ellos"[5] ("accumulation of themes, surely, but also of the successes obtained by them"). Jitrik's observations are somewhat typical of more modern views of *Las montañas del oro.* Part of the present study, however, will examine this supposed orthodoxy and suggest a different type of reading of these accumulated themes, successes, and excesses.

The opinions of two of Lugones' contemporaries, Amado

Nervo and Rubén Darío, show more clearly the special position
this volume represented when it was first published. Their com-
ments are similar; while praising the force and dynamism of the
poetry, they also note the multiple influences and the disparity
of tone produced by the avalanche of mixed forms. Nervo
states:

> ¿No flota, por ventura, sobre el haz de citas . . . , sobre el deseo
> mismo infantil de hacer saber que se sabe, sobre el imitado
> artificio . . . , la inspiración más activa y consciente, el estilo más
> personal, el sabor lírico más intenso, el espíritu más lúcido e
> imperioso del Nuevo Continente Latino?[6]

> (Does there not float, by chance, over the surface of quotes . . . over
> the same childish desire to show how much he knows, over the
> imitative artifice . . . the most active and conscious inspiration, the
> most personal style, the most intense lyrical flavor, the most lucid
> and imperious spirit of the New Latin Continent?)

Nervo finds the richness of accumulation to be the greatest trait
of the poet of the "New Continent." What Nervo praises, how-
ever, is as much the role of the poet expressed in *Las montañas
del oro* as the poetry itself. The volume is structured loosely
around the progression of the poetic journey, falling from the
summit to the dark, interior depths, rising again to the sunlit
peaks. The journey exalts the role of the poet and calls atten-
tion to those who have previously followed the path, the poet's
models—Homer, Dante, Whitman, and Hugo. The comments
of Lugones' contemporaries praise not only the work itself but
the poetic process it described, reflecting the importance they
assigned to their poetic role.

Rubén Darío views the Lugones of *Las montañas del oro* from a
later perspective (1913): "Ya en la tarea de ideas revélase la
inagotable mina verbal, la facultad enciclopédica, el dominio
absoluto del instrumento y la preponderancia del don principal
y distintivo: la fuerza"[7] ("Within the framework of ideas one
finds the inexhaustible verbal mine, the encyclopedic authority,
the absolute power over the instrument and the preponderance
of that principal and distinctive gift: force"). These are the
traits most often attributed to Lugones' work, but Darío adds a

new perspective in viewing the derivative nature of *Las montañas del oro.* He compares the process of assimilation to a "rápido choque de miradas" (a "swift clashing of glances").

> Hay allí, sobre todo, un infuso conocimiento de cosas inmemoriales que se ha transmitido a través de innumerables generaciones, y que hace vagamente reconocerse, apenas, con algún rarísimo *contemporáneo,* en un rápido choque de miradas, o en la similitud de interpretación de un gesto, de un signo, de una palabra.[8]

> (There is, above all, an infused knowledge of immemorial ideas that has been handed down through countless generations, which is vaguely recognized, by some strange contemporary, in a swift clashing of glances or in the similar interpretation of a gesture, a sign, or a word.)

Darío sees Lugones' work as clearly derivative, but it is the process of selection that impresses him. Of his work Dario declares, "háceme pensar en las adolescencias proféticas, en una pérdida y un encuentro, no en el templo de los doctores, sino en el bosque entre los leones" ("[it] makes me think of prophetic adolescences, about loss and recovery, though not in the temple of the sages, but in the forest among the lions"). In the statements of both Nervo and Darío there is a hesitancy to use the label "original," yet both stress the impact and novelty of the volume.

STRUCTURE OF A BIZARRE JOURNEY

In *Las montañas del oro* one can see the beginning of Lugones' curious joining of technological prowess to erotic imagery, forecasting his adaptations of Laforgue's stress on the urban, scientific element and its relationship to the dissolution of traditional social and poetic patterns. Though the first two *ciclos* of the volume have their share of "rosas ultrajadas" ("defiled roses"), and "amor blasfematorio" ("blasphemous love"), the anthropomorphized landscapes take on a more jolting profile in the third *ciclo,* or cycle, where they are juxtaposed to Lugones' incongruous list of scientific and historical events. Although this volume is usually considered romantic in tone, its variations suggest some unusual twists. The "potro del viento" ("colt of the wind") earlier associated with the searching poetic *persona,* becomes the crashing locomotive, the "Gran caballo nego al cual no se ve sudar"[9] (the "Great black stallion whose sweat is not seen"). In this third *ciclo* Lugones sets this new beast next to more familiar constructions, mixing the organic and the technological with poetry's favored symbolic groupings:

> Y mira cómo se llena de amor el metal, tocándole el alma por medio del rayo; y cómo se ordena la armonía de los átomos; y cómo en la carne de los seres se modela la futura estatua que ha de ser el coronamiento de los Reinos: la triple estatua de talones de piedra, cintura de árbol y cabeza elocuente; y cómo en el sereno mar de sangre de las matrices está de la maternidad la flor callada, en el sueño de su corola de nueve pétalos; y cómo los carros sonantes corren por la paralela de hierro, en pos del corcel de hierro, cuya alma es un trueno de hierro, y cuyos bronquios de hierro tosen el huracán, y cuyo corazón de hierro va tempestado de brasas.(*OPC,* 99)

> (And see how the metal swells with love, its soul touched by lightning; and how the harmony of atoms is ordered; and how in the flesh of beings the future statue, to be the crown of the Kingdoms, is modeled: the triple statue with heels of stone, treelike waist and eloquent head; and how in the serene sea of the blood of the wombs lies the silent flower of maternity in its dreamy corolla of nine petals; and how the noisy cars speed along the iron parallel, in pursuit of the iron stallion, whose soul is of thunderous iron and whose iron bronchia cough up the hurricane, and whose iron heart goes forth stormed by hot coals.)

Even the quickening rhythm here signals an increasing fascination with the fabricated objects of an increasingly technological world.

Modernismo's extremes of beauty had to call forth their underside, the grinding gears that keep the machine going. Organic form, so highly praised in part of Lugones' early work, finds its corruption in these new hybrid forms, but most significant is the changing vision of the female figure. Taking his case to extremes, he singles out the figure of the Virgin to exemplify the horrors of fleshly decay:

Entonces, ¡oh armonía de los santos cielos!, parece como si sobre una herida vieja se derramara un ungüento de perlas finas; como si cada pecho estuviera lleno de música . . .

Y una voz se levanta diciendo: he aquí la Virgen que ha roto su prisión de seis mil años, para ofrendar a la Vida el jardín codiciado de su seno; he aquí sus cabellos, he aquí su carne que el horror de la esterilidad marchita, y que en la gloria de la germinación florecen, como divinos adornos, del trance luminoso . . . (*OPC,* 102)

(And then, Oh harmony of the sacred heavens!, it appears that a potion of fine pearls has been poured over an old wound; as if each breast were filled with music. . . .

Then, a voice rises speaking: behold the Virgin who has broken her prison of six thousand years, to offer to Life the coveted garden of her breast; behold her hair, behold her flesh withered by the horror of barrenness, and in the glory of germination they flourish, resembling divine adornments, of the luminous trance . . .)

The visceral nature of the passage leaps to the forefront, despite the slight taming effect of the accustomed setting. Even more startling is the reappearance of the "Rosa resplandeciente" (the "Blazing rose") to close the cycle of *Las montañas del oro* as the crowning image of the "Torre de Oro" (the "Golden Tower"). The triumvirate includes "el AMOR, la ESPERANZA, . . . y más alta, más alta, sobre todas las oraciones, sobre todas las liras, vestida con el fulgor de todos los soles, saludada por el fervor de todas las alabanzas, como un corazón de oro fundiéndose en llamas, más alta, más alta, la Rosa resplandeciente: la FE, en un formidable despedazamiento de astros" (*OPC,* 103), ("LOVE, FAITH, . . . and higher, higher, above all the prayers, above all the lyres, dressed with the splendor of all the suns, hailed by the fervor of all praise, like a heart of gold melting in the flames, higher, the Blazing Rose: FAITH in a splendid eruption of stars"). Like many other strange groupings in Lugones' poetry and prose, this grouping seems to thwart the allegorical summing-up that Lugones often resorts to. The bizarre mixture at the close of the volume, added to other extreme pairings, calls into question the journey of the "alma golondrina" (the "swallow's spirit") who seeks to ascend to the heights of the "cima pura" (the "pure crest").

Las montañas del oro's structure reinforces its thematic polarities. It constantly presents thematic opposites and then explores the unknown territory lying between them. The book's format, with divisions clearly marked by titles and its obvious assemblage as a **unified** work, struggles to maintain the coherent conceptual framework. It is composed of a lengthy introduction and three cycles. The three cycles, which differ thematically, are separated from one another by two "Reposorios" ("Responses") that return to the journey theme of the introduction. Loosely connecting all the sections is the journey of the poet, whose presence, although sometimes dispersed and displaced, gives the volume its coherence and direction.

Las montañas del oro has been interpreted as Lugones' attempt to recreate Dante's journey through the struggles of mankind; yet, without the aid of the introduction, epigraphs, and sections of the last cycle, this interpretation seems unlikely. The circuitous passage is perhaps more the record of Lugones' experimentation with new metrical forms and patterns of imagery than with an epic message. Certain patterns of imagery are developed extensively with different techniques, apparently for their own sake. The extent of their elaboration becomes the focus of the work, and not their value as bearers of intention. The mention of "pasos dantescos" ("Dantesque steps") in the introduction gives way to other forms of exploration. In the book's three cycles, the journey is not through the introduction's ordered realm of panoramic description but is a fragmented passage through the realm of the senses ("Primer ciclo"), through anthropomorphized landscapes ("Segundo ciclo"), and to the ascent and return to the panoramic view from the tower ("Tercer ciclo"). The final passage of the cycle marks a return to the ideal concepts of *Amor, Esperanza,* and *Fe* presented in the introduction, a discovery finally viewed from the summit of the "Torre de Oro."

The fall into darkness and the depths from the summit of light and faith, followed by the upward return to light, is a projection of an interior journey. In the interior cycles the organizing, rational poetic consciousness presented in the introduction is metonymically displaced onto surrounding nature or undergoes an inversion process when the rational, intellectual forces confront sensuality or eroticism. The opposition and divisiveness of the conflict of conscious and unconscious desires is projected outward onto nature, animal and human—especially female—forms. The idea of infinite expansion or progression through outward forms has its parallel in the expanding forms of consciousness, a concept forming the basis of much romantic poetry.[10] The two modes of examination of humanity—one outwardly and socially directed, the other inward-turning—form the base of the poetry of Lugones' favored models. The poetry of Edgar Allan Poe, Walt Whitman, and Victor Hugo is reflected in the different forms of *Las montañas del oro* and in its abrupt jumps from one direction of conscience to another.

INTRODUCTION TO *LAS MONTAÑAS DEL ORO*

The introduction to *Las montañas del oro* presents a poetic journey that strays from its contrasts of sublimity and degradation to give a tour of *modernismo*'s monuments built for social awareness and redemption. In Lugones' scheme of universality, the "Nuevo Mundo" ("New World") is not only an allegorical realm but a very present, endangered Spanish American frontier. The shift of focus, here ponderous and clearly drawn, from the personal spiritual journey to the exhortative mission of the prophet shows the same mixture of solipsistic viewpoint and messianic vision seen earlier in the prose journalism. The attack on positivism, the call to the People (el Pueblo), and the warning against the Herculean "Tío Sam" ("Uncle Sam"), repeat *modernismo*'s emphasis on the mixture of aesthetic and social battles.

The last section of the introduction provides the rationale for the beginning of the poetic journey and also establishes the thematic link to the first two cycles. In the midst of a cataclysm of darkness, faced with "esas formidables alarmas del abismo" ("those formidable alarms from the abyss") in the apocalyptic night that sets the poles of the earth against each other, the narrative voice establishes the path of ascension:

> La Cruz austral radiaba desde la enorme esfera
> Con sus cuatro flamígeros clavos, cual si quisiera
> En sus terribles brazos crucificar al Polo.
>
> . . . yo estaba solo

Entre mi pensamiento y la eternidad. Iba
Cruzando con dantescos pasos la noche . . .

(OPC, 60)

(The Southern Cross radiated from the enormous sphere
with its four flaming spikes, as if it desired
to crucify the Pole in its terrible arms

. . . I was alone

between my thoughts and eternity. I was
crossing with Dantesque steps the night . . .)

Although this passage suggests the possibility of descent and
impending danger, the movement into the first cycle is so
abrupt that the previously established unifying perspectives are
totally dissolved. Despite the introduction's last passage, which
mentions "bestias luminosas" ("luminous beasts"), "heridas / En
el flanco" ("wounded in their sides"), and unbridled movement,
the eroticism of the first cycle moves to the forefront so sud-
denly that its very appearance seems to dissolve the rational
consciousness that ostensibly directs it. The first cycle's epi-
graph, "HIC SUNT LEONES (Anotación geográfica de un
antiguo mapamundi)" ("HIC SUNT LEONES [Geographical
notations on an ancient map of the world]"), carries a connota-
tion of danger and bestiality, which will be developed almost
completely in terms of sexuality, darkness, and punishment.
The epigraph also announces the intention of removal to dis-
tant places and epochs, as if it were a journey into some savage
land long ignored.

Earthly physicality in the introduction serves a purpose dif-
ferent from that of the first two cycles. There its presence is
integrated into a symbolic system and its claims for attention are
denied in favor of an ideal scheme. The suggestiveness of frag-
ments of an earthly order is circumscribed within the enclosure
of the polarized scheme. In the first two cycles, however, the
repercussions of fragments of a more sensual natural order will
begin to overtake the ideal scheme and dislocate the balancing
system. The quest for poetic knowledge eventually must en-
counter its "cavernas" ("caverns"), and its "abismo" ("abyss")—a
reversion to primitivism—as the inevitable counterpart of the

unrestrained elevation.[11] Many symbols in the first two *ciclos* are drawn from the same network of classical and biblical motifs often used for erotic suggestion. The constant mingling of "castigo" ("punishment") with "lujuria" ("lust") shows a dangerous pleasure in transgression.[12]

"PRIMER CICLO": THE EROTIC LANDSCAPE

The system of imagery in the first cycle allows for greater freedom of associations and suggestion than the structures of the introduction. It is, however, monotonously continuous, and explicit similes thunder out analogies. At times the terms that compose and announce the analogies are startling in their association. For example, in "Metempsicosis" the unification of animal traits and natural landscapes presents striking contrasts: "Una luna ruinosa se perdía—con su amarilla cara de esqueleto—en distancias de ensueño y de problema;—y había un mar, pero era un mar eterno,—dormido en un silencio sofocante—como un fantástico animal enfermo.—Sobre el filo más alto de la roca,—ladrando al hosco mar, estaba un perro" (*OPC*, 72), ("An evil moon was losing itself—with its yellow skeleton face—in distances of dream and problem;—and there was a sea, but it was an eternal sea,—asleep in a suffocating silence—like a sick, fantastic animal. Upon the highest rocky ridge,—barking at the dark sea, was a dog"). The association of animal traits with the poetic persona is a constant in the first two cycles, and it gives a nebulous framework to the savagery and victimization that accompany the theme of sexuality.

The subjects of the first cycle are descriptions of mental states or of objects—"Oda a la desnudez," "A histeria," "Los celos del sacerdote," "La rima de los ayes," "Nebulosa Thule," "La vendimia de sangre," "Rosas del Calvario," "Metempsicosis," and "Antífonas." Eroticism, heavily laden with sadistic or macabre overtones, constitutes the major thematic material. The universal, impersonal religious imagery used in the introduction is here distorted to produce a satanic scheme of darkness, with the redemptive elements of light and ascension largely absent.

In a work where everything reverses the earlier stated

pattern—a spiritual underworld which is "la infinita latitud de mi alma—con silenciosas noches de seis meses" (*OPC,* 66) ("The infinite latitude of my soul—with its silent nights of six months")—even the mountain peaks represent a reversal of the earlier order. The mountain is a crypt, and the attention is directed to its interior, the fall from the peak to the caverns: "—Que allí ruge una mar de ondas acerbas—que enturbian los asfaltos y las naftas;—y que en ella las almas desembocan—los tristes sedimentos de sus llagas" (*OPC,* 67), ("There roars a sea of scathing waves—that obscure the asphalts and naphthas;—into it the souls empty—the wretched sediments of their sores").

The figure of the woman and the presence of eroticism abruptly enter this cycle. The break in the patterns of imagery and changes in the typographical format which accompany the theme of eroticism point out its transgressive, disruptive nature. Antitheses are no longer clearly outlined and conducive to soothing mediation. Even the all-inclusive vision of the central poetic figure breaks down, for the evasion of explicit erotic description leads to dissymmetry of expression. Here the female images are the favored ones of the decadents: the pale, spectral beauty and the cruel and distant *femme fatale* with androgynous characteristics.[13] Lugones mixes several types in his cast, from Poe's romantic heroine to the cadaverous image of necrophiliac passions in decadent fiction. The choice of the night as a temporal setting, with its countering effect to the rational forces of light, reinforces the transgressive nature of the theme.[14]

Traditional symbols relating to the female—those of Christian iconography as well as simple physical description—contribute to the unification of all the elements, for example, *flores, rosas, seno, luna, azucena, manzanas, del Edén* (flowers, roses, breast, moon, lily, apples, of Eden). Far from being an idealized conception of woman, however, these terms are used for degradation. The women are the "mujeres de mis noches" ("women of my nights"), and the feminine imagery is charged with degeneration: "Las llagas de las flores" ("the wounds of my flowers"), "rosas ultrajadas" ("defiled roses"), "las pálidas nupcias de la fiebre—florecen como crímenes" ("the pale wedding of the fever—flourishes like crimes"), "la media luna, como blanca uña—apuñaleando un seno" ("the half moon like a white fingernail—stabbing a breast"), "tus uñas, dagas de oro" ("your fingernails, golden daggers"). The idea of possession is that of profanation: "Quiero que ciña una corona de oro—tu corazón . . . y que brille tu frente de Sibila—en gloria cirial de los altares,—como una hostia de sagrada harina:—y que triunfes, desnuda como una hostia, en la pascua ideal de mis delicias" (*OPC,* 62) ("I want a golden crown to encircle— your heart . . . and I want your Sybilline brow to shine—in the glory of the altar candles,—like a host of sacred flour:—and I want you to triumph, naked like a host, in the ideal Easter ceremony of my pleasures").

Liturgical terms linked to eroticism are a constant in much of *modernista* poetry, as in Darío's *Prosas profanas* and much of Herrera y Reissig's verse. The iconography of medieval Christianity and mysticism provided an ideal source for mixture with the sensual images of Byzantine and Greek mythology. Yet Lugones is often more sexually explicit and violent than either Darío or Herrera y Ressig, as in "A Histeria": "—la selva dolorosa cuyos gajos—echaban sangre al golpe de las hachas,—como los miembros de un molusco extraño . . .—Y era tu abrazo como nudo de horca,—y eran glaciales témpanos tus labios,—y eran agrios alambres mis tendones,—y eran zarpas retráctiles mis manos,—y era el enorme potro un viento negro—furioso en su carrera de mil años" (*OPC,* 63) ("—the aching jungle whose limbs—spurted blood at the blow of the axe,—like the limbs of a strange mollusc . . .—And so your embrace was like the knot of a noose,—and like glacial floes were your lips,—and bitter wires were my tendons,—and so the enormous stallion was a black wind—furious in its thousand-year race"). The link between sexuality, victimization, and the woman is especially explicit in "Los celos del sacerdote" in the "deseado crucifijo de las bodas": "—y la gracia triunfal de tu cintura,—como una ánfora llena de magnolias,—y el hermético lirio de tu sexo,—lirio lleno de sangre y de congojas" (*OPC,* 65) ("desired crucifix of the weddings":—"and the triumphant grace of your waist,—like an amphora filled with magnolias,—and the impenetrable iris of your sex,—iris full of blood and anguish"). These combinations of suggestion and explicitness, especially here in the first cycle with its repetition and exclamations, sometimes strain the poetic associations to the point of creating a perhaps unwitting and grotesque parody on Lugones' part.

Profanation, linked with the macabre, is present in almost all the poems of the first cycle. The imagery patterns, established in the introduction (heridas, abismos, cavernas, larvas de los vicios [wounds, abysses, caverns, larvae of vices]) depart from the ideological frame of reference provided by the introduction. The human link is made explicit: "en la hipnótica selva de mi alma" ("in the hypnotic jungle of my soul") ("Rosas del Calvario" [*OPC,* 69]). The messianic prophet is transformed into his opposite: "Ése es mi corazón, el Maldiciente,—el que canta a los cielos tenebrosos—donde lloran en fuego las estrellas. . . . Ése es mi corazón hinchado de odios,—como un estuche de terribles joyas—ávidas de punzar tu cuerpo de oro" (*OPC,* 69) ("That is my heart, the slanderer,—who praises the dark skies—where blazing stars shed tears. . . . That is my heart swollen by many hatreds,—like a box of terrible jewels— anxious to stab your golden neck"). The sadomasochistic element is one of the most powerful sources of thematic material, for the frequent repetition of "castigo," "herida," "llagas" ("punishment," "wound," "sores") constantly parallels scenes of sensuality: "Y cuando hundido en la imponente noche—como el escombro de una altiva estatua,—naufrague mi cerebro en el ensueño,—yo exaltaré el cariño de tus garras,—como aprieta el cilicio a sus riñones—el lujurioso asceta en sus batallas" (*OPC,* 70) ("And when in the imposing night—like the ruins of a proud statue,—my brain awash in fantasy,—I shall praise the affection of your embrace,—just as the lecherous ascetic in his battles pulls tight the hairshirt around his kidneys").

In the nocturnal settings only one side of the cosmos outlined in the introduction is developed, the realm of darkness combined with shrouded as well as explicit eroticism. Erotic imagination adopts negative connotations by its description in terms of delirium, darkness unredeemed except for the reflected, spectral light of the moon seen in the pallor of the female amid skeletal ruins, and the repetition of wounding. The thunder of proclamation gives way to the voices of the nocturnal forest, carried by the wind and the poet's lyre.

The animal most closely associated with the wind and the night is the stallion or colt, linked to the masculine poetic voice. Its association with sexuality is made explicit by its link to "yeguas" ("mares") while the mystery of the feminine is involved with the night's invasiveness and the wounding power of nocturnal eyes. The moon's reflection is cold and deathlike, as in "Rosas del Calvario," and its connotation is always negative within this section; it is deathly pale and merely reflective in "Metempsicosis": "Una luna ruinosa se perdía—con su amarilla cara de esqueleto—en distancias de ensueño y de problema" (*OPC*, 72) ("An evil moon was losing itself—with its yellow skeleton face—in distances of dream and problem"). Its very mention accompanies an unusual pairing of terms, "de ensueño y de problema" ("of dream and of problem"), which prefigures the use of the moon theme within a constant scheme of dislocation and fragmentation, as in the *Lunario sentimental.*

Repetition of the same nuclear elements often carried to extremes is one of the most important stylistic devices in the first cycle. Apparently borrowing from Poe, and even more clearly from José Asunción Silva's *Nocturnos,* rhythmic repetition at times produces the desired incantatory effect, but also creates a numbing sensation by pounding out the same element in a repetitive syntactical arrangement, as in "Oda a la desnudez":

—Mira la desnudez de las estrellas;—la noble desnudez de las bravías—panteras del Nepal, la carne pura—de los recién nacidos; tu divina—desnudez que da luz como una lámpara—de ópalo y cuyas vírgenes primicias—disputaré al gusano que te busca,—para morderte con su helada encía—el panal perfumado de tu lengua,— tu boca, con frescuras de piscina. (*OPC*, 62)

—Look at the nakedness of the stars;—the noble nakedness of the savage panthers of Nepal, the pure flesh—of the newborn; your divine nakedness which shines like a lamp—of opal and whose virgin first fruits—I shall dispute with the worm that seeks,—to bite with its frozen gums,—the perfumed honeycomb of your tongue,—your mouth with the freshness of a pool.)

The same technique of repetition can produce a seemingly conscious parody of itself, as in "Rosas del Calvario." In extending the description of deathly pallor and frigidity, the reduction of elements to a parenthetical expression is as deflating an operation as a footnote in a poem: "Mi novia yerta viene:—es un callado lirio—que nació en la bondad de los sepulcros—(Flor, Virgen, Alma, Espuma, Nieve, Símbolo),—¡lo frágil!" (*OPC*, 71) ("My beloved, so rigid, comes;—she is a silenced iris—born in the kindness of the sepulcre—(Flower, Virgin, Soul, Foam, Snow, Symbol) O so fragile!"). Rather than extending the comparison, this shortcut ends with the word "símbolo" ("symbol") followed by the summary "¡lo frágil!" ("so fragile!"). In the same poem, the words "símbolo" or "simbólico" are repeated three times, drawing attention to the artificial nature of the scene created. The heaping up of nouns in one stretch, compressing the extended previous description, serves the same purpose.

"SEGUNDO CICLO": VIOLENCE AND NATURE

Extraordinary landscapes form the background of the second cycle, whose dominant characteristics are the hostile, embattled forces that surge through nature's forms—trees, mountains, sea, coal, cattle, clouds, and wind. The first cycle's presentation of eroticism in terms of physical wounding (for example, "llagas," "heridas" ["sores," "wounds"]) is here transformed into a more generalized anthropomorphic landscape, the cycles of nature itself. It is as if individual passions were mirrored by scenes from nature (a reflecting technique made much more explicit in *Los crepúsculos del jardín*). In the second cycle of *Las montañas del oro* the passionate quality of natural forces is physically agonizing and destructive, as in "Las montañas": "¡Oh, cuán fríos son los besos de las nieves,—de las nieves que ensangrienta la agonía de las tardes, . . ." (*OPC*, 82) ("Oh, how cold are the kisses of the snows,—of the snows that are bloodstained by the agony of the afternoons! . . ."). Similarly, in "Los árboles" clouds are dissolved into martyrdom: "como yeguas desgreñadas que se agolpan . . .—como pira de amazonas degolladas—que confunden las heridas desnudeces de sus cuerpos" (*OPC*, 80) ("like rumpled mares who crowd together . . .—like a pyre of slaughtered Amazons—confusing the naked wounds of their bodies").

Repetition is even more pronounced in the second cycle than in the first. Descriptive passages are extended at great length by the use of the conjunction *y* (and), while apostrophe and exclamation, present in the first cycle, are almost totally absent. The absence of the first-person voice, combined with an extremely lengthy sentence structure, creates a distancing, impersonal effect. In this cycle, which describes the elemental forces of nature, the distancing effect contributes to the enormity and grandeur of the scenes described. Although the specific human element is absent, the thematic elements are anthropomorphized—*el desierto, los árboles, las montañas, el mar, el carbón, las vacas, las nubes, el viento* (the desert, trees, mountains, sea, coal, cattle, clouds, wind). These natural scenes are described in terms of the dichotomy of the sexes, with veiled mythological references and the language of esoteric religions.

In the nocturnal world of pulsating movement and sound, the elements are victimized by devouring, unspecified primal forces. Without the aid of an explicit thematic link, the martyrdom of "El hijo del hombre" is repeated in the forms of nature. Even light can appear in "Los árboles" as a disruptive image: "—se esfuma la Vía Láctea cual la sutura de un cráneo—negro" (*OPC*, 8) ("—the Milky Way disappears as if it were the suture in a black cranium"). Nowhere is the erotic aspect of nature's processes more pronounced that in "La Mar." The sea is "la hembra jadeante" ("the panting female") whose "grandes pechos—de sirena echa a la orilla,—y los muerden los peñascos,—y las ásperas arenas los lastiman" (*OPC*, 84) (great siren breasts,—she throws to the shore,—and the rocks bite them,—and the rough sands bruise them"). The sea's eternal flux, "sus pulsos acordes como octavas gigantescas" ("its flux in harmony like gigantic octaves") occurs on another level, the cyclic passage of the sun into night, yet another martyrdom, where the sun is also battered about and is like "una gran rosa deshojada" ("a great deflowered rose"). The sea as it approaches the coast resembles the enveloping approach of the night; both are procreative, and at the same time threatening:

—y el confuso advenimiento de las vidas—riega su matriz de flores,—y de fósforos rielantes la ilumina,—y el misterio de los gérmenes en los plácidos silencios—de las aguas, tiene nupcias de amatista. (*OPC,* 84)

—and the confusing arrival of lives,—drenches her womb with flowers,—and with shimmering matchlights illuminates her,—and the mystery of germs in the placid silences—of the waters, celebrates amethyst nuptials.)

The sea throws itself against the rock, "—destrozándose . . . en las hondas convulsiones del insomnio de su gran cuerpo de víctima" (*OPC,* 84) ("—destroying itself . . . in the deep convulsions of insomnia of its great victim's body"). A mention of ecstasy is always associated with violence. The fate of all nature is to devour and be devoured. Therefore everything is described in terms of physical martyrdom. Even silence takes on corporal form in "Las vacas." Dream is also like a physical presence: "Flota el sueño de los bosques—impregnado de la gran extenuación de las aromas—en el seno de la noche como un feto agonizante" (*OPC,* 86) ("The dream of the forests floats—impregnated with the great weakening of the aromas—in the heart of the night like an agonizing fetus"). Cattle do not appear framed in the usual placid picture of a pastoral setting. Their sound arrives first, "como el lívido sollozo de una viudez herida—que lancea el largo flanco de la sombra" (*OPC,* 86) ("like the pale wimper of wounded widowhood—that spears the long side of the shadow"). In the second *reposorio,* "Laudatoria a Narcisco," the poetic voice again emerges as a unified presence. Even though the combative *yo* of the introduction and first *reposorio* is directed toward a public and carries a social message, the two interior cycles dissolve this unifying voice in a solipsistic projection onto a multitude of earthly and unearthly presences. In "Laudatoria a Narcisco" the return of the unifed voice is not accompanied by the same concerns. Leaving behind the messianic stance of the prophet in the wilderness, this *yo* (I) is directed to itself alone. No more fitting image of self-contemplation could be found than that of Narcissus. Exterior reality fades from view as the soul contemplates itself, losing itself in the rites of communion with solitude, no longer striving to gain an outside audience nor to push it to action. The passage of time is no longer perceived and the rite of mirroring is endlessly repeated.

The act of self-enclosure, whose ultimate aim is self-knowledge, must not look toward exterior forms for its expression. Therefore the images of this rite are taken from liturgical or magical forms, whose purpose is to draw the unifying conscience together again. Removing associations of punishment and wounding from sexual pleasure, the rite is a sensual one, "en el completo / Deleite de la consunción" ("in the complete / Pleasure of consummation"). In the address to Narcissus, natural elements are no longer devouring but are bound together in an animating, vital structure: "Y la virtud del fuego que animó tu estructura / Carnal, hecha de sangre, de lirio y de amargura" (*OPC,* 91) ("And the virtue of the fire that gave life to your carnal / Structure made of blood, of iris and of bitterness"). With the combination "de sangre, de lirio y de amargura" ("of blood, of iris and of bitterness"), one begins to see the condensing or foreshortening process that will occupy a major role in many of the poems of *Los crepúsculos del jardín.* The very image of the soul's duality, as it is reflected in the water, will be expanded in the second volume to an almost constant process of reflection, self-enclosure, and introspection. The narcissistic focus subsumes all things viewed under its self-reflexive nature.

The second *reposorio*'s final salute to Verlaine, although fitting within the context of this poem, hardly announces what is to come in the third cycle. As if pressing on in his "titanic epic," Lugones pays homage to another poetic model and seeks yet another revelation of the perfect model of the poetic spirit. The "suaves clavicordios" ("soft clavichords") of the second *reposorio* are scarcely fitting for the proclamations to modernity that will be made in the final cycle: "El himno de las torres" praises "la gloria de las buenas artes de hierro y la de piedra" ("the glory of the good arts of iron and stone") and leaves behind the fluidity and measure of the rites of Narcissus. Making a complete about-face, the poetic voice once again thunders out to the multitudes, and the poetic soul, now the "golondrina ideal . . . desde su torre sigue mirando" (*OPC,* 95) ("the ideal swallow . . .

continues to keep watch from her tower"). The previous passage through the cosmos, the interior darkness, and contemplation has led to this—a bird's eye view of human evolution and future progress. Absurd in its grandiosity and conception and rapid jumps, the logic of the poetic journey is yet undeniable. In Nervo's terms, "el mismo deseo infantil de hacer saber que se sabe" ("the same childish desire to show how much he knows") reaches its highest point in the third cycle. Ending the whirlwind tour of the universe with a flourish, the last cycle resembles a catalogue of the events of humanity, a compressed history lesson. Saúl Yurkiévich has pointed out the resemblances between this cycle and the poetic practices of juxtaposition by Huidobro and the *modernistas*.[15] Notable also is the forecasting of elements to come in *Los crepúsculos del jardín* and especially in *Lunario sentimental*. Despite its partial justification in terms of the journey of ascent and descent, the eclecticism and exaggeration bring forth a self-deflating movement. The long lists of names and places produce a loss of perspective under the weight of their sheer abundance.

The last cycle does, however, thematically bring together the previous elements of the volume. It establishes a retrospective continuity between the "Introducción," and the two intermediate cycles. Surveying all of the physical world from the "Torre de Oro," the voyager poet again finds opportunity for the ascent to the heights and can survey the day's cyclical passage from day to night and then to a new dawn.

"TERCER CICLO": MYSTICISM AND TECHNOLOGY

Just as the "Introducción" begins with "una gran columna de silencio y de ideas en/marcha. / El canto grave que entonan las mareas / Respondiendo a los ritmos de los mundos lejanos. . . ." ("a great column of silence and ideas / march forth. / The deep song harmonized by the tides. / Responding to the rhythms of faraway lands . . ."), so the third cycle is initiated with a mention of song and sound. Topics of modernity and of the conflict of science and nature again enter, and from the elevated perspective the aims of faith and reason are to be resolved. Mythic aspects of antiquity mingle with the discoveries of the present, while the treasures of antiquity are contiguous with the rhythmic cycle of nature, just as modernity discovers a new nature. New realms of discovery will create new pathways of understanding. Lugones gives a new twist to the organic metaphor:

> Y hay no obstante otros hombres, sabios, que hacen libros, como quien siembra una selva, para tener maderos con que arbolar naves futuras: Darwin y Claudio Bernard, Crookes y el profesor Roentgen, Pasteur, Edison, Ernesto [sic] Hello y Nietzsche, Karl Marx y Fabre d'Olivet y Eliphas Lévi, Champollion, Augusto Comte, Maury, Vogt y Ralph Waldo Emerson. (*OPC*, 99)

> (And there are nevertheless, other men, sages, who write books like someone who plants a jungle, in order to produce wood to outfit future ships: Darwin and Claude Bernard, [etc.] . . .)

Paying tribute to his century, this eclectic list praises the unification of science and vision:

> Y mira cómo se llena de amor el metal, tocándole el alma por medio del rayo; y cómo se ordena la armonía de los átomos; y cómo en la carne de los seres se modela la futura estatua que ha de ser el coronamiento de los Reinos: la triple estatua de talones de piedra, cintura de árbol y cabeza elocuente. (*OPC*, 99)

> (And see how the metal swells with love, its soul touched by lightning; and how the harmony of atoms is ordered; and how in the flesh of beings the future statue, to be the crown of the Kingdoms, is modeled: the triple statue with heels of stone, treelike waist and eloquent head.)

The same descriptive opulence earlier applied to the elements of nature is present, though less frequent. The newly explored continents are set forth in terminology similar to that of the first cycle's erotic descriptions. The new lands are:

> tierras negras donde el Sol se acuesta entre palmeras; donde hay serpientes que parecen joyas venenosas y flores más bien pintadas que los tigres; y bisontes, y elefantes, y jirafas, y pájaros del Paraíso, y luciérnagas, y resinas, y esencias, y bálsamos, y corales, y perlas—

éstas en conchas de valvas rosadas, como hostias intactas entre labios que comulgan—, y dulces nueces, y polvo de oro. (*OPC,* 97)

(black lands where the Sun sets among palm trees; where there are snakes that resemble venomous jewels and flowers more vividly colored than tigers: and bisons, and elephants, and giraffes, and birds of Paradise, and fireflies, and resin, and essences, and balsams, and corals, and pearls—these in shells with rosy valves, like hosts, intact, between lips receiving communion—, and sweet nuts and powdered gold.)

In the penultimate section, the passage of night into day is resolved by the descent of God to the "Torre de Oro." The appearance of celestial beings explains and gives coherence to the succession of earlier states. Even the appearance of the Virgin is described in terms earlier used for erotic description. In conjunction with the first cycle, this last section is obviously meant to tie together the previous erotic passage with the rising of the soul from night to day: "Porque ya es la Pascua sobre tu noche de seis mil años" (*OPC,* 102) ("Because it is finally Easter over your night of six thousand years").

The final section concludes the cycle with an ascension and the appearance of the virtues: *el Amor, la Esperanza,* and *la Fe.* The poetic voyager, authenticated through the passage of the poetic journey, has now returned to the position of heights and self-knowledge forecast in the introduction. While in the introduction the conflict between faith and doubt is seen in stark terms of rigid dichotomies, with faith represented as ascetic purity rising out of darkness ("La cima es el esfuerzo visible del abismo / Que lucha en las tinieblas por salir de sí mismo" [*OPC,* 57] ["The peak is the visible effort of the abyss / That battles in the darkness to overcome itself"]), in the final passage of the third cycle its nature changes. It is opulent, fiery, and acclaimed, "como un corazón de oro fundiéndose en llamas, más alta, más alta, la Rosa resplandeciente: la Fe, en un formidable despedazamiento de astros" (*OPC,* 103) ("like a golden heart being melted in flames, higher, higher, the blazing Rose: Faith, in an astounding eruption of stars"). The sensual imagery once confined to darkness and sexuality is elevated and greeted with acclaim. In conjunction with the description of the Virgin, the

"Rosa resplandeciente" takes on mystical and sensual associations. Like the rest of the third cycle, here many traits once codified into dichotomies are now combined in multivalent symbols, unstable as they may be.

One of the most significant elements of the third cycle is its praise of progress and technology. The names of contemporaries from all professions are given along with those of musicians, spiritual leaders, and explorers from the past. The eclectic mix foreshadows the juxtaposition of ancient and modern mythology that will be used in *Lunario sentimental*. Elements from the second cycle, which there describe psychic states, are here used to name technical realities. The railroad, prime symbol of technology and expansion, is described in animated form:

> ¡gran caballo, negro, negro, negro, gran caballo comedor de fuego, gran caballo en temblor de enormes músculos lanzado, con una nube en las narices, a los jadeantes trotes del millar de leguas: gran caballo negro, gran caballo negro, gran caballo negro al cual no se ve sudar! (*OPC*, 99)

> (Great black, black, black horse, great fire-eating horse, great horse thrown forth in a trembling of enormous muscles, with a cloud in its nostrils, to the panting, thousand-league trots: great black horse, great black horse, great black horse that never sweats!)

These symbolic groupings are mixed to the point of incongruity, and if these last passages of the third cycle were not contained within the structure of the volume as a whole, their hybrid appearance would seem to be a parody of the fanciful and often bizarre mixtures *modernismo* created with its inherited symbols.

CONCLUSION

In no other selections from Lugones' early work does his avid desire to be in the forefront of artistic endeavors show more clearly than in *Las montañas del oro*. Still under the spell of *modernismo*'s rush into territories to conquer and assimilate, Lugones attempts to scale the heights in record time. The furious rush of assimilation leaves little time for careful arrangement and measured gradation from one style to the next. Experimenting with practices that would become more apparent in later poets (such as the *ultraístas* and Huidobro), Lugones' first major work reflects his age's anxiety to move into the mainstream.

The poetic journey, through the leaps among the poet's models—Homer, Dante, Hugo, Poe, Whitman, Verlaine, and countless unnamed ones—does indeed constitute an allegory, an unsteady and paradoxical one. Although Lugones' original scheme of dichotomies is rearranged and fractured to such an extent that only fragments can be seen toward the end (despite the last-ditch effort in the third cycle at summing up his purpose), the remnants of his model texts crop up along the way to orient his followers. If not an allegory with universal meaning, the particular outlines of this rite of passage do have special relevance for the poetry in the *modernista* context. Darío's earlier mentioned comment, comparing Lugones' process of assimilation to "un rápido choque de miradas" ("a swift clashing of glances"), points out the rapid, jolting, and all-encompassing nature of the volume. Not only does he strive to include all the great figures of poetry, Lugones also wants to include thinkers, inventors, mystics, and magicians of the past and present in his *opus*. Since the original framework cannot accommodate all this within its scheme of polarities, a final flourish of lists climaxes his survey from the towering stance of encyclopedic knowledge and vision. Attempting to surpass *modernismo*'s foremost poet, Rubén Darío, who searched for a path to incorporate "toda la lira" ("all of the lyric tradition"), Lugones attacks other realms—science and technology—in his effort to expand his poetic empire.

Modernismo's and Lugones' excesses, so flagrant in *Las montañas del oro,* will undergo a condensation and taming in later collections. Having traveled the poetic circuit of his day, Lugones will no longer be so flamboyant in his proposals. The massive ensemble will undergo a refining process, and as the inventory focuses in on reduced expanses, so the poetic subject will be reduced in perspective and presence. Nevertheless, although scale is being reduced, the particular traits of *Las montañas del oro*—its overt exaggerations, monumental excesses and overloadings, willful twistings of form and content, and elements of grotesque humor—will continue and be intensified in different functions in *Los crepúsculos del jardín* and *Lunario sentimental.*

4

Los crepúsculos del jardín:
Subversion, Irony, Parody

Los crepúsculos del jardín (1905) is usually considered to be the work of Lugones which exhibits most completely the conventions of *modernismo*, especially with its attention to stylized scenes, exotic detail, and erotic description. Although it presents many similarities with *modernismo*'s conventions, it also includes a masked but critical commentary on them. By his excesses of elaborate stylization. Lugones deflates the self-enclosure of *modernismo*, its arcane symbols and resistant formal structures. The publication of *Los crepúsculos del jardín* in 1905 corresponds to a waning in the poetic movement of *modernismo*, which now begins to intersect with other literary tendencies such as realism. Its conventionality as a mode of writing now becomes more clearly visible because of the abundance of productions that make its mechanisms more apparent. Just as *la poesía gauchesca* at this time reveals itself as a code of constructions that simulates frankness and "simple" language,[1] so *modernismo*'s ubiquitous presence allows for its own deciphering as a code and enlarges its circle of initiates.

Although *modernismo* does not postulate a world vision in the same way that the social prophecies of romanticism do, its inward expansion creates a type of muted message. Although its rhetoric is not the "Romantic megaphone" of Hartman's description, its plethora of euphonic devices and striking visual images assertively push forward its conceptual framework. *Modernismo*'s foundations in symbolism propose correspondences between the sensory world and a transcendent reality, and since this system privileges a certain array of objects in the sensory world to symbolize inner states, its intensification process is often one of decoration, a heaping up of stylistic devices and

109

visual details until its very excesses make it vulnerable to parodic attack. When the conceptual framework supporting the code of *modernismo* begins to fade, when it becomes accessible to a wider public as a set of easily understood signs, then the writing itself becomes more visible as an act of construction, a craft or work rather than a revelation of transcendent meaning.

The poetic self-enclosure of *Los crepúsculos del jardín* alternates between fragility and tonal shading on one hand, and violent dislocation and cacophony on the other. In the same manner, *Los crepúsculos del jardín*'s major themes, eroticism and crepuscular landscapes, bounce back and forth between extremes. For Lugones, a pattern of pristine intactness apparently invites an invasive transgression. In *Los crepúsculos,* however, rather than breaking *modernismo*'s patterns of mysterious rites and consistent beauty from the outside, Lugones subverts them from within. Exaggeration is one of Lugones' favored methods of making his models more visible. He exaggerates certain themes by extending their development too far, or points out certain techniques by explicitly commenting on their use within the poems themselves. One swan will not suffice, there must be three; each facet of the sunset's fading glory must be catalogued, and the detailed presentation of the desired woman detracts from its totality by a listing of the separate parts of her decor, including even her stocking color. The overflow of odds and ends, the *bibelotisme* of the poems, begins to take on prosaic tones of realism rather than the enchanted sketches for which *modernismo* was striving.

In his second volume Lugones violates the mysteries of *modernismo* by exaggerating the methods of producing the aura, by disclosing its secrets and allowing the uninitiated to participate. The elements he selects from the code's iconography of eroticism and beauty are not contained within a relationship of impassibility and self-containment. Lugones' didacticism reemerges as he strives to point out, with a heavy hand, his production methods. In doing so, he releases its secrets and exposes its rites. As the models become explicit, he adds a distancing commentary on the construction process which deflates the aura. Time and again, the deflation is apparent and the self-reflexive world of *modernismo* changes into a commentary on the process of construction. Yet, unlike the deflation in *Lunario sentimental,* here one cannot see as clearly the impulses behind the dismantling of *modernismo*'s world view.

Is this transgression and subversion of *modernismo*'s norms by exaggeration and overloading a completely conscious act on the part of Lugones? Given the context of his preceding and subsequent writings, this interpretation seems unlikely. All of Lugones' early writings, including the journalistic prose and the poetry of *Las montañas del oro,* exhibit the celebratory style and the overloading process that triggers its own parody.[2] By exalting the nature of his models, he overvalues their use for his own purposes and clings very tightly to culturally approved models. The awareness of the end result of this process, the dissolution of the image of the poet as *vidente* (prophet), although suggested in the poetic preface to *Los crepúsculos del jardín,* is acknowledged fully only later, in the preface to *Lunario sentimental.* And when he does bow to the image of the poet as simply a craftsman or maker, rather than a prophet or seer, Lugones replies with a vengeance and, in effect, retreats instead of advancing farther into new territory.

Evidence of the presence or absence of intentionality in creating the parodic effect is given by the opinions of Lugones' contemporaries. The excesses of *Los crepúsculos del jardín* created an impact lost to later readers. Within its frame of reference, the poetry of the surrounding epoch, *Los crepúsculos del jardín* strained but did not destroy *modernismo*'s conventions. A non-ironic reading of its poetry would presuppose a stability of contexts, that is, a reading without a parodic double imposed by an explicit knowledge of the poetic code it illustrates.[3] Since *Los crepúsculos del jardín* was produced within a transition period, not only of literary conventions but of Lugones' society as a whole, it must be remembered that many of the codified signs still carried their evocative power, without being perceived as out of context.[4]

CONTRASTS WITH *LAS MONTAÑAS DEL ORO*

Los crepúsculos del jardín contrasts in many ways with the message-oriented *Las montañas del oro.* Not structured as an allegorical progression, as is *Las montañas del oro,* its divisions are based more on internal thematic unity than on their relationship to the volume as a whole. There are, however, two main unifying elements of the collection. First, it is characterized by the attention to visual aspects, especially those associated with the volume's title. Its formal or rustic gardens and the play of fading light on static scenes serve as settings on which to project emotion or memory. The second element is the highlighted presence of the woman, an ideal the *modernistas* transformed into a special symbolic code. These two elements are present in most *modernista* poetry and usually suggest nostalgia and sensuality within a self-contained world far removed from that of everyday objects and trite settings. Their recurring presence in *Los crepúsculos del jardín* gives an apparent unity to the collection; however, some variations in treatment constitute a departure from established *modernista* patterns, even to the point of dismantling *modernismo*'s common precepts.

The preface of *Los crepúsculos del jardín,* in contrast to the introduction to *Las montañas del oro,* stresses the volume's lighter nature. Offered to reader as a *ramillete* (collection), its aim is diversion rather than instruction:

> Pasatiempo singular
> Tal vez, aunque harto inocente,
>
> . . . .
>
> Epopeya baladí
> Que, por lógico resorte
> Quizá sirva a tu consorte
> Para su *five o'clock tea* . . .
>
> (*OPC,* 107)
>
> Singular pursuit
> Perhaps, although quite innocent
>
> . . . .
>
> Trivial epic
> That, as a logical resort
> Might be of use to your consort
> For his five o'clock tea . . .

A mixture of levels is signaled early in the Preface by the use of deflationary adjectivization, such as "flaqueza vencedor" ("victorious weakness"), and the use of everyday words. The role of the poet is no longer a godlike or martyred one; he is but a simple worker who expects earthly rewards:

> Mas yo sudé mi sudor
> En mi parte de labranza.
> Y el verde de mi esperanza,
> Es primicia de labor.
>
> Obrero cuya tarea
> Va sin grimas ni resabios,
> Mientras a flor de sus labios
> Un aria vagabundea . . .
>   (*OPC,* 108)
>
> (But I have toiled in my sweat
> At my part of the cultivation.
> And the green of my hope,
> Is the first fruit of my labor.
>
> Worker whose task
> Goes on, unresisting,
> While upon his lips
> An aria idly meanders . . .)

Gigantism, present in *Las montañas del oro,* is replaced in *Los crepúsculos del jardín* by watercolor landscapes and formal gardens. It is poetry ostensibly in the tradition of Verlaine or of Rubén Darío's *Prosas profanas,* whose search was for musicality in verse and the suggestive nuance instead of overt comparison. Figures from Greek mythology, swans, ephemeral twilights, *femmes fatales,* and exotic coloration—the unmistakable stamps of *modernismo*—are clearly present. There are derivations from Albert Samain's *Au jardin de l'infante,* and the precision of detail follows Gautier's Parnassian precept, "Sculpte, lime, cisèle" ("Sculpt, polish, chisel"). Character, like that of the poet–speaker in *Las montañas del oro* or of the beautiful woman prized by the *modernistas,* is dispersed in a series of functions that negate total identity. The metonymical description of the woman ranges from vague suggestion to fetishistic contemplation. At times religious language expresses eroticism, similar to the practice of many *fin de siglo* poets, and most importantly, the poetry of Rubén Darío. The treatment of eroticism, always linked with darkness, punishment, and wounding in *Las montañas del oro*, is much less consistent here. Lugones sometimes changes the *femmes fatales* into laughing schoolgirls and the ardent young suitors into aging bachelors.

The function of nature's imagery has a different purpose in *Los crepúsculos del jardín*, for no coherent structure in nature is traced. Although natural settings are favored, they are viewed from a fragmented perspective. Leaving the *tableau* presentation in favor of a close-up focus on individual elements, the vision of the poetic eye is narrowed. No longer does nature serve as an ordered symbolic background from which an allegory can be constructed, as it did in *Las montañas del oro*. The favored scene is an interior space, a garden, a landscape reflected in a mirror, or moonlight gazing back from the water. The extension of the twilight moment aids in giving a nebulous quality to the scenes, which are usually detached from an historical frame of reference.

LOS CREPÚSCULOS DEL JARDÍN: A VISUAL PERSPECTIVE

With the close-up focus, it is difficult to keep in view a hierarchy of nature. Just as the temporal scheme is broken, the panoramic gaze breaks into fragments, with special emphasis on objects seen out of context, especially luxurious or exotic materials. Baudelaire's remarks on pictorial art have special relevance for a discussion of *Los crepúsculos del jardín*, for attention is shifted more to visual elements in this volume. In his art criticism, Baudelaire remarks on the results of this shift of focus: "Plus l'artiste se penche avec impartialité vers le détail, plus l'anarchie augmente. Qu'il soit myope ou presbyte, toute hierarchie et toute subordination disparaissent"[5] ("The more the artist tends impartially toward detail, the more anarchy increases. Whether he is near-sighted or far-sighted, all hierarchy and all subordination disappear"). An important change within *Los crepúsculos del jardín* is the inversion of the practice of landscape/emotion reflection. The mirror image, which catches a fragment of a landscape and contains it within an enclosed space, restructures the relationship of human reflection in nature. It points up the mechanical manipulation of scenic space, and provides a visual image for the poetic process of duplication and refraction of sight. The use of reflection, either in pools of water or mirrors, is an important element that repeats on a visual level the process of authorial duplication by refraction from many angles. The sky, the water, and human eyes participate in this merging, identification, and subsequent awareness of dissimilarity.

As the images of nature in *Los crepúsculos del jardín* are dispersed or fragmented, the all-encompassing poetic voice that frames the diverse poems of the volume dissolves. Instead of possessing grandiloquence, the lyrical voice is diminished and dispersed in a variety of functions. The run-on alexandrines separated by dashes of *Las montañas del oro* disappear, and the sonnet form dominates the collections. Although verse forms are often mixed, rhyme always remains. Owing to the conciseness the sonnet requires, extended similes (as in *Las montañas del oro*) virtually disappear, and the syntax becomes more fluid with the extensive use of enjambment. Neologisms and unexpected modifiers transmit a playful, more humorous tone; and the formal gardens grow in complexity until they become a mockery of themselves. Comments inserted about the construction of these scenes give some of them a conversational tone, as in "New Mown Hay." Lugones treats not only the love theme more lightly, but comments implicitly on the type of poetry that he and others had been writing.

DESDOBLAMIENTO AND THE SUBJECT'S ROLE

The process of double vision, or *desdoblamiento* of the braided helix of signifier and signified, rests on the interruption, or *découpage*, of the construction process. *Los crepúsculos del jardín* is not only an assemblage of different sets of icons; as a representation of the process of textual production, it presents as well an act that metaphorizes its own procedures. If we hunt for revealing signs of the fissure of a poetic text, the narrow entrance that helps us understand the shrouded mechanics of construction, what we find in Lugones is an anticipation of this intrusion. Rather than be discovered, with the startled look over the shoulder, by the intruder who peers into the circle, Lugones makes great whacks in the circle, jolts that open it wide. He invites the voyeur to enter the circle, like the circus barker who drums up business. The defined poetic voice stands back as interpreter or summarizer, the parodist who breaks the identification between the representation of the scene and its observer. This interruption, or distancing, may be caused not just by parody but by the insertion of the deflating or disquieting moment, the wrong word, the colloquial turn of phrase into the fixed scene.

The directing speaker's voice, although not necessarily identified as such, may be present in the binding and encircling presence of rhyme and meter, a note of knowing irony, an outlining of scenic space, or the way it parcels out the presentation of the body. In the case of the presentation of the female figure, an image prized for possession, status, and, above all, rich possibility, a fetishistic or metonymical dispersion of the figure invites a destructive gaze, an invitation to participate in dividing it up, and therefore in a total possession and directing dominance on the part of the observer. The challenge is to sort out the shifting relationship of this subject–object pattern, to show when the directing hand loses control and allows, consciously or unconsciously, another subversive voice to enter on its own terms. As Gilles Deleuze defines this relationship in writing, it is language's **reflexive** nature that parallels the physical and creates analogies between speaking, seeing, and hearing:

> Si le langage *imite* les corps, ce n'est pas par l'onomatopée, mais par la flexion. Et si les corps imitent le langage, ce n'est pas par les organes, mais par les flexions. Aussi y a-t-il toute une pantomine intérieure au langage, comme un discours, un récit intérieure au corps. Si les gestes parlent, c'est d'abord parce que les mots miment les gestes.[6]

> (If language *imitates* the body, it is not by onomatopoeia, but by flexion. And if bodies imitate language, it is not by the organs but by flexions. Thus, there is a whole interior pantomime to language, like a discourse, an interior narrative to the body. If gestures speak, it is first because words mime gestures.)

The introduction of prosaic or urban elements in the tableau presentation of a crepuscular landscape, so favored by the *modernistas,* threatens its enclosure. The presence of prosaic elements invites metonymical displacement, breaking the circle of metaphoric enclosure, leaving the emblematic scene open to multivalent interpretations. For Lugones the emblem (icon, gathering together, metaphor, composure) is coded in terms of the evocative power of language in relation to its place in the heritage of literature, important as a social institution. Enclosure, or closure, must always be reasserted by an identification of the speaking subject. In an individual poem this assertion may be present as a narrative voice, the binding and encircling presence of rhyme, or the deflationary movement of conscious parody. More generally, within the structure of the volume itself, this reassertion may take the form of an attached prologue, an arrangement of poems in a thematic progression, or knowing titles and dedications. Yet given the verbal mastery of a poet such as Lugones, the binding process must be strong to contain deviations inherent in the nature of language itself with its multivalent associations and resonance. For us as modern readers, therefore, Lugones is only interesting when he steps outside the circle, when encircling repression snaps and the body of language reasserts its primal will.

In the poetry of Lugones the coded thematic systems of eroticism, the night, and urban living provoke this slip and fall. Whenever introduced, these elements are either parodied, transformed into a larger didactic text, or linked very carefully with the obvious imitation of another text, such as those of Samain and Laforgue. Yet in *Lunario sentimental, Los crepúsculos del jardín,* and parts of *Las montañas del oro,* the figure of the representing subject loses ground. In each case meter, rhyme, and metaphoric progression are distorted and never totally recaptured. The rhyme scheme and sound patterns become agitated, calling attention to themselves as a distancing countermeasure to the introduction of these themes.

THE HERITAGE OF SYMBOLISM

Au Jardin de l'infante by Albert Samain is considered to be the direct inspiration of *Los crepúsculos del jardín,* as well as of Julio Herrera y Reissig's *Los éxtasis de la montaña.* There are similarities, especially thematic ones. The toning of colors, the settings,

and a frequent presence of malevolence associated with eroti-
cism are common to all three works. The first and last stanzas of
"Dilection" from *Au Jardin de l'infante* illustrate Samain's poetic
preferences:

> J'adore l'indécis, les sons, les couleurs frêles,
> Tout ce qui tremble, ondule, et frissone, et chatoie.
> Les cheveux et les yeux, l'eau, les feuilles, la soie,
> Et la spiritualité des formes grêles:
> . . . .
> Et tel coeur d'ombre chaste, embaumé de mystère,
> Où veille, comme le rubis d'un lampadaire,
> Nuit et jour, un amour mystique et solitaire.[7]

> (I adore all vagueness, sounds, fragile colors,
> All that trembles, undulates, shivers, shimmers.
> Hair and eyes, water, leaves, silk,
> And the spirituality of slender forms;
> . . . .
> And such a heart of chaste shadow, embalmed in mystery,
> Where a mystical and solitary love,
> Keeps vigil, like the ruby of a candelabrum.)

Robert M. Scari cites three procedures he considers to be derived
from Samain's poetry: animistic adjectivization, metaphors cre-
ated by means of prepositional phrases, and verbs that end in
-izar (*iser*) which create instantaneous metaphor, for example,
histerizar.[8] Although there are indeed unmistakable thematic
similarities, Samain uses explicit equivalences that are found
much less frequently in *Los crepúsculos del jardín* and he adheres
much more closely to the landscape/emotion equivalence:

> Mon coeur est un beau lac solitaire qui tremble.
> Hanté d'oiseaux furtifs et de rameaux frôleurs . . .
>   ("Invitation")[9]

> (My heart is a beautiful, solitary lake that trembles.
> Haunted by darting birds and rustling branches . . .)

> La vie est une fleur que je respire à peine.
>   ("Extrême Orient, II")[10]

> (Life is a flower that I scarcely breathe.)

> Mon coeur, tremblant des lendemains,
> Est comme un oiseau dans tes mains,
> Qui s'effarouche et qui frisonne.
>
> ("Viole")[11]
>
> (My heart, trembling with tomorrows,
> Is like a bird in your hands,
> That flutters and shivers.)

In contrast to Samain, Lugones often condenses this process of creating explicit equivalences, or provides enough elliptical expressions to leave any such equivalence ambiguous, as in "Hortus deliciarum" in which the night, the woman, and the flowers are united and compared by a transposition of attributes. Or a mere listing of objects may suffice to create a setting by contiguity, rather than by an outline of its contours, as in the attention given the fading state of different fabrics in "El solterón."

The influences of poets such as Verlaine, Samain, and Rubén Darío are clearly apparent among the wide and eclectic range of techniques and themes of *Los crepúsculos del jardín*. Lugones, however, seems to resist the maintenance of mystery and musicality, choosing to deflate patterns of suggestiveness and intrigue with the unexpected term or the incongruous image. In his critical writings, Lugones even presents ambivalent views about theories and practices of symbolism. In the prologue to *Castalia bárbara* by Jaimes Freyre in 1899, Lugones applauds the poet's production because he demonstrates the most important of poetic talents, an individual poetic rhythm.[12] Lugones discusses also the poetic concept behind Jaimes Freyre's poetry, where solitude and contemplation reveal the innate correspondences between man and the universe. This concept determines the techniques of his poetry; specific figures are not presented since the poems' subjects are collective:

> Es poesía enteramente subjetiva la suya y sólo aspira a producir estados de alma, dejando que el lector se coloque en el medio más apto para cultivarlos o refinarlos, una vez producidos.[13]
>
> (His poetry is entirely subjective and only aspires to produce spiritual states, letting the reader place himself in the most fitting me-

dium so that once these spiritual states are produced he may culti-
vate or refine them.)

According to Lugones this method also has disadvantages: "la
primera una completa inaccesibilidad para el público, y la
segunda, entre otras, una vaguedad lindera a veces de la confu-
sión y del extravío"[14] ("the first is its total inaccessibility for the
public, and the second, among others, a vagueness that occasion-
ally borders on confusion and deviation"). He notes, however,
that its primary advantage is the force of its powers of evocation.

Lugones' main objection to the theories and practices of the
symbolists is not so much a question of technique, but a more
basic issue, the essential lack of unity that it reflects: "He aquí lo
que este poeta practica. Yo no estoy conforme ni con sus ideas ni
con sus tendencias en general . . ."[15] ("Here is what this poet
practices. I do not agree with his ideas nor with his tendencies in
general . . ."). For Lugones the essential poetic elements are
rhythm and harmony, which are reflections of the unified con-
science that produces them: "Sentir la Belleza es percibir la
unidad del Universo en la armonía de las cosas. De este
postulado se desprende una consecuencia que antes de ahora
tengo expresada así: el estilo es el ritmo"[16] ("To feel Beauty is to
perceive the unity of the Universe in the harmony of objects.
From this postulate one can derive the consequence that I have
previously expressed in this manner: style is rhythm"). In theory
as well as in practice, Lugones shows himself to be resistant to
many of symbolism's practices. Thus, despite the fact that *Los
crepúsculos del jardín* has usually been judged as Lugones' most
typically *modernista* work, and the one that most clearly approxi-
mates the techniques of symbolism, it is impossible to view it as
consistent in this respect. It does include many *modernista* traits,
but its mixture of levels, including parody and satire, violates the
symbolist canons of self-enclosure and the primacy of suggestive-
ness. Despite the strength of visual aspects, Lugones' tendency
toward depersonalization disrupts the harmony of scenes and
sounds.

Even with its departures from *modernismo, Los crepúsculos del
jardín* most closely resembles the work of the *modernistas* by its
exhibitions of spectacular accumulations and learned allusions.

It shows its author's knowledge and mastery of specialized forms, poetic treatments, and current standardized images. By varying and combining so many types of poems, it flaunts its erudition and then dismisses it by satire and comedy, a process that will be extended and heightened in *Lunario sentimental*. Alternating with *modernista* sonority is disruption into cacophony and comic play.

One of the major aims of symbolism, to suggest and not to explain, is carried to extremes by Lugones, for he forces into view the possibilities of manipulation of the signs themselves. The inclusion of vocabulary outside the *modernista* code—such as a colloquial turn of phrase "así fue el caso," ("that's how it was") of "Tentación"—points up the special code in contrast to everday usage. Although in some poems the trivialization of caricature of established practices can only be viewed as authorial intention, as in "Los cuatro amores de Dryops," in others the search for novelty and accumulation may be the unconscious process that leads to parody. Many poems, to varying degrees, include distancing signals that interrupt the progression of scene–emotion correspondence. "Romántica," which is tightly united by parallels of the loved woman with the beauty of the afternoon and flowers, includes unlikely combinations such as:

> Fúnebre es tu candor adolescente
> Que la luna sonámbula histeriza,
> Y el perfume de nardo decadente
> En que tu alma pueril se exterioriza.
>
> > (*OPC*, 138)

> (Funereal is your adolescent candor
> Which the sleepwalking moon excites to hysteria,
> and the decadent perfume of the tuberose
> in which your puerile spirit manifests itself.)

The melancholy progression of memory follows many traditional paths, but there are departures even in the most unified poems.

By exalting convention Lugones undermines it. The focal points of his perspectives dissolve as he focuses in on his models with an ever-narrowing gaze. Metaphors are sustained to such an extent that their center is displaced, while words and sounds are used like objects whose original function has been forgotten. Here the convention of *modernismo* intersects with that of realism, where the actual naming of objects, a fascination with filling up spaces in an effort to evoke the presence of a certain mood or personality, goes unrestrained. As pointed out earlier, even the most closely unified poems suggests a deflationary intent by their excesses. In a poem such as "El solterón," parody makes the model obvious and the new creation has its own strength.

DIVISION OF *LOS CREPÚSCULOS DEL JARDÍN*

Although somewhat arbitrary, the following classification of poems in the work *Los crepúsculos del jardín* allows for a discussion of its poetic construction, based on the degree of deflationary or parodic elements within each poem. The first group includes poems that proceed by means of progressive imagery development beginning with a landscape scene. These poems are "Cisnes negros," "El buque," "Hortus deliciarum," "Romántica," "Melancolía," "El crepúsculo de los cóndores," and "Ave Mía, gratia plena." Along with specific visual detail of the landscape their symbolic nature is at least partially explained by explicit comparison. The second strophe of "Ave Mía, gratia plena" presents the formula for such scene and memory equivalents:

> El paisaje, algo adusto en su atonía,
> De nuestro grave amor fue el emblema;
> Los crepúsculos visten todavía
> Un raso gris de distinción suprema.
>
> (*OPC*, 182)
>
> (The landscape, somewhat austere in its lassitude,
> was the emblem of our grave love;
> The twilights still don
> A grey satin of supreme distinction.)

The extended length of many of these poems allows also for the fuller development of a narrative.

In the second group (including the twelve sonnets of "Los doce gozos" and the three sonnets of "Ramillete") there is more condensation due to the use of synecdoche and metonymy instead of more complex metaphors created by parallel constructions. The narrative element is much less pronounced because of the emphasis on separate details, and because of the poems' brevity. Although there is no blatant mocking of poetic conventions here, there are still some digressive and disrupting elements. This is usually due to the use of a single term out of context or to unusual juxtaposition of key elements. The major part of the discussion of *Los crepúsculos del jardín* will concentrate on this second group.

The third group (including "Endecha," "Aquel día," "Coqueta," the poems of "Los cuatro amores de Dryops," "Las loas de nuestra servidumbre," and "El mal inefable") resemble the first by their similarities in theme and imagery development. Parallelisms, however, are overemphasized to such an extent that they clearly present examples of caricature. The greater length of most of these poems also allows for the development of comic scenes.

The poems of the fourth group ("El solterón" and "Emoción aldeana") are quite different from the other poems. Although the outline of *modernista* topics and treatments is still visible, they widen perspectives and begin to include themes and terms from other poetic codes. The inclusion of provincial and urban settings is no longer for parodic effect, but for its own sake. "Emoción aldeana," which closes the volume, illustrates the complete transformation of the *modernista* code. These two poems are especially important because they suggest the new directions taken by the later *sencillista* and even *vanguardista* poets.

"LOS DOCE GOZOS": VOYEURISM AND THE SPEAKING SUBJECT

The role of seduction, not only in *Los crepúsculos del jardín* but in *modernismo*'s creations in general, offers a focal point that provides an almost infinite array of stances for the speaking subject. In *Los crepúsculos del jardín*, the role of *voyeur* is often domi-

nant. In the work of later female poets, for example, Delmira
Agustini and Alfonsina Storni, the constructive apparatus of
the poem is redesigned so as to negate the authority of the
voyeuristic gaze.[17]

What creates the impact in Lugones' poetry is the physicality
of the language itself, its very malleability, as in the abundance
of *esdrújulos* (that is, words with stress on the antepenultimate
syllable), and of difficult and often cacophonous rhyme. The
dense verbal texture is paralleled by an emphasis on the physi-
cal, tangible aspects of imagery. A physical detail often spins out
all its possibilities. In Lugones' work there is also a thematic
emphasis on physical violence, especially in connection with
eroticism. With the cutting apart of the imagery system, the
dismembered parts of language's evocative structure float to
the surface. Violence is apparent first by fetishism—the ex-
treme metonymical dispersion of the figure of the female in
"Los doce gozos," and is followed in *Lunario sentimental* by a
violent dissection of the lunar imagery of dreams, poetry, and
the feminine image. The nexus of contiguity in "La alcoba
solitaria," for example, is a closed one. The gestures that might
provoke further reflection, such as the "gota de sangre" ("drop
of blood"), are blocked, just as the reflection from the mirror is
stunted: "El espejo opalescente / Estaba ciego" (*OPC*, 122–123)
("The opalescent mirror / Was blind"). The distracting and jar-
ring rhyme, along with the presence of the "corsé de inviolable
raso" ("corset of inviolable satin") which does not fit smoothly
into the elements of the room and clashes in its pairing with
"una magnolia" ("a magnolia"), tips the poem so off balance
that the web of suggestiveness is torn through by the attention-
getting gestures of the not-so-distant speaking subject, the inter-
rupter, the summarizer.

In defining the "speaking subject," Gilles Deleuze in *Logique
du sens* asks the question, "Who speaks?" In his answer he de-
scribes the subject's wayward appearance, for we find it where
we do not seek it:

> Ce qui est impersonnel et pré-individuel, ce sont les singularités,
> libres et nomades. Ce qui est plus profond que tout fond, c'est la
> surface, la peau. Ici se forme un nouveau type de langage ésotér-

ique, qui est à lui-même son propre modèle et sa réalité. Le devenir-fou change de figure quand il monte à la surface, sur la ligne droite de l'Aiôn, éternité; de même le moi dissous, le Je fêlé, l'identité perdue, quand ils cessent de s'enfoncer, pour libérer au contraire les singularités de surface.[18]

(That which is impersonal and pre-individual, these are the singularities, free and nomadic. That which is deeper than all depth, is the surface, the skin. A new type of esoteric language is being formed here, which is its own model and its own reality. The figure of madness changes when it rises to the surface, on the straight line of Aiôn, eternity; likewise the dissolved me, the cracked I, the lost identity, when they stop sinking, in order to free, on the contrary, the surface singularities.)

The static landscapes of "Los doce gozos," which seem to offer the reader a single, directed point of engagement, are engineered with other possibilities. With their constant reshuffling of a received idiom and visual icons, these scenes are less a mimesis of prized commodity pleasures, the "bazares de cosmos" in Lugones' term, than an invitation to intrusiveness and the temptation of dismantling and destruction.

"Los doce gozos," a grouping of twelve sonnets, is dedicated to José Juan Tablada. The dedication is significant, for the subject matter of the sonnets resembles Tablada's collection "Hostias negras" from *Florilegio*. More clearly than in the other poems of *Los crepúsculos del jardín*, with the possible exception of the three poems joined in "Las loas de nuestra servidumbre," eroticism is emphasized in its relationship to mystery. The temporal setting for these poems is twilight or night, and scenes of silence and isolation dominate the section. The most famous section of the volume, "Los doce gozos," is notable for its striking, largely static imagery and for its thematic uniformity.

The titles of the individual poems—"Tentación," "Paradisíaca," El astro propicio," "Conjunción," "Venus victa," "En color exótico," "El éxtasis," "Delectación morosa," "Oceánida," "La alcoba solitaria," "Las manos entregades," and "Holocausto"— suggest different stages of a mysterious rite. Frequent mention of God, death, suspension, crucifixion, along with the emphasis on eroticism, links sexuality to mystery, transgression, and to the night. The presentation of the female figure, never in fully outlined form, heightens the feeling of mystery. Nevertheless, the combination of scenic setting, mythological references, and fleeting glimpses of human form does not completely enmesh to sustain the air of mystery, for the creation of mystery seems to invite its own deflation. The use of a term out of context, the overspecific description down to cataloguing of every fabric, the introduction of domestic animals in a love sonnet, or the occasional use of colloquial phrases, strike discordant notes in these sonnets.

The essential development of the poems is the movement toward unification—nature interpenetrates with the *yo* and the *tú*, as well as the sexual union. By a nexus of contiguity, the feminine elements are entwined with nature's forms. Whereas in the first cycle of *Las montañas del oro* the eyes of the woman are transposed onto the night and the forest, here the night is described in terms of the woman, moon, and stars. In "Los doce gozos" subject matter loses primary importance; the treatment of the scene takes priority over any message.

In "Tentación" natural elements express sexual ecstasy or union by displacement of modifiers from one category to another. The afternoon is identified with the woman by "suspiro" ("sigh"), "de amor" ("of love"), and "raso" ("satin"): "Se extenuaba de amor la tarde quieta / Con la ducal decrepitud del raso" (*OPC,* 117) ("The still afternoon wasted away in love / With the ducal decrepitude of satin"). Just as the light of the afternoon stretches out, the slow movement of the poem is reinforced by the associations with languorous quietness. The mention of "ducal decrepitud," "palidez dorada," and "silenciosa golondrina" ("ducal decrepitude," "golden paleness," and "silent swallow"), along with "éxtasis impuro" ("impure ectasy") establishes an ambiguous tone. The pairing of a noun with an unexpected but not completely contradictory modifier is one of the most important features of "Los doce gozos," and, like the presence of elements such as the "media negra" ("black stocking"), it contributes to a jarring and dislocating of the synthesis of mysterious elements. The mention of the sunset reinforces the association with the woman by its attribute "palidez dorada" ("golden paleness"). In contrast to the evening skies, the countryside spies on and envelops the feminine element:

> El campo en cuyo trebolar maduro
> La siembra palpitó como una esposa,
> Contemplaba con éxtasis impuro
>
> Tu media negra; y una silenciosa
> Golondrina rayaba el cielo rosa,
> Como un pequeño pensamiento oscuro.
>
> *(OPC,* 117)

> (The countryside, in whose ripe clover
> The seed trembled like a wife,
> Observed with impure Ecstasy
>
> Your black stocking; and a silent
> Swallow skimmed the rose sky
> Like a small, dark thought.)

Since the sky is already associated with the woman, the fetishistic contemplation of her as a transgression is reinforced with "pensamiento oscuro" ("dark thought") and "impuro" ("impure").

In "Paradisíaca" suspension and union are more explicitly expressed, as is the transgressive nature of the union. The poetic *I* enters in the first strophe, along with an invasive intent:

> Cabe una rama en flor busqué tu arrimo:
> La dorada sepiente de mis males
> Circuló por tus púdicos cendales
> Con la invasora suavidad de un mimo.
>
> *(OPC,* 118)

> (By a flowering bough I sought your affection:
> The golden serpent of my evils
> Slithered through your chaste silks
> With the invading softness of a caress.)

The second quatrain adds another disquieting note: "Sutil vapor alzábase del limo / Sulfurando las tintas otoñales / Del Poniente . . ." ("A subtle vapor rose from the lime / Sulphuring the autumn hues / of the West . . ."). In contrast to the prosaic and nonlyrical "mimo" ("caress") and "sulfurando" ("sulphur-ing"), the third stanza returns to the title theme of paradise, and to union:

> Sintiendo que el azul nos impelía
> Algo de Dios, tu boca con la mía
> Se unieron en la tarde luminosa.
>
> (*OPC*, 118)

> (Feeling that the blue thrust upon us
> Something from God, your mouth with mine
> Joined in the luminous, early evening.)

In the last tercet a statue of a satyr is introduced—"Bajo el caduco sátiro de yeso" ("beneath the decrepit, plaster satyr")—which cancels out the earlier "algo de Dios" ("something from God"), and the mythological reference resolves the ambiguity of the poem. In Darío's "Leda" of *Cantos de vida y esperanza,* the myth of Leda and the swan serves as the organizing principle. In Lugones' poem only a fragment of the mythological setting remains; his satyr is a decrepit one, a plaster cast of a once-vital image. As in all the poems of "Los doce gozos," here many elements are twisted and transformed to heighten their unusual or nontraditional placement. Whereas Darío organizes all the elements consistently within the natural setting, Lugones de-naturalizes the setting with the clash of archaic ("Cabe" ["By"]) and colloquial ("mimo" ["caress"]) Spanish terms.

In other sonnets, a physical union or suspension is associated with natural elements by a metonymical process. In the first examples, distance and illusion are emphasized by the reflec-tion in eyes:

> Y desde el cielo fraternal, la misma
> Estrella se miraba en nuestros ojos.
>
> ("El astro propicio," (*OPC*, 119)

> (And from the fraternal sky, the same
> Star gazed at itself in our eyes.)

> Una resurrección de primaveras
> Llenó la tarde gris, y tus ojeras,
> Que avivó la caricia fatigada,

> Me fantasearon en penumbra fina,
> Las alas de una leve golondrina
> Suspensa en la ilusión de tu mirada.
> ("Conjunción," OPC, 119)

> (A resurrection of Springs
> Filled the grey evening, and your deep-shadowed eyes,
> That the tired caress revived,

> Appeared to me in fine shadow,
> The wings of a small swallow
> Suspended in the illusion of your gaze.)

Here Lugones again overloads the poem with elements from different contexts. The woman's figure, described only by separate physical traits, is presented ambiguously. The "little white shoe," with its movement of "grace," suggests the lighter presence of a young innocent, especially in combination with "small swallow." Yet the mention of "deep shadows under the eyes," more appropriate to a worldly siren, abruptly changes the female's nature and confuses the impact of "the illusion of your gaze."

In "Venus victa," a personal article, "collares" ("necklaces"), replaces the female, and her violation is expressed in terms of her jewels, while her total identity is fragmented and displaced onto inanimate objects:

> Pidiéndome la muerte, tus collares
> Desprendiste con trágica alegría
> Y en su pompa fluvial la pedrería
> Se ensangrentó de púrpuras solares.
> (OPC, 119)

> (Asking me for death, your necklaces
> You removed with tragic joy
> And in their liquid pomp the jewels
> Were blood-stained by purple suns.)

In the last two tercets, the violence of sexuality is presented in similar terms:

Y cuando por tu seno entró el estoque

   Con agucia feroz su hilo de hielo
Brotó un clavel bajo su fina punta
En tu negro jubón de terciopelo.

(OPC, 120)

(And when through your breast the rapier entered

   With fierce subtlety its icy thread
Sprouted a red carnation under its fine point
On your black velvet bodice.)

The last section of "En color exótico" also explicitly links the observer and the observed, even though the feminine figure is only seen in terms of synecdoche:

   Se apagó en tu collar la última gema,
   Y sobre el broche de tu liga crema
   Crucifiqué mi corazón mendigo.

(OPC, 120)

   (The last gem in your necklace died away,
   and on the clasp of your ivory garter
   I crucified my beggar's heart.)

Although in the two preceding stanzas definite persons are established, emotions associated with *tú* are projected onto the landscape.

   Hería en los musgosos surtidores
Su cristalina tecla el agua clara,
Y el tilo que a mis ojos te ocultara
Gemía con eclógicos rumores.

   Tal como una bandera derrotada
Se ajó la tarde, hundiéndose en la nada,
A la sombra del tálamo enemigo.

(OPC, 120)

   (In the moss-covered fountains
The clear water wounded its crystalline key
And the lime tree that hid you from my eyes
Moaned with the murmurs of eclogues.

Like a defeated flag
The afternoon crumpled, sinking into nothing
Under the shade of the hostile marriage bed.)

Surrender involves repercussions of taboo and is shown as a defeat by the use of "Hería," "gemía," "derrotada," "Se ajó," "hundiéndose," "enemigo," and "se apagó" ("Wounded," "moaned," "defeated," "crumpled," "sinking," "hostile"). Taboo also extends to the *yo,* for "crucifiqué" ("I crucified") in the last strophe is in function of the musculine element.

"Delectación morosa" (*OPC,* 121) presents its message through decor. Nonnatural elements are weighted with iconic messages, and the human presence is reduced to the mention of "nuestro asilo" ("our asylum"), "tus rodillas" ("your knees"), and "nuestros pies" ("our feet"). Just as the female in other poems is metonymically represented by clothing or jewels, here the emphasis on the artificiality and rareness of the scene sets a tone of sterility and preciousness. A series of discordant effects links the "delicia inerte" ("inert delight") and the river's silent passage "hacia la muerte" ("toward death"). Perspectives are reversed by the mixture of detail and abstraction, and silence itself becomes the dominant force (as in "El solterón"). Lugones emphasizes the artificial nature of the scene's construction with the "ligera pincelada" (light brushstroke") of the afternoon light, the "matiz crisoberilo" ("greenish-yellow hue"), "una sutil decoración morada" ("a subtle purple decoration"), the subdued colors, and the "combo / Cielo, a manera de chinesco biombo" ("bent / Sky, like a Chinese screen") which shows the artist's hand. Here the manipulation and subduing of natural elements serve as significant decor rather than as univocal symbols.

Lugones' "Oceánida" carries the linkage of natural elements with masculine or feminine identification further than any other of the twelve sonnets. Here the explicit observer is absent, but the sea is clearly defined as masculine and the feminine presence is clearly drawn: "El mar, lleno de urgencias masculinas, / Bramaba alrededor de tu cintura . . ." (*OPC,* 122) ("The sea, full of masculine urgencies / Raged around your waist . . ."). Again, declining light and stars are reflected by feminine elements:

En tus retinas,

Y en tus cabellos, y en tu astral blancura,
Rieló con decadencias opalinas
Esa luz de las tardes mortecinas
Que en el agua pacífica perdura.

(*OPC,* 122)

(In your retinas,

And in your hair, and in your starry whiteness
Shimmered with opaline decadence
That light of fading afternoons
Which lingers in the peaceful water.)

"La alcoba solitaria" (*OPC,* 122–123) differs more from the
other poems of "Los doce gozos" than any other. Its setting (an
empty room) is not from nature, and the poem prefigures the
more frequent juxtaposition of prosaic, static elements that will
be used in poems such as "El solterón" and "Emoción aldeana,"
as well as in much of *Lunario sentimental.* Its consonantal rhyme
is also more noticeable, moving to the forefront as an indepen-
dent element. Reflected light here is not from the moon, but
from a murky mirror—"El espejo opalescente / Estaba ciego"
("The opalescent mirror / Was blind"). Human actions are trans-
ferred to inanimate objects: "El diván dormitaba" ("the divan
napped"); "un antiguo silencio de Cartuja / Bostezaba en las
lúgubres rendijas" ("an ancient silence of Cartuja / Yawned in
the dismal cracks"); "Sentía el violín . . . / Flotar su extraña
anímula de bruja / Ahorcada en las unánimes clavijas" ("Felt the
violin . . . / Floating its strange witch anima / Hanging by the
unanimous pegs"). The only presence of the woman is "una
gota / De sangre pectoral, sobre la rota / Almohada" ("a drop /
Of blood from the breast, on the ripped / Pillow"). The femi-
nine element is associated with fetishistic items: "Y en el fino
vaso, / Como un corsé de inviolable raso, / Se abría una magno-
lia dulcemente" ("And in the fine glass, / Like a corset of inviola-
ble satin / a magnolia opened sweetly"). The terms "fino vaso"
("fine glass") and "inviolable raso" ("inviolable satin") seem un-
defiled, yet are linked by contiguity with "oxidada aguja"

("rusty needle"), "gota de sangre" ("drop of blood"), and "rota / Almohada" ("ripped pillow"), not to mention the "corsé" ("corset"). The entire poem is structured around the injection of off-key elements, such as "corsé" and "magnolia." The static and lugubrious nature of the scene is thrown off balance by the diminution or deflation of its languorous elements. "Bruja" ("which") rhymes with "burbuja" ("bubble"), and the poem's final word, "dulcemente" ("sweetly") trivializes the poem's "prolijas sugestiones" ("prolix suggestions") in much the same way that the infelicitous floral analogy does. Elements of scenic decor dominate the poem's construction, and all the scene's conflicting suggestions are made to mingle in one setting.

CARICATURESQUE POEMS AND THE SELF-REFLEXIVE DESTRUCTION OF LYRICISM

In contrast to "Los doce gozos," poems such as "Endecha," "New Mown Hay," "La sola," "A tus imperfecciones," "Las loas de nuestra servidumbre," and "Los cuatro amores de Dryops" often parody the exalted comparisons between the natural setting and human actions. Within the poems themselves Lugones deflates his comparisons, inserts comments about his metaphor construction, and judges their success and appropriateness. Here, in contrast to "Los doce gozos," dislocating elements make their models stand out, thus producing overt parody. The poetic vocabulary includes colloquial expressions and technical terms which deflate the sensuousness of adjacent lyric images.

In "Endecha" the inclusion of the trivial and the ridulous deflates the lament for lost love into a "parodia venusina" ("Venusian parody"), including even the worn rhyme *tul / azul* (*tulle / blue*) and jumping fleas. The lilting rhyme and the presence of lighthearted elements (reminiscent of the poetry of Gutiérrez Nájera) give this remembrance of young love the tone of a nursery rhyme. The presence of "dulzura sin moscas" ("sweetness without flies"), "pulgas locas" ("crazy fleas"), "gatitos / enguantados" ("gloved kittens"), and "cosquillas" ("ticklings"), as well as a recurring use of diminutives, overcomes the listing of exotic flowers and jewels. The combination of the everyday,

with the vengeful disavowal of a former love, signals Lugones'
growing attachment to blatant dislocation and destruction of
idyllic scenes. In few other poems is the departure from a poetic
style so explicit. The loved one is changing, and in maturity the
wine "hipocrás" no longer attracts:

> ¿Por qué ya tu seno blando
> No me atrae al suave arriendo
> De otros días;
> Y yo voy llora llorando
> Y tú vas ríe riendo
> Tus folías?
>
> (*OPC*, 143)

> (Why is it that your soft breast
> No longer leads me on
> As before;
> And I keep on weeping
> And you keep laughing at
> Your trifles?)

No longer will the poetic quest be the same. The "dulce
enemiga" ("sweet enemy") now provokes destruction: "A mal-
quererte provoca / Tu desvío" (*OPC*, 140) ("Your indifference /
Provokes me to hate you").

The subject of the love poem "A tus imperfecciones" diverges
from the "canón adusto" ("austere canon") of the perfect beauty
of convention. She is unlike the "literaria muñeca de los sonetos
clásicos y postizos" ("the literary doll of the classical and artificial
sonnets"), and even the moon shining on her refers to the act of
writing. The deflationary motive in "La coqueta" is made clear by
the commentary on the authenticity of her description:

> A la frágil gracia de su figulina,
> Une casi auténtico, un aire de esplín;
> Y con incentivo carmín ilumina
> La falacia irónica que huye en su mohín.

(*OPC*, 135)

> (To the fragile grace of her figurine,
> It joins, almost authentic, an atmosphere of spleen;

And with ruby incentive it illumines
The ironic fallacy that flees in its gesture.)

Diminutives and unexpected adjectives, as well as extensive use of *esdrújulos* emphasize the infidelity to convention: "breve seno" ("small bosom"), "sucinto prado de azucenas" ("brief field of lilies"), "poco fatuo" ("not foolish"), "leves insomnios de té" ("slight insomnias of tea"), and "abanico lánguido y burlón" ("languid and mocking fan") (*OPC,* 135–136).

The caricaturesque elements in "El mal inefable" and "Aquel día" are based on an amplification of situations from "Los doce gozos." By extending a metaphor to ridiculous lengths, Lugones stresses the incongruity of his mixtures, as in the comparison of the day's passing to a melancholy state:

> La certidumbre de tu amor lejano,
> Que a fúnebres azares se encomienda,
> Trocó a mi corazón, trivial Fulano,
> En un excelso prócer de leyenda.
> ("El mal enfable," *OPC,* 163)

> (The certainty of your far-away love,
> Which gives itself over to funereal chance,
> Changed my heart, a trivial Nobody,
> Into an exhalted, legendary grandee.)

"Aquel día" presents now-familiar metaphors in abbreviated fashion. The "tarde de muaré" ("watered-silk evening") drowns in the fountain, and an extended metaphor, such as that of "El buque," is suggested by the mere presence of "muaré." The spill of tears that follows is likewise a drowning:

> Y con mi alma lloré; y era tu encanto
> Lo que lloraba en mí con ese llanto.
> Y era mi alma el escuálido reflejo.
>
> .   .   .   .
>
> Mojamos el silencio gota a gota
> En esa angustia; . . .
>
> (*OPC,* 165)

(And with my soul I wept; and it was your spell
That wept in me with that lament.
And my soul was the squalid reflection.

.   .   .   .

We wet the silence drop by drop
In that anguish; . . .)

Lugones mocks the poem's excesses not only with its "fácil agonía" ("facile agony") but also in the "neblinas impostoras" ("imposter mists"). The bleating of a lamb, being slaughtered with a "débil grito de agonía" ("weak of cry of agony"), stops the mourning process. Handkerchiefs are folded, the crying ends, and prosaic reality with love's "estériles consuelos" ("sterile consolations") stops cold the process of excessive "poetic" emotions.

The three poems of the "Loas"—"Canto de la vida y de la mañana," "Canto del amor y de la noche," and "Canto de la tarde y de la muerte"—are marked by a freer metrical scheme. Verses of different length are mixed without specific patterning, although the rhyme scheme is fixed. The first of the poems maintains a lyrical tone more consistently than the latter two. Irregular versification gives flexibility, and the luxuriant images surrounding the description of the dove offer an example of the extended image, painting a scene of radiant light:

> En tanto el sol puebla de espejismos las dunas,
> Inflama esmaltes carmesíes,
> Y en las rizadas lagunas
> Amoneda cequíes,
> Devastador como
> Una áurea fiebre, cae su rayo a plomo,
> Esponjando la gola,
> Sobre su chalet de una teja, el palomo
> Bullente de arrullos gira y se tornasola.
>
> (*OPC*, 169)

> (While the sun peoples the dunes with mirages,
> Inflames crimson enamels,
> And in the rippling lagoons
> Coins sequins,
> Devastating like

A golden fever, its ray plummets,
soaking the gorge,
Over its linden tree chalet, the dove
Bubbling with murmurs, circles and iridesces.)

With the rhyme "como / plomo" Lugones accentuates his capricious methods. The contrast between the length of the two verses, the obvious rhyme filler "como" and the vertical plummet "a plomo" serve to point out the arbitrary, leaden touch that can destroy harmonious progression with acrobatic swings of movement. Later in the poem, the mention of the dove is returned to in relation to the female figure, while alliteration with *l* and *n* plays a role in the establishing of the sensory elements:

Esparce tal beatitud en torno,
Que en una laxitud llena de dicha,
Sin un delirio,
Sin un anhelo,
Se siente uno bajo el cielo
Como una mosca en un lirio.
(*OPC*, 169)

(It spreads such blessing all around,
That in a happy lassitude,
Without a delirium,
Without a yearning,
Beneath the sun one feels
Like a fly in an iris.)

The number of neologisms and rarely used words is striking in the second and third poems of this tryptich, for example, "histerizando," "sobrenaturalizando," "normalizáronse" ("hystericizing," "supernaturalizing," "normalizing"). In addition, elements outside the tradition of poetic sonority and preciosity, especially urban or technological terms, draw attention to the departures from previously established schemes, as in the following examples:

El musical insomnio de los casinos . . .
(*OPC*, 172)

(The musical insomnia of the casinos . . .)

Tu corazón desborda, populoso
Como una metrópoli de fiesta.

(*OPC*, 172)

(Your heart overflows, populous
Like a metropolis of celebration)

Tu carne aguza su delicia
Con felina electricidad de terciopelo.

(*OPC*, 172)

(Your flesh quickens its delight
With feline, velvet electricity.)

El brillo carnicero de tus dientes.

(*OPC*, 173)

(The butcher brilliance of your teeth.)

Even the night, the moon, and the stars are trivialized by unexpected modifiers:

La luna, trivial como un plato. . . .

(*OPC*, 172)

(The moon, trivial like a plate . . .)

. . . el astro, con amarillez de pena

(*OPC*, 174)

(. . . the star, with the yellow of grief)

Tiende la Vía Láctea su malla gigantesca,
Como una red a la pesca
De pececitos de oro.

(*OPC*, 174)

(The Milky Way stretches out its gigantic coat of mail,
Like a net fishing
For little golden fish.)

"Los cuatro amores de Dryops" illustrates most clearly the fall into bathos created by extending to the utmost the same scheme. In *alejandrinos* (fourteen-syllable lines) with paired consonantal rhyme, the jaded expressions and the inevitability of rhythm and rhyme lead to monotony. The four stories that compose the poem provide an essentially caricaturesque commentary on this poetic convention used by Darío in "Recreaciones arqueológicas." The lovers share "caricias inciertas" ("uncertain caresses"), "bocas inexpertas" ("inexperienced mouths"), "ilógico llanto" ("illogical lament"), and "estériles delicias" ("sterile delights"). The poetic process is commented on within the poem itself, as in "Rompía nuestro encanto como un hiato a un verso" ("It broke our enchantment like a hiatus breaks a verse") or by summary description: "Tal revive la escena de nuestro amor. . . . Y ya nada recuerdo de sus otros hechizos . . . / Nada sé de sus labios, nada sé de sus rizos" ("Such revives the scene of our love. . . . And now I remember nothing of her other charms / I know nothing of her lips, I know nothing of her curls").

"EL SOLTERÓN" AND "EMOCIÓN ALDEANA"

The presentation of the afternoon in "El solterón" ("The Old Bachelor") does not serve as a panoramic background, but instead faintly glimmers in through the window as a "crepúsculo perplejo" ("bewildered twilight"). It does not overpower the scene, flooding it with color, but is weakly reflected in a tarnished mirror. As in "La alcoba solitaria" and "Emoción aldeana," the mirror diminishes the importance of the landscape and emphasizes, along with the loneliness and alienation of the old suitor, the self-reflexiveness in the poem. Nature scenes are replaced with descriptions of the musty room, and the fabrics of the furniture and clothing show the age and inefficacy of the old suitor. Instead of the decorative presence of richly colored and exotic materials found in much *modernista* poetry, the fabrics and other objects here illustrate a harsher reality. The "grandes años / con sus cargas de algodón" ("great years / with their cargo of cotton") are reflected in the "felpa azul" ("blue plush"), "crucificado frac" ("crucified frock coat"), "desusado cancel" ("unused partition"), "cretona centenaria" ("centenary cretonne"), "estufa precaria" ("precarious heater"), "otoño de gró" ("grosgrain autumn"), and "tenebroso crespón" ("dark and dismal crepe") which mark the passing of time.

The lyrical voice is not included within the recounting of the

scene. Distanced, like an outside observer, it places the seeing
eye at even another remove by commenting on the poem itself:
"A inverosímil distancia / Se acongoja un violín . . ." (*OPC*, 130),
("At an unlikely distance / A violin sobs . . .") References to the
poem's literary convention within the poem itself, as well as the
term "tragedia baladí" ("trivial tragedy") serve as deflationary
techniques. Space and time cross categories as the coming of the
night and the advance of death are presented from the perspec-
tive inside the room:

> El crepúsculo perplejo
> Entra a una alcoba glacial,
> (*OPC*, 128)

> (The bewildered twilight
> Enters an icy bedroom)

> En el fondo de sus días
> Bosteza la soledad.
> (*OPC*, 129)

> (At the end of his days
> solitude yawns.)

> Sobre su visión de aurora,
> Un tenebroso crespón
> Los contornos descolora,
> Pues la noche vencedora
> Se le ha entrado el corazón.
> (*OPC*, 133)

> (Above his vision of dawn,
> A dark crepe
> Discolors the contours,
> For the conquering night
> Has taken over his heart.)

The transposition of the theme of unrequited love to the old
bachelor allows for the parodic use of elements usually associ-
ated with the love theme. Contradicting all expectations of a love
poem, the dislocation from one order to another parodies the

poetic conventions as well. A comparison of verses from "Hortus deliciarum" with those from "El solterón" illustrates the dislocation. On the one hand, in "Hortus deliciarum" the interpenetration of the elements of the afternoon, the decor, and the woman provide some disquieting notes, such as "La breve arruga de tu media lila" ("slight crease in your lilac stocking") and "Tu integridad estéril de camelia" ("your sterile integrity of a camelia"). However, most of the poem's elements are taken from a consistent context. In "El solterón," on the other hand, the delicacy and sterility of its heroine come into jolting relief by the addition of advanced age. Now the "integridad estéril" of "Hortus deliciarum" is transformed into "su leve/ Candor de virgen senil" ("her fragile / Innocence of a senile virgin"). In the selections from "El solterón" the use of rhyme and alliteration is obviously used for parodic effect also, for example *senil/abril* (senile/April). The exaggeration of the woman's descriptions invites laughter, not the slight questioning of "Hortus deliciarum." Nonetheless, despite the disparity between the poetic convention and its displacement in "El solterón," the elements are not totally heterogeneous but are derived from similar paradigms. True to the nature of caricature or parody, the poem resembles its convention in most ways. The combination of different elements is not a juxtaposition of fragments from different contexts. Patterning remains constant within a homogeneous spatial and temporal context. Only one context, that of old age and decrepitude, is substituted for a context of youth and beauty.

"Emoción aldeana" ("Village Emotion") closes the volume with a synthesis of many of the themes and techniques interspersed within the collection. It combines the delicate recounting of the first meeting of timid young lovers, the introduction of everyday scenes, internal commentary, irregular versification, and an expansion of the mirror image. The poetic *I* is faithful to the stated characterization, a country boy with "timidez urbana y ebrio de primavera" ("urban shyness and drunk with Spring"). No disruptive notes enter to provide parodic commentary. He surrenders himself to the barber's hands, leans back in the barber's chair, and sees the chipped mirror reflecting the landscape:

Absorbiendo el paisaje en su reflejo,
Era un óleo enorme de sol bermejo,
Praderas pálidas y cielos azules.
Y ante el mórbido gozo
De la tarde vibrada en pastorelas,
Flameaba como un soberbio trozo
Que glorificara un orgullo de escuelas.

                                                   (*OPC*, 187)

(Absorbing the landscape in its reflection,
It was an enormous oil canvas with a reddish sun,
Pale meadows and blue skies.
And faced with the soft pleasure
Of the evening vibrating with pastourelles,
It flamed like a magnificent fragment
That would glorify a pride of schools.)

Sounds and smells are mingled without an attempt to weave an explanatory pattern. Mixed with the conversational patter of the barber are other elements: "un perfume labriego / De polen almizclado las boñigas" ("a peasant perfume / Of pollen mixed with dung"), "una ráfaga de agua de colonia" ("a gust of eau de cologne"), "En insípido aroma de pradera pobre" ("In the insipid aroma of a poor meadow"), "Un maternal escándalo de gallinas" ("A maternal scandal of hens") (*OPC*, 187–188). The focus of his amorous dreams is the barber's daughter—"doncella preclara / Chrisporroteada en pecas bajo rulos de cobre" (*OPC*, 188) ("illustrious damsel / Sprinkled with freckles under copper curls"). Absent is the languid, exotic woman of "Los doce gozos." Rather than possessing the dangerous eyes of the siren, hers are "ojos de gata / Fritos en rubor como dos huevecillos" ("cat eyes / like two little eggs fried in her blush"). All exoticism of setting is experienced indirectly by means of the mirror. In the last stanza, the mirror image returns, and the metonymical interchange between the scene and the girl standing next to it resolves the disparate elements of the poem:

Sobre el espejo, la tarde lila
Improvisaba un lánguido miraje,
En un ligero vértigo de agua tranquila.

Y aquella joven con su blanco traje
Al borde de esa visionaria cuenca,
Daba al fugaz paisaje
Un aire de antigua ingenuidad flamenca.
                                        (*OPC*, 188)

(On the mirror the lilac afternoon
Improvised a languid mirage,
In the faint whirl of peaceful water.
And that young girl dressed in white
At the edge of that visionary basin
Gave the elusive landscape
An air of old-fashioned Flemish ingenuity.)

"Emoción aldeana" stands in contrast to most of the other poems of the volume by its transformations of *modernista* elements. Their presence is faint; meanwhile another code of meaning, composed of provincial scenes and everyday characters, begins to take precedence. This new code is not used to point out the artificiality or constraints of another one. It establishes its own dominance and needs no exaggeration to make itself visible.

While Lugones generally operates in *Los crepúsculos del jardín* with several codes at once, other poets will concentrate more on this last-mentioned code of the provincial or the prosaic. As mentioned earlier, Ramón López Velarde's joining of eroticism with an often abbreviated inclusion of the prosaic shows a direct inheritance of part of Lugones' work. This use of the prosaic for its own sake also found development in poets such as Enrique Banchs and Baldomero Fernández Moreno. Their poetry in the *sencillista* current uses this element not simply as a method of providing contrasts. Their emphasis on the everyday, the colloquial, took a very different turn from that of Lugones' later works. Their calmer tone contrasts with his heightened use of shock elements within works such as the *Lunario sentimental*, where the contrasts are heightened to cacophony and stridency. While Lugones continues to manipulate several codes at once, the *sencillistas* develop this single element more consistently.

5

LUNARIO SENTIMENTAL AND THE DESTRUCTION OF *MODERNISMO*

No attack on the spirit and practice of *modernismo* made by succeeding generations of poets has been as complete as that of Lugones' in *Lunario sentimental*. For Lugones the poetic world of *modernismo*, no longer a secret code to be deciphered only by its initiates, had to be left behind, since its arcane symbols and transformations were now immediately apparent as visible signs of an established order. Having pushed this system to its limits in *Los crepúsculos del jardín*, often to the point of overstepping its boundaries, Lugones recognized the futility of continuing in this vein and moved on to new territories, the mockery of archetypal patterns that he found in the poetry of Jules Laforgue. Despite the great strides forward into unaccustomed territory, there is a sense in the work of uneasy footing, a reluctance to relinquish every vestige of the older order. Despite *Lunario sentimental*'s allowance of broken and mingled hierarchies and long stretches of ambiguity, the guiding hand of the poet reasserts its presence in the form of parodic humor and cleverly fashioned rhyme.

LUNARIO SENTIMENTAL IN HISTORICAL PERSPECTIVE

No better evidence for the importance of Lugones' *Lunario sentimental* exists than the vehement commentary it provoked. Impossible to ignore, succeeding generations have either attacked it or incorporated many of its elements into their own work. Octavio Paz points out the volume's nature as a point of departure in the breakup of *modernismo:*

Después de *Prosas profanas* los caminos se cierran; hay que replegar las velas o saltar hacia lo desconocido. Rubén Darío escogió lo primero y pobló las tierras descubiertas; Leopoldo Lugones se arriesgó a lo segundo. *Cantos de vida y esperanza* (1905) y *Lunario sentimental* (1909) son las dos obras capitales del segundo modernismo y de ellas parten, directa o indirectamente, todas las experiencias y tentativas de la poesía moderna en lengua castellana.[1]

(After *Prosas profanas*, the paths close; one must either trim the sails or leap into the unknown. Rubén Darío chose the first possibility and inhabited the discovered lands; Leopoldo Lugones risked following the second one. *Cantos de vida y esperanza* [1905] and *Lunario sentimental* [1909] are the two major works of the second *modernismo*, and from them come, directly or indirectly, all the experiences and attempts of modern poetry in the Spanish language.)

In *Lunario sentimental* the grand scheme of totalities and organic coherence crumbles. Objects, memories, multiple voices, and stock images intermingle without an organizing framework to bind them together. The eclectic mixture of names and places, the blend of past, present, and future in the *Lunario sentimental* has been forecast in the third cycle of *Las montañas del oro*. Like Huidobro's "collar de imágenes" ("necklace of images"), the images in parts of the *Lunario sentimental* will be strung together with seemingly little plotting of a total design. The *Lunario sentimental* represents the culmination and explosion of the impulse of *modernismo*. Its excesses do not sink under their own weight, as in "Los cisnes negros" of *Los crepúsculos del jardín,* but seem to rebel from within. Instead of clustering images even more tightly and intricately, as in *Los crepúsculos del jardín,* or balancing them along polar lines, as in *Las montañas del oro,* Lugones in the *Lunario sentimental* dismisses the laws of gravity and eliminates the tension of balancing widely ranging elements within obvious formal constraints. A type of parody or caricature is also present, but in an altered sense in comparison to *Los crepúsculos del jardín.* Lugones modifies the outlines of models in an elusive way. Left with only fragments of an earlier order, the reader is left to join together new patterns from the images flung out. Yet one pattern or model does remain constant, that of rhyme. Consciously or unconsciously, it generates its own parody through extravagance. Accentuating an earlier trait, Lugones in *Lunario sentimental* emphasizes the use of words for their sound value. It is not just the clash of meanings that suprises; the constancy of incongruous juxtaposition gradually becomes an accustomed experience for the reader, and the rhyme's drift becomes nonreferential to any pattern outside its own sonority.

The *Lunario sentimental* has been both praised as a high mark of originality in Spanish American poetry and derided as a misguided copy of the work and intentions of Laforgue. In straining the excesses and formal experimentation beyond *modernismo*'s aesthetic basic, that of the underlying harmony of spirit and universe, the *Lunario sentimental* released a flow of energy into poetry by means of its break with previous poetic norms. Given the prior evidence of *Los crepúsculos del jardin,* it is unlikely that Lugones planned to continue in the *modernista* vein. He was reluctant, however, to dismiss the claims this movement made for the power of poetry, as is shown in his prologue. In 1909, the same year as the issuing of the first manifesto of Futurism by Marinetti, Lugones published the poems of the *Lunario sentimental.* To them he attached a prologue that exalts innovation in poetry while scorning the public appetite he served. In this prologue he laboriously constructed yet another framework—this time one leaning on historical, not natural, precedents—as a justification for his continued exaltation of the poetic idiom. The "sagrada prenda de la lengua" ("the sacred treasure of language") is indeed an "espada de dos filos" (a "double-edged sword"). Lugones, in his devouring appetite for novelty in construction, proposes in his poetry a world view that he denies in his prologue, as well as in his continuation of some of poetry's formal constraints within the poems themselves.

To understand the importance of the *Lunario sentimental* requires not only a knowledge of the nature of the work itself, but also of the nature of the poetic conventions it assimilated and transformed. In the same manner, its critical reception and later influence are important for an understanding of subsequent poetry in Spanish America. Not only the text itself, but the perceptual and artistic patterns it embodies, had resonance for many years. the next discussion deals with these issues in the following manner: first, an examination of the work's prologue in relation to Lugones' previous writings; second, an overview of the background and themes of the *Lunario sentimental;* third, an examination of its structure and techniques; and fourth, a review of the *Lunario sentimental*'s critical reception.

THE POLEMIC PROLOGUE

In the "Prólogo" to *Lunario sentimental,* Lugones address himself to two audiences, "la gente práctica" and "los literatos" ("the practical people" and "the literati"). To the first, he defends poetry as a pragmatic and functional good. Renewing language with new metaphors is a way of enriching society because "el idioma es un bien social" (*OPC,* 192) ("language is a social good"). Poetry is a luxury commodity: "Se llama lujo a la posesión comprada de las obras producidas por las bellas artes" (*OPC,* 192) ("Luxury is defined as the ownership by purchase of works produced by the fine arts"). Functional by virtue of its civilizing nature, it can be bought and sold like any other manufactured product. If language itself is no longer privileged as metaphor, then its very elements—words—may be scattered without danger of disrupting a transcendental scheme of significance. If it is indeed merely malleable material, then its craftsmen are no longer prophets or *videntes,* and a "buen libro de versos" ("good book of verse") is no more than a "sala elegante" (an "elegant parlor") whose furnishings may be bought and sold as any other commodity. The Promethean martyrdom of the poet is no more than a day's labor or carnival performance, and the stolen fire is no more than a fireworks display (an idea powerfully developed in "Los fuegos artificiales"). In his address to the second audience, however, Lugones defends innovation in literature, especially the *verso libre* or *free verse* he espouses here, by showing its continuity with classical tradition. He defines poetry as music and compares its changing forms to the evolution of musical harmony. Unwilling to divest poetry of its superior nature, he scorns the triumph of the commonplace as "el envilecimiento del idioma" ("the debasement of language") (195). In comparison to those who do not understand the special nature of poetry's appeal, the poet' work will always be an elevated one: "Homero, Dante, Hugo, séran siempre más grandes que esa persona, sólo por haber hecho versos" (*OPC,*

192) "Homer, Dante, Hugo will always be greater than that
person, simply because they have written poetry").

Paradoxically, Lugones advocates artistic innovation as a lib-
eration from outworn and degraded patterns of perception and
expression, but insists on the continuity of its formal aspects, a
paradox revealed within the poetry itself. In freeing his poetry
from many constraints of the past—in themes, metrical pat-
terns, and the types of construction of metaphor—Lugones'
emphasis on innovation in metaphors and the importance of
formal aspects in maintaining the musical nature of poetry does
mark a departure from *modernista* tradition. Although the *mod-
ernistas* called for innovation in imagery and metrics, the images
were usually selected from a commonly consented range. In
Lunario sentimental Lugones widens the field of imagery to in-
clude topics of urban life and prosaic objects, in contrast to the
archetypal images of beauty and timelessness. The subjects of
poetry are removed from the realm of supernal existence and
beauty to everyday life. For Lugones the use of any image is
legitimate by virtue of its creative force in jolting the reader into
new patterns of thinking, into making new analogies.

What is most striking in Lugones' statements in the "Prólogo"
is their consistency with his earlier pronouncements on art. Al-
though the poetic production in *Lunario sentimental* belies some
of the points in the "Prólogo," Lugones insists on the civilizing,
systematic nature of poetry and of art in general. Poets are the
caretakers of language who guide its evolution and protect it
from lapses into mediocrity. No longer claiming for the poet
the role of genius or martyred hero, the poetic vocation for
Lugones still occupies a rung on the human ladder several steps
up from the masses. Although Lugones, unlike other *modern-
istas,* never truly participated in a cult of pure poetry, he was
still unwilling to dismantle all of poetry's traditional rules and
precepts, because doing so might change its stature as a noble
influence. While bowing to a new audience and to a changed
standard, he adopts a distanced attitude and an ironic posture
before the nature of the change.

Toward the close of the prologue, Lugones specifically refers
to the verse of the *Lunario sentimental* as an exteriorized creation
resulting from interior conflicts, as if to deny all utilitarian so-

cial claims made earlier for the volume and its innovations. He
expresses a purpose of intimate rancor: "¿Existía en el mundo
empresa más pura y ardua que la de cantar a la luna por
venganza de la vida?" (*OPC*, 196) ("Did there exist a more ardu-
ous and pure enterprise in the world than that of singing to the
moon as a revenge on life?"). The volume is not to be a mirror
image of interior conflict, but a new creation, as different from
interiority as light is from dark:

> ¿Habría podido hacerlo mejor, que manando de mí mismo la
> fuerza oscura de la lucha así exteriorizada en producto excelente,
> como la pena sombría y noble sale por los ojos aclarada en cristal de
> llanto? (*OPC*, 196)
>
> (Could I have done it better than drawing from myself the dark
> force of the struggle thus exteriorized in an excellent product, the
> way that somber and noble sadness springs from the eyes, cleared
> in a prism of tears?)

The terms "producto excelente" ("excellent product") and "cris-
tal" ("prism") are important in relating the prologue to the
poems of the volume. The process of transforming dark, amor-
phous sensations to sparkling and hard-edged prisms suggests
refraction. In *Los crepúsculos del jardín* the mirror image serves
the purpose of self-duplication by the reflection of emotions in
nature, yet in the *Lunario sentimental* the prismatic image creates
a distancing effect. Its facets allow for a distancing of the self
from the "fuerza oscura de la lucha" ("dark force of the strug-
gle") and the "pena sombría y noble" ("somber and noble sad-
ness"). The prism not only duplicates but also multiplies the
self. With dramatization and multiple roles, the I can comment
on the scenes presented and even participate without sacrificing
distance. In *Lunario sentimental* the dramatic function—the use
of many voices, the attention given to masks, multiple Pierrots,
and dramatized scenes—provides techniques for the process of
duplication and self-reflection. The term "producto excelente"
also points up the technical nature of the works. As excellent
fabrications, the poems point up the technical prowess of their
creator. The accustomed automatized roles of stock images are
made more clearly visible by displaying their new and unex-

pected possibilities in different contexts. Instead of being deadened, significant coded terms—"luna," "sol," "rosas," "amor," "poeta" ("moon," "sun," "roses," "love," "poet")—will be pulled out of their accustomed hierarchies and forced to mingle with others that give them different connotations.

Since once-familiar poetic signs are now freed from their previous constraints, the stated role of the poet must change also. In *Las montañas del oro* the figure of the poet was one of extremes. As chosen prophet leading the multitudes, or as Lucifer cast down into the dark underworlds of the spirit, his fate had universal meaning and importance. His role in *Los crepúsculos del jardín* was a diffused one, functioning as a recurring, organizing voice to draw together disparate elements of the scene presented. In *Lunario sentimental,* all these roles are present, but from another vantage point. The exaltation of the poet derives from his defensiveness and his awareness of the inherent falseness of all things observed. From this superior position he can afford the frankness, comedy, and exposure of the once-sacred by his distance from it. Removed from the mountain summit, no longer supplicant before the powerful loved one, the poet can mingle on all levels, protected by his secret knowledge. The use of multiple roles, like the use of multiple Pierrots, provides a wide variety of vantage points, as well as a defense.

In "A mis cretinos," the first poem of the volume, the poet takes on the role of entertaining clown. Along with "A Rubén Darío y otros cómplices," the second poem of the volume, "A mis cretinos" deals with the role of the poet. A direct address to the public by the poet, it is structured like the opening lines of a *commedia dell'arte* performance. He dedicates the "lírico proyecto" ("lyric project") to the moon, "Astronómica dama, / O íntima planchadora" (*OPC,* 197–198) ("astonomical lady, / Oh intimate laundress"). He mocks his tribute and his own role as well. It is significant that Baudelaire, in defining comedy, uses the Pierrot figure as his exemplar. Pierrot's traits are "insouciance and neutrality, and consequently the accomplishment of all the greedy, rapacious fantasies. . . . It was the vertigo of hyperbole." Pierrot's act of pantomine "is the purification of comedy; it is its quintessence; it is the pure comic element, disengaged and concentrated."[2] In different essays, the themes of artifice and laughter are mixed. The only protection against the trickery of the outside world is the construction of an alternative wall of artifice, an ironic duplication of sense: "Obviously, in an age full of dupery, an author installed himself in complete irony and proved that he was not a dupe."[3] Baudelaire's exaltation of the *dandy,* a figure developed even more fully by later writers, is also seen as a response to surrounding decadence. "Dandyism is the last burst of heroism amid decadence."[4] The nature of artifice and caricature is not sheer play; it is a defiant assertion of individuality in a world of appearances.

SOURCES AND THEMES OF *LUNARIO SENTIMENTAL*

The poetic world in *Lunario sentimental* is formed from the accumulation of the most prized images of earlier verse. Just as Laforgue imposed a different treatment on the metalanguage of romantic and symbolist poetry in his work, Lugones breaks and disperses the metalanguage of *modernista* poetry in *Lunario sentimental. Modernista* contexts cannot accomodate the everyday paraphernalia found in the *Lunario sentimental*—bicycles, cold cream, tangos, or neuralgia; nor can they accommodate the middle class as they move about on the street.

Patterning his work on Laforgue's *L'Imitation de Notre Dame la Lune* and *Derniers Vers,* Lugones draws on a rich fund of literary tradition in selecting his materials.[5] He mixes ancient lunar mythology with the nineteenth-century treatment of the theme in the poetry of Laforgue, Verlaine, Théodore de Banville, Darío, and countless other writers. To the array of traditional literature concerning the moon he adds the figure of Pierrot, the tragic clown of the *commedia dell'arte* who is enamored of the moon. By using a figure from pantomime, Lugones brings the aspect of artifice into full attention. The recurring presence of Pierrot and his feminine counterpart Colombina, figures both farcical and tragic in many guises and settings, represents human passions and weaknesses in caricaturesque poses. Their embodiment as thematic constants of the eternal masculine and feminine allows for distancing and farce. Other characters, more closely allied to conventional reality, share in their pathos and ridicule by absorbing their traits and by proximity.

Laforgue's poetry had great impact on later poets by his use of romantic themes and stylized metaphors for ironic effect.[6] An admirer of the fanciful, the bizarre, and the extravagances of the theater, he countered both rationalism and idealism with an ironic pessimism. He used the patterns of popular songs and poetry, colloquial speech, and Christian ritual for parodic effect. Combining archetypal images and religious and scientific terminology with ballad measures and refrains, as well as with more traditional verse forms, his playful irreverent tone appealed to many as the essence of anarchism. He not only refused systematic theories but mocked their most treasured values—love, idealism, mythology, and the ideal of artistic superiority: "I would forget the mind that the centuries have made for me."[7] Laforgue's work anticipates a surrealist or stream of consciousness technique by its dissolution of rational hierarchies, but more importantly, because it concentrates on the inherent illogic of many metaphors prized for their symbolic value. His eclectic choices from the images of nature, legend, poetry, and art enter in his verse without regard for their space or time logic.

Experimental in form, as well as in his themes, Laforgue was one of the first French poets to use free verse in his collection *Derniers Vers*. His playfulness extended to deflating not only his subjects but himself, "Moi-le Magnifique," who is like the buffoon of farce or the mournful Pierrot. One of the first poets in French to extensively use technical and scientific words in lyric verse, he coined new words, combining latinisms with the wordplay of children. When applied to the great topics of philosophy or religion, his neologisms, alliterative rhymes, and internal poetic commentary ironically mock his own poetic aims, as in "Complainte de Sage de Paris."[8]

Laforgue's treatment of the moon theme mocks almost all traditional associations. The strength of the mockery is an indication of its pervasive influence as a symbol. Like the Pierrot character who is powerless against the misfortunes that befall him and whose only defense is an air of nonchalance, so all of humanity is defenseless against the moon's forces. The moon contrasts with the beneficent powers of the sun by its sterility, passiveness, and ability only to reflect, not to create. Its aspects are ambivalent. Although cold and sterile, it regulates the cyclic changes of the earth and biological rhythms. Although it represents the passage from life to death, it also provides the passage to immortality and fosters introspection. Most importantly, the moon represents the feminine principle in opposition to the solar, masculine principle, with goddesses such as Isis, Ishtar, Artemis or Diana, and Hecate associated with the moon. The lunar zone of the personality is traditionally the area of night, the unconscious, and the animal instinct. In contrast, the sun represents the rational, active, and conscious realm linked with fire.

Laforgue's juxtaposition of morbidity and humor, urban life and pastoral scenes, preciosity and colloquialism, is a reflection not only of a personal sense of division but of a more generalized response of the poets of his era to the change of the times. His poetic experiments find parallels in those of Tristan Corbière, who extended ironic mockery to more overt black humor, and in the prose of Huysmans, who used urban imagery to create grotesque scenes. It is apparent that Laforgue's treatment of traditional poetic symbols derives from Baudelaire, whose view of urban life surrounding him fused with pessimism to create powerful images reflecting the grotesqueness of modern life.[9] Laforgue's poetic rendering of human alienation and sense of trivilization influenced a whole generation of English and American poets through the work of T. S. Eliot, whose adaptations of Laforgue's verse formed the nucleus of the portrayal of modernity in "The Wasteland."

It is in this sense of tradition that Borges' remarks concerning the importance of *Lunario sentimental* in Spanish American verse may be understood:

Lugones publicó ese volumen el año 1909. Yo afirmo que la obra de los poetas de "Martín Fierro" y "Proa"—toda la obra anterior a la dispersión que nos dejó ensayar o ejecutar obra personal—está prefigurada, absolutamente, en algunas páginas del *Lunario*. En "Los fuegos artificiales," en "Luna ciudadana," en "Un trozo de selenología" en las vertiginosas definiciones del "Himno a la luna" . . . Lugones exigía, en el prólogo, riqueza de metáforas y de rimas. Nosotros, doce y catorce años después, acumulamos con fervor las primeras y rechazamos ostentosamente las últimas. Fuimos los herederos tardíos de un solo perfil de Lugones.[10]

(Lugones published that volume in 1909. I affirm that the work of the poets of *Martin Fierro* and *Proa*—all the works to the dispersion that allowed us to try out or execute our own work—is definitely foreshadowed in some pages of the *Lunario*. In "Los fuegos artificiales," in "Luna ciudadana," in "Un trozo de selenología," in the vertiginous definitions of "Himmo a la luna," . . . Lugones required, in the prologue, a richness of metaphors and rhymes. We, twelve and fourteen years later, passionately collected the former and ostentatiously rejected the latter. We were the heirs of only one side of Lugones.)

It is significant that Borges singles out the four poems of the collection which focus on urban life and on the indignities of everyday existence. These poems also eliminate, to the greatest extent, the process of discursive thought, substituting transitional phrases and qualifying remarks with snatches of colloquial language or abrupt shifts to another perspective.

It is not just the ubiquitous presence of the moon as symbol of the sterility of aspirations or of lost religions which ties Lugones' poetry to that of Laforgue. It is his seizing on the visceral nature of automized images and renewing them by their introduction into new contexts, totally disassociated from prior constraints, which distinguishes the relation of adaptation. This is the perceptual element that Lugones most clearly adapted from Laforgue, as well as the elements of urban imagery. Even though Lugones copied many verses, rhymes, and neologisms almost intact from the earlier writer, what emerges most clearly is the emphasis on the changed perspectives and lack of continuity in modern life. Lugones was extreme in his appropriation of this element. Even in the rhyme techniques, it is not usually the "petit bonheur de la rime" of Laforgue that dominates through sonority but the aggressive contrast of cacophony, as in "lucha"/"flacucha," "dieciocho"/"bizcocho,"

"botella"/"doncella," "fotográfico"/"seráfico," and "pícara"/
"jícara" ("struggle"/"skinny," "eighteen"/"biscuit," "bottle"/
"maiden," "photographic"/"seraphic," and "rogue"/"bowl").

Lugones' aggressive insistence on cacophonous rhyme and
abrupt and startling contrast is not a new element in his verse. It
appears previously in sections of *Las montañas del oro* and in the
sometimes not-so-subtle deflations of *Los crepúsculos del jardín*,
generally used for caricaturesque effects. In the *Lunario senti-
mental*, however, this element is stressed as its own referent, and
the self-reflexive nature of the poems is heightened by the stri-
dent calls for attention the rhyme schemes provoke.

IRONY IN *LUNARIO SENTIMENTAL*

The sarcastic, rougher tones of Lugones' work, an important
element of the *Lunario sentimental*, contrast with the gentler
strains of Laforgue. Paradoxically, the more aggressive tone
appears in the poems that most clearly are adapted from La-
forgue, with their confrontations of archetypal images and
their prosaic counterparts. Yet where Lugones most clearly
strikes on ironic tone, and thus touches a note of knowing loss,
is the section "Lunas," which corresponds most clearly to his
own *modernista* poetry. The presence of authorial intrusion,
overt or covert, is diminished, and the unspoken or muted con-
frontation of the old and the new allows for ambiguity. The
reader, not the directing poetic voice, must question the con-
struction. This juncture of the old and the new, with its allow-
ance for ambiguity (noted previously in the interior cycles of
Las montañas del oro and in "El solterón," "Los doce gozos," and
"Emoción aldeana" of *Los crepúsculos del jardín*), is one of the
striking elements of the *Lunario sentimental*. While the *ultraístas*,
later adapting some of the same techniques, concentrated on
metaphor development by joining disparate categories—the
"solo perfil" ("single side") of which Borges speaks—poets such
as Ramón López Velarde and Ricardo Molinari seized on the
less apparent but more intense aspect of Lugones' verse, its
ambiguity.

Startling contrast here in the *Lunario sentimental* still depends
on recognition of symbolic structures, but evasion, the indefi-
niteness of nostalgia, and repressed longing create a dislocation

of perception, a knowledge of loss without its former outline. Only in this sense is Lugones a true ironist in the *Lunario sentimental.* The poet may point out and openly berate or celebrate the changes in a modern world and lament the loss of the goals of romanticism, but this is frank exposure or simple sarcasm. Irony involves not only a double vision, but a paralysis of the ability to set the two perspectives apart, to decode the message in its final form. Irony's intrinsic fall is not the plummet from summit to abyss, nor the opposition of noon to midnight, but the crepuscular, indefinite, split-second moment of the passage from night to day, when perceptions are uncertain. Once its message is decoded or apparent, irony becomes static, and its message leads to a single sign, not to double vision.[11] When this occurs in the *Lunario sentimental,* as it often does, the poetic voice has resolved the question and dissolved the possibility of ironic surprise, as in many caricaturesque poems and in the "Teatro quimérico." In the fifteen poems comprising "Lunas," however, and in other poems such as "Los fuegos artificiales," "Pescador de sirenas," and "Divagación lunar" (all of which possess moments of caricature also), the ironic mode presents itself by the absence of overt balancing, message proclamation, or the framing authorial voice. These poems recall Lugones' earlier poetry and ideals by their reminiscences and formal manipulations, but their models are diffused by a metonymic displacement that leaves undefined the total scheme from which its fragments are drawn. In this fusion, not only signs of the physical universe are displaced and rearranged, but signs of a past poetry mingle on several planes. In this metonymical displacement and fusion the physical rather than the symbolic nature of its component parts is stressed (as in "Los fuegos artificiales") to the extent that the lexicon itself—seen as infinite array rather than as structured order—begins to seem part of malleable physicality, as the plasticity of the rhyme exhibits. Once begun, the process is like a chain reaction and continues to reverberate until the postulated self that views it cannot be conceived of as an absolute. Therefore in its inception and its effect, the force of irony is disconcerting and dislocating, like the process of metonymy carried to extremes, where no totalizing referent can be ascertained.

The way to stop irony is to understand it, expose it, to separate the true from the false. Humor or caricature may perform this function, as it often does in the *Lunario sentimental.* Both modes hasten the process of *desengaño,* of setting up a distancing effect. According to Baudelaire, this impulse has its root in self-defense: "one will find at the bottom of the laughing man's thought a certain unconscious pride. That is the point of departure: *I* do not fall, *I* walk straight, *my* foot is firm and sure."[12] Just as the self-enclosure and projection of subjectivity onto the natural world in romantic and symbolist poetry once provided an elevation of the poet an artist, creator or *vidente (seer)* now the buffoon or clown embodies the secret knowledge that is the poet's.

POETIC CONSTRUCTION IN *LUNARIO SENTIMENTAL*

In its mixture of different levels *Lunario sentimental* is an uneven volume. It resembles a series of experiments, first tentative, then daring. Its very unevenness and unexpectedness at the time of its publication explain its mixed reception. It has been called by critics both a powerfully original work and a mere copy. These critics take their cues not only from their individual perspectives but from the volume itself. The poetic tension is created by a willful insistence on destroying archetypal categories of meaning, and a reluctance to leave their fragmented vestiges dispersed and unbound by the constraints of an earlier poetics. Although the scheme of polar oppositions is completely dismantled, its framework is hinted at through the constant strain of ambiguity in the *Lunario sentimental.* "Divagación lunar" shows, perhaps more clearly than any poem of the collection, the outlines of the dichotomy between the old and the new. It presents a constant dismantling of its own precepts and its stated intention—"Si tengo la fortuna / De que con tu alma mi dolor se integre, / Te diré entre melancólico y alegre / Las singulares cosas de la luna" (*OPC,* 240) ("If I have the good fortune / Of joining your soul with my pain, / I will tell you half sadly and half joyfully, / The unique things about the moon"). Its description of a lovers' encounter might well be the recounting of the passing of an illusion, like "el ritmo de la dulce violencia" ("the rhythm of sweet violence"). its rhyming of "poema" ("poem") with "sistema" ("system") is not merely a verbal fit, for by undoing the themes of an earlier poetry its entire system is revealed, and its echoes resemble "el rizo anacrónico de un lago" ("the anachronic ripple of a lake"). The light of the moon, at once "fraternal" but with an intimacy of "encanto femenino" ("feminine charm"), does not clarify but passes "indefiniendo asaz tristes arcanos" ("undefining rather sad mysteries").

The unexpected confrontation of mixed levels of speech along with an irregular metrical scheme, gives many of the *Lunario sentimental*'s poems a close link to popular speech or song instead of to conventional *modernista* poetic lyricism, for example, "cold cream," "sportswoman," "ridiculous," "bric-a-brac," "alkaline," "hunchback," "gelatine." The element of poetic diction that is not sacrificed is rhyme. Not only is it retained, but its presence is accentuated. Stereotyped rhymes are blatantly repeated, as if parodying the old combinations, for example "tul–azul" "amor–dolor" ("love–pain"). Yet, more frequently, unexpected rhyme words are paired, a lyrical word sometimes rhymed with a scientific expression or neologism, with different areas of experience forcefully brought together ("fotográfico"/ "seráfico" ["photographic"/"seraphic"]). "El Pierrotillo" exemplifies the experimental nature of much of the rhyme. Its last quatrain involves a rhyme with a monosyllabic verse:

> Un puntapié
> Le manda allá
>   Y se
>   Va . . .
>   (*OPC*, 243)
>
> (A kick
> Sends him off
> And there he
> Goes . . .)

The constancy of innovative rhyme shows the importance assigned to its function. Rhyme for Lugones is important because it preserves for poetry the quality of artifice, since strict rhythmic patterns are no longer binding.

In regard to rhythm and rhyme, Carlos Navarro has thoroughly examined the use of *esdrújulos* in the *Lunario sentimental,* and he finds there is an even higher count in the caricaturesque poems.[13] By making the rhythm a more textured, difficult process, the use of *esdrújulos* increases the awareness of the specifically literary nature of the work, drawing attention away from the word as denotation of concrete objects or experience. On many levels—rhyme, theme, individual metaphor, and rhythm—the disparity between literary convention and Lugones' unexpected transformations of it call attention back to the "life of words." The space between reader expectation and its reversal is the place of irony or surprise.

A constant in the poetry of *Lunario sentimental* is the transposition of qualities from antithetical categories.[14] The opposing categories of animal/human, divine/human, sun/moon, maker/destroyer, speech/silence, creator/reflector, nature/technology are intermingled in a process of multiple metonymies. Opposites are often united without causal explanation, and the outcome is not resolution but an ever-increasing awareness of dissimilarity. To emphasize even more forcefully the irreconcilable oppositions and lack of harmony, the essential fictional nature of unifying hierarchical categories is stressed. By revealing the mechanics of the process of illusion making, especially poetic illusions, the sense of manipulation and trickery is heightened, as in "Los fuegos artificiales." Incoherence emerges through metonymic displacement, and the simplest way of doing this is by attributing a physical nature to the nature of illusions, and then by parceling out and dividing the pieces among other categories. Natural processes, inversely, are accorded fictional qualities. In these manipulations, language itself is shown to be part of the body of things. The obvious manipulation of rhyme points up the guiding hand behind the disintegration of customary arrangements.

PHYSICAL PRESENCE IN *LUNARIO SENTIMENTAL*

The treatment of the sirens in "El pescador de sirenas" is like an epiphany of the fetishistic contemplation of the female in earlier verse:

Bogan muy cerca de la superficie
Blancas y fofas como enormes hongos,
O deformando en desconcertante molicie
Sus cuerpos como vagos odres oblongos.
                                        (*OPC*, 227)

(They float near the surface
Soft and white like giant mushrooms,
Or deforming in disconcerting masses
Their bodies like vague, oblong wineskins.)

With the erotic vision now completely dismembered, corporeal parts float to the surface "Con fosfórica putrefacción de molusco" or "En lenta congelación de camelias" ("With phosphoric putrefaction of the mollusc" or "In the slow freezing of camelias"). The search for the perfect poetic form, the hunt for the sirens, parallels the parceling out of physical images in its destructive intent toward poetic form itself. Attempting and discarding methods of approaching the perfect method, the fisherman seeks the sirens' songs, yet, "como ha seguido el método de Ulises, / Nunca pudo oír el hechicero canto"/ (since he has followed Ulysses' method, / He could never hear the bewitching song"). His ludicrous fate, on finally hearing the sirens' song, is to be thrown to the "agua sinfónica" ("symphonic water") without being able to record the perfect sound.

Like the description of an empty room in "La alcoba solitaria," in which the inventories of an interior suggest the presence of life by its absence, or the listing of fabrics in "El solterón," in which musty smells and threadbare conditions reflect the characteristics of the old suitor, the vitality of illusion as opposed to reality is shown in the listing of sterile forms in the *Lunario sentimental*.[15]

"Himno a la luna" offers numerous examples of images deprived of their former symbolic value by association with degrading or colloquial words. Previously, in *Las montañas del oro* and in *Los crepúsculos del jardín*, the rose was associated with the desirable and often mysterious woman. In "Himno a la luna" they are: "las rosas ebrias de etileno / Como cortesanas modernas" (*OPC*, 205) ("the roses drunk with ethylene / Like modern courtesans"). The sun, symbol of the summit of human aspiration in *Las montañas del oro,* is an automaton that hatches the dead moon: "Mientras redondea su ampo / En monótono viaje / El sol, como un faisán crisolampo, / La empolla con ardor siempre nuevo" (*OPC,* 207) ("Circling her dazzling whiteness / In monotonous voyage / the sun, as striking as a pheasant / Hatches her with a passion always new"). The moon, once the "ilustre anciana de las mitologías" ("illustrious lady of mythologies") is now only a skeleton, "ese luminoso huevo" ("that luminous egg") which "Milagrosamente blanca, / Satina morbideces de *cold cream* y de histeria / Carnes de espárrago que en linfática miseria, / La tenaza brutal de la tos arranca" (*OPC,* 27) ("Miraculously white, / glazes the softness of cold cream and of hysteria / Asparagus flesh that in tired misery, / the brutal tongs of a cough tear out"). Associated with the woman, the moon is presented with all its sinister qualities that are the inverse qualities of the prized feminine image in much *modernista* poetry—the *femme fatale* or gentle innocent. Her passion changes to cruel compulsion and her gentle innocence to ineffectual sterility:

> Trompo que en el hilo de las elipses
> Baila eternamente su baile de San Vito;
> Hipnótica prisionera
> Que concibe a los malignos hados
> En su estéril insomnia de soltera;
>
> (*OPC,* 209)
>
> (Spinning top forever performing
> Its Saint Vitus' dance within the lines of the elipsis;
> Hypnotic prisoner
> Who from within her sterile spinster's insomnia
> Conceives evil fates;)

The moon's influence is the cause of suffering and excess. Her followers are the night's victims—"¡Pobre niña, víctima de la felona noche, . . . Mientras padece en su erótico crucifijo / Hasta las heces el amor humano" (*OPC,* 215) ("Poor little girl, victim of the felonious night, . . . Suffering the very dregs of human love / on her erotic crucifix"). For Lugones, the modern woman, divided into her composite parts, reflects the shattering of sentimental ideals into fragmented bits and pieces.

"LUNAS": INTRUSION OF THE CITY AND THE COMMONPLACE

"Himno a la luna" occupies a place of central importance in the collection. Its possibilities of forming new metaphors are further explored in most of the other poems, especially in the division "Lunas," fifteen poems that illustrate the possibilities of manipulating the moon theme. The first, "Un trozo de selenologia" ("A piece of selenology"), illustrates the series of associations that can arise from a single image or a picturesque analogy of speech. The clear moon is visible from the window "a tiro de escopeta" ("a gunshot away"). The mention of the gun sparks a digressive monologue:

> No tenía rifle,
> Ni nada que fuera más o menos propio
> Para la caza; pero un mercachifle
> Habíame vendido un telescopio.
> Bella ocasión, sin duda alguna,
> Para hacer un blanco en la luna.
>
> (*OPC*, 271)

> (I had no rifle.
> Nor anything that would be more or less suitable
> For the hunt; but a huckster
> Had sold me a telescope.
> Fine chance, without a doubt,
> To hit the mark on the moon.)

Continually interrupting the description of the moon is the frequent intrusion of the inside room and its concerns. Mixing parenthetical statements—"La vida resulta desconcertadora / De esta manera" ("Life seems disconcerting / this way") with the panoramic view from the "perspectiva teatral de palco escénico" ("theatrical perspective of the stage box")—abstractions mix with minute descriptions and are materialized. Metaphor construction is in shorthand:

> Así en símiles sencillos,
> Destacábase en pleno azul de cielo,
> Tu cuerpo como un arroyuelo
> Sólo contrariado por dos guijarrillos.
>
> (*OPC*, 274)

(So, in simple similes,
Your body stood out against the deep blue sky,
A brook
Ruffled only by two pebbles.)

The process of the poem is interrupted by pointing out that the functionality of a term is only its rhyme value: "Te vi a ti misma— ¿por qué ventana? . . .— / En tu bañadera de porcelana" (*OPC*, 273) ("I saw you, yourself—In which window? . . — / In your porcelain bathtub").

"El taller de la luna" accentuates the self-reflexiveness of its production. It alternates between serene, geometrical progression ("con vertical exacta," "Tiene por tema un ángulo de blanca noche" ["with exact verticality," "It has as its subject an angle of white night"]) interspersed with the disequilibrium and resistance of physical materials ("Trueca el percal de la palurda / En increíble tisú de dama fatua" ["It converts the yokel's percale / Into the incredible tulle of a fatuous lady"], "Un inconcluso fauno a quien no cupo / En el magro pernil el pie de cabra" [*OPC*, 275] ["An incomplete faun on whose lean haunches / The goat's foot did not fit"]). Its verses prefigure the changes to come within the poem. The work of the "luna artista" ("artist moon") will be interrupted by that of another poet whose "cráneo, negro de hastío, / Derrocha una poesía rara, / Como un cubo sombrío / Que se invierte en agua clara" (*OPC*, 276) ("skull, black from boredom / Pours out strange poetry / Like a somber barrel / That is inverted in clear water").

"Claro de luna" continues the process of materializing abstractions. The moonlit cityscape, with the moon as its "cima de calma" ("crest of calm") and "El casto silencio de su nieve" ("The chaste silence of its snow"), is interrupted by the croaking of the frog, whose asymmetrical description within the scene heightens its presence "como un isócrono cascanueces" ("like an isochronous nutcracker"), juxtaposed with a silent guitar. From the "eclógico programa / De soledad y bosque pintoresco" (the "eclogic program / of picturesque forests and solitude"), the prosaic movement below is transposed onto the impassive sky. Like the process of the poem itself, the "noche en pijama, . . . se dispersa y restaura" ("night in pyjamas, . . . is dispersed and

restored") with the comings and goings of the night, as the
neighbor's punctual key in the lock marks out time.

Instead of the moon's regular circling of the earth in her
orbit, in "Luna ciudadana" an unexciting "fulano" ("John Doe")
crosses through the city in his "consuetudinario / Itinerario"
("habitual itinerary") by streetcar. The contrast between his
daily routine and its more exciting transformation in a "versátil
aerostación de ideas" ("versatile airstation of ideas") points up
the bleakness of urban life. Reality gives him little to work with,
but remnants of a distant poetry allow him to reconstruct some-
thing other than "la muda / Fatalidad de una vulgar tragedia, /
Con sensata virtud de clase media" (*OPC*, 287) ("the mute /
Fatality of a vulgar tragedy, / With sensible, middle-class vir-
tue"). The physical presence of the young woman seated across
from him in the tram "Con su intrepidez flacucha / De insti-
tutriz o de florista" ("With the skinny intrepidness / Of a govern-
ess or a flowergirl") serves him well as the nucleus of his medio-
cre dreams. The sum of her physical parts is only united by his
imaginative additions—"Lindos ojos, boca fresca" ("Pretty eyes,
fresh mouth") with "Un traje verde oscuro" ("A dark green
dress"—down to the detail of her glove size. After she leaves the
tram, "Fulano," who is "vagamente poeta" ("vaguely a poet"),
reconstructs the scene in terms of a tragic lost love, to the
rhythm of "Y monda que te monda / Los dientes" ("And pick,
pick / your teeth,") and the sound of a street organ. The sounds
and scenes are in accord with his meager reality and not his
richer dreams.

"Luna campestre," like the other poems of "Lunas" has fram-
ing narrative elements, which, although disjointed, do not leave
multiple and contradictory images totally unresolved. The most
common frame is the presence of snatches of an earlier land-
scape poetry, with tales of lost loves and the moon's changes as
constants. "Luna de los amores" eliminates to a great extent the
lyricism that could provide the contrast to its suburban setting.
It is largely consistent in taking all referents from the same
context, that of the house and its objects. The house merges
with its inhabitants, and outside elements enter the scene only
on their own terms—"El plenilunio crepuscular destella, / En el
desierto comedor, un lejano / Reflejo, que apenas insinúa su

huella" (*OPC*, 298) ("The full moon glimmers in the twilight / In the deserted dining room a distant / Reflection barely hints at its passage"). The moon is also a domesticated one, "abollada / Como el fondo de una cacerola / Enlozada" (*OPC*, 300) ("dented/ Like the bottom of a cooking pot"). The clock's tick repeats the exchange of categories, "Anota el silencio con tiempos immemoriales" (*OPC*, 299) ("Notes the silence with time immemorial"). The metonymical interchange in terms of the physical nature of the house reflects the "hastío de las cosas iguales" ("boredom of the same things") and the tameness of its measured life. The clock, with "espíritu luterano" ("Lutheran spirit") marks out the slow beat of the lives of its inhabitants. The young girl's dreams of love contrast with the prosaic movement of the kitchen—"La joven está pensando en la vida. / Por allá dentro, la criada bate un huevo" (*OPC*, 299) ("The young girl is thinking about life. / Back inside, the maid is beating an egg"). The lyricism of unrequited love is confined to the young girl's dreams and appearance:

> Rodeando la rodilla con sus manos, unidas
> Como dos palomas en un beso embebecidas,
> Con actitud que consagra
> Un ideal quizá algo fotográfico,
> La joven tiende su cuello seráfico
> En un noble arcaísmo de Tanagra.
>
> (*OPC*, 300)
>
> (Clasping her knee with her hands, joined
> Like two doves lost in a kiss,
> With an attitude that confirms
> An ideal perhaps somewhat photographic,
> The young girl stretches her seraphic neck
> In an noble archaism of Tanagra.)

Despite the frequently prosaic tone of the poems of "Lunas" and their unusual juxtapositions, they possess coherence by the continual reappearance of landscape description. It is as if the appearance of everyday humans were a jolting presence in the midst of cosmic forces. Yet the moon theme allows for the combination of a natural setting and disruptive agents. Unsettling events may or may not be malevolent in themselves; it is their continuity with the setting which determines the degree of their disturbance. In the same way, the moon in all its phases absorbs and reflects human passions and cruelties.

TECHNOLOGY AND "LOS FUEGOS ARTIFICIALES"

"Los fuegos artificiales," more than any other poem, best represents the explosive destruction of the iconography of previous poetry. The swarming mass of humanity, with its "alma de tribu que adora un fuego augusto" ("tribal spirit that worships a majestic fire") is rapt before the fireworks at a patriotic festival. The spectacle's "bazares de cosmos" ("cosmic bazaars") and its "astronómica feria" ("astronomic fair") constitute a technical caricature of past creations which will foreshadow a future model:

> Y ¡con qué formidable caricatura,
> Tu policroma incandescencia
>   Destaca a la concurrencia
> En un poema de humanidad futura!
> (OPC, 260)

> (And with what formidable caricature
> your polychrome incandescence
> Displays the crowd
> In a poem of future humanity!)

Formed from a mixture of "un poco de mixto, de noche y de mal gusto" ("a bit of fire, night and bad taste"), the spectacle is a fitting work of art for its audience, who are described in animalistic terms. The plaza that contains then "hormiguea / De multitud, como un cubo de ranas" ("swarms / With the crowd, like a bucket of frogs").

Free from any reminiscence of traditional poetry, "Los fuegos artificiales" accentuates the speed, movement, and color of a changed technique. Its title is a metaphor of itself. It celebrates a new technique that does not reproduce the dimensions and perspectives of nature. Yet there is ambivalence in the presentation of this celebration. The crowd reflects the other face of technical prowess. The appeals to instinct and elementary violence are reflected in the crowd watching the cannons, bombs, and bright lights of the artificial explosions. Its "mil-lionario tesoro de colores" ("rich treasure of colors") awakens "arrobos / De paganismo atávico, en cursivas alertas, / Es la pura majestad de los globos / Sobre la O vocativa de las bocas abiertas" (*OPC*, 255–556): ("Amazement / from atavistic pagan-ism, in alert cursives, / Is the pure majesty of the balloons / Above the open mouths formed by the vocative O"). Its dizzy-ing spin "hace babear los éxtasis del tonto; / Trocando ab-surdamente su destino / En el sautor regular de un molino" (*OPC*, 258): ("Makes the fool drool in ecstasy; / Absurdly ex-changing his destiny / In the ordinary crosspiece of a mill").

Technology, praised in *Los montañas del oro* as a force equiva-lent to nature's own ("el gran caballo negro") must here con-tend with its results. The bourgeois family, grotesque in its presentation, is transfigured beneath the artificial lights. The exaggeration of physical traits once applied to erotic subjects is extended here to form a picture of macabre juxtaposition:

> A su lado el esposo, con dicha completa,
> Se asa en tornasol, como una chuleta;
> Y el bebé que fingía sietemesino chiche,
> No es ya más que un macabro fetiche.
> La nodriza, una flaca escocesa,
> Va, enteramente isósceles, junto a la suegra obesa,
> Que afronta su papel de salamandra
> Con una gruesa
> Inflación de escafandra,
> Mientras en vaivén de zurda balandra
> Goza sus fuegos la familia burguesa.
>
> <div align="right">(<i>OPC</i>, 260)</div>

(By her side the husband, totally content,
Roasts on both sides like a chop;
And the baby who acted out his scrawny cuteness,
Is nothing more than a macabre fetish.
The wet nurse, a skinny Scotswoman,
Stands, all isoceles angles, next to the obese mother-in-law,
Who faces up to her salamander role
With a swollen inflammation of her headgear.
While in the clumsy rocking of a sloop
The bourgeois family enjoys the fireworks.)

The narrative point of view also changes. Not just a spectator of the crowd, the narrator himself is caught up in its movement, changing the relationship of distanced observer—"Donde mi propia persona / En coloreado maleficio, / Adquiere algo de sota y de saltimbanqui / Yanqui . . ." (*OPC,* 261), ("Where my own self / In colorful wickedness, / Becomes something of a spade and of a Yankee / Jester . . ."). Like the spectacle's audience, he himself becomes grotesque.

In the four romantic tales and the "Teatro quimérico," the process of inversion is much more explicit. Not just characteristics but entire roles are switched. Here exaggeration is carried to explicit satire. The theme in the four romantic tales is impossible love. In almost every way imaginable Lugones satirizes the traits of romantic lovers. In "Abuela Julieta" the aristocratic pretensions of romanticism are the object of attack. A forty-year unrequieted love is "una migaja de tragedia en la impasibilidad de los astros eternos" (*OPC,* 269) ("a crumb of tragedy in the impassibility of the eternal stars"). In "Inefable ausencia" the luxuriant description usually reserved for the heroine is lavished on Roberto:

> El era mucho más bello. Una dulzura de niño pensativo inundaba su rostro; y como las vírgenes, tenía cuello de lirio. En la oscuridad azul de sus ojos se aterciopelaban melancolías. (*OPC,* 217)

> (He was much more beautiful. The sweetness of a pensive child flooded his face; and like a virgin, his neck was like a lily. In the blue depth of his eyes melancholy turned to velvet.)

The lovers' situation, so trivialized by exaggerating their narcissism and delicacy, cannot be contained even within traditional literary patterns: "Y el silencio era tan grande afuera, que ambos retrocedieron en el balcón" (*OPC,* 218) ("So great was the silence outside, that they both stepped back into the balcony").

In *Lunario sentimental* Lugones not only mocks previous texts but, with a vengeance, attacks the ideals that inspired them. He confronts the aristocratic ideals of romanticism and symbolism, with their enclosed, self-reflexive worlds and the nostalgia of the sublime, and counters them with new standards. The old models must face their aggressive counterpart, the world of modernity, with its technology, urban life, rational identities, and new mythologies. Cosmological forces, mythical figures, and archetypal lovers are ceaselessly paired with their unkind reflection. The canonized forms remain in the foreground, but their main purpose is to display the vitality of their conquerors.

Continuing in a vein begun in the "Tercer ciclo" of *Las montañas del oro*, Lugones juxtaposes ancient idols with the heroes of his own time, but with a different emphasis. There is no aim of redemption set forth, and he caricatures the heroic nature of the old and new idols. The figure of the poet again takes explicit shape, but not as a victorious promethean figure at the summit who surveys the world from the "Torre de oro." Now as the buffoonlike figure of Pierrot or "fulano," his only superiority is his distance, his character a succession of masks. The poet appears directly in view of his public, not the mythicized and glorious "Pueblo," but before the masses, "mis cretinos" ("my cretins"). In these poems Lugones departs from the aristocratic ideal that he and others—"Rubén Darío y otros cómplices" ("Rubén Darío and other accomplices")—had previously espoused. The poet will descend to the popular stage.

What is vital in the *Lunario sentimental* is the nature of artifice. A representative natural world loses ground as linguistic play moves to the forefront. Verse and prose are mixed to point up the automatized roles that traditional forms usually play. Lugones, in reaching toward a new fund of imagery and rhythms that he found in writers such as Laforgue, helped to change the nature of poetry in Spanish. At the time of its publication in 1909, the *Lunario sentimental* evoked both applause and derision, and its example served as a model for future poets, either as a standard to combat or as an invitation to experiment with new forms.

6

THE FRENZY OF *MODERNISMO:*
HERRERA Y REISSIG

Lugones' preoccupation with the meaning and mechanics of style is a constant among other *modernistas.* Julio Herrera y Reissig, in "El círculo de la muerte," discusses the concept of beauty and asks for a fitting of form and concept that pleases the reader "sin violencia" ("without violence") yet which moves with the glistening duplicity of a mirror's reflection:

> Es una duplicidad armónica y semejante; trátase de que la idea tome inmediatamente la forma del vocablo, como un perisprit la forma del cuerpo donde mora, confundida con él y fraternizando hasta parecer tangible; y a su vez de que la palabra se imprima en el pensamiento y entre en él, de un modo ágil, ni más ni menos que como en un molde preciso y pulcro la cera caliente. El gran estilo es el que brilla y corre como un agua primaveril, espejo moviente de sombras movientes y vivas que erran por la página y se hunden en ella, cual pececillos traslúcidos, color del cristal . . . [1]

> (It is a harmonic and similar duplicity. It is a question of the idea immediately taking the form of a word, in the same way that a spirit takes the form of the body that it inhabits, blending and fraternizing with it until it seems tangible; and it is, in turn, a question of the word impressing itself upon the mind and entering it, nimbly, exactly as hot wax enters a clean, precise mold. A great style is one which shines and leaps, like spring water, a moving mirror of lively, mobile shadows that wander along the page and are submerged in it, like little translucent fish, the color of crystal . . .)

The later productions of Herrera y Reissig, Lugones, and other *modernistas,* less seemingly stylized, illustrate the "minus devices" or "simplicity" of which Yuri Lotman in *Analysis of the Poetic Text* speaks:

The concept of simplicity as an aesthetic value comes with the following stage and is invariably connected with the rejection of ornamentality. Perception of artistic simplicity is possible only against a background of "ornamental" art whose memory is present in the consciousness of the viewer–listener. . . . Consequently, simplicity is structurally a much more complex phenomenon than ornamentality.[2]

An analysis of aspects of the work of Julio Herrera y Reissig can illustrate the force of the subversive movement in *modernista* poetry. As a late *modernista*, Herrera y Reissig exemplifies many of the contradictions of this period that would serve as inspiration for other poets of the twentieth century.

On presenting Pablo Neruda at the Facultad de Filosofía y Letras in Madrid in 1935, Federico García Lorca singled out three Spanish American poets who represent "el tono descarado del gran idioma español de los americanos" ("the brazen tone of the great Spanish American language"). Along with the voices of Rubén Darío and the Uruguayan-born Lautréamont, he named another, "la extravagante, adorable, arrebatadoramente cursi y fosforescente voz de Herrera y Reissig"[3] ("the extravagant, adorable, wrenchingly vulgar and phosphorescent voice of Herrera y Reissig"). In one of the early studies of *modernismo*, Arturo Torres Rioseco distinguishes Herrera y Reissig from authors notable for their obvious American heritage, calling him "absolutamente desprendido del ambiente"[4] ("absolutely detached from his surroundings"). Torres Rioseco uses the same type of adjectives as Lorca in differentiating Herrera y Reissig from his *modernista* contemporaries and from other models: "La figura grandiosa de Julio Herrera y Reissig— más loco que Verlaine, menos que William Blake—nos afirma que debemos confiar en nuestra fuerza cerebral"[5] ("The grandiose figure of Julio Herrera y Reissig—more insane than Verlaine, less so than William Blake—affirms for us that we should trust in the strength of our brain").

Julio Herrera y Reissig filled his short life of only thirty-five years with a dazzling output of verse and prose which startled its early readers and continues to evoke astonishment even among contemporaries. Exceptionally able in his mastery of verse forms, Herrera y Reissig's command of his lyrical instrument is overshadowed by his daring lexicon and the abrupt juxtapositions of decadent and classical formulas. The modern world of science and technology, especially its darker undertones, invades a pastoral world of nymphs, shepherdesses, and goddesses. Herrera y Reissig's novelties of language, however, and the inheritance of exotic aspects of decadent literature, left some critics and admirers with a more ambivalent opinion. Rubén Darío, praising Herrera y Reissig's poetic mastery, is reluctant to give total approbation:

> En Herrera y Reissig lo artificial, el virtualismo, se penetra de su vibración si queréis *enfermiza* de la verdad de su tensión cordial, de su verídico sufrimiento íntimo.[6]

> (In Herrera y Reissig artificiality, virtuosity, is penetrated by its sickly vibration, if you will, of the truth of his heart-felt tension, of his very real inner suffering.)

Yet Darío points to *Los éxtasis de la montaña,* a series of sonnets published in 1904, as products of a masterful visual and auditive inspiration, "con el giro innovador, el verbo inusitado y el adjetivo sorprendente"[7] ("with innovative turns, unusual verbs, and surprising adjectives"). He calls "La muerte del Pastor: 'Balada Eglogica,' " " . . . de lo más suavemente encantador, de lo más musicalmente sentimental, y de lo más simplemente fino que se haya escrito en nuestra lengua"[8] ("The Shepherd's Death: 'An Eclogic Ballad,' " " . . . the most smoothly enchanting, the most musically sentimental, the most simply fine ballad of its kind that has ever been written in our language").

Contemporary readers have found appeal in the fantastic and allegorical treatments of death and eroticism in Herrera y Reissig's poetry. His syntactical compression, his neologisms, and the startling combinations of classical and scientific terminology went farther than those of Lugones' *Lunario sentimental.* Although it may have been difficult for his contemporaries to separate the decadent iconography from the innovative treatment of language (as well as his flamboyant personal proclamations and polemics), Herrera y Reissig's example affected several major writers of the twentieth century (notably César

Vallejo) with his foreshortened focus and syntactical experiments. Combining the prosaic rural village with its Greek or Roman evocation in eclogues, Herrera y Reissig drops the framing fiction that makes the transition between the two codified worlds. The resulting jolt or ambiguity and the unsettling intrusion of subversive notes give access to twentieth-century experiments in poetic diction. Federico de Onís singles out the influence of Góngora on Herrera y Reissig in the creation of difficult and elusive metaphors, and affirms Herrera y Reissig's novelty: "aprendió mucho de Góngora y se adelantó a sus más recientes intérpretes, siendo la suya una de las influencias capitales que llevaron el modernismo hacia el ultraísmo"[9] ("he learned much from Góngora, and he surpassed that poet's most recent interpreters, his being one of the principal influences that carried *modernismo* toward *ultraísmo*"). Some of the adjectives most often used to describe Herrera y Reissig's poetry are "surprising," "jolting," or even "vulgar." Even amidst discussion of the derivative nature of his poetry—specifically, the influences of Samain and Lugones—the outstanding features of his poetry are judged as its surprise elements and its not always pleasant energy. Herrera y Reissig's poetry resists easy classification. His startling metaphors, noisy alliteration, and surprising rhymes struck his contemporaries as disruptive. From a later point of view, however, the same experiments often sound trite, or "cursi," as both his admirers and detractors have stated.[10] The following discussion will attempt to give a more specific definition of the nature of this "energy" so often attributed to Herrera y Reissig, and will place him within the context of his epoch.

As late *modernista* poets, both Lugones and Herrera y Reissig obviously borrow from certain traditions, and the overlapping of their works derives from a sharing of many of the same models of traditions. Although the similarities are immediately obvious (especially their borrowings from Samain), down to the development of images similar even in minute details, the articulation of these elements is often strikingly different. In the *modernista* spirit, accumulation from the outside was seen as an enrichment to the general wealth. The ideal of the writer as a solitary genius, although expressed in their works, was obviously not a motivating force in their respective productions. On the contrary, both writers accentuate the presence of prestigious "foreign" elements.

The poetry of Lugones and Herrera y Reissig belongs to a stage of late *modernismo* marked by the stillness and heavy ornamentation of its rites. Severo Sarduy's description of the work of Giancarlo Marmori, written in roughly the same period, could apply as well to the final stages of *modernismo:*

> La retórica de lo accesorio convirtiéndose en esencial, la multiplicación de lo adjetival sustantivado, el ornamento desmedido, la contorsión, lo vegetal estilizado, las estatuas y cisnes, y lo cosmético como instrumento de sadismo mediatizado.[11]

> (The rhetoric of what is really secondary becomes essential, the proliferation of adjectives used as nouns, excessive ornamentation, contortion, stylized plant forms, statues and swans, and cosmetic elements used as instruments of a mediatized sadism.)

The rites of ornamentation and of breaking the silence are very different in Lugones and Herrera y Reissig. Both poets carry *modernismo*'s landscapes and stylized language to extremes and then dismantle their productions in a single stroke.

In Lugones' *Los crepúsculos del jardín* and Herrera y Reissig's *Los parques abandonados,* their two most similar works (with the direct stamp of Samain's influence introduced to Herrera y Reissig by Lugones' poems),[12] even the books' titles suggest the exhaustion of *modernismo*'s ritual ornamentation. They twist their models to the breaking point, with their heraldry, sunsets, and deserted gardens where cruel and perverse lovers enact their studied rites. By syntactical compression and metonymical interchange, both Lugones' and Herrera y Reissig's sonnets prefigure later artistic techniques, for example Herrera y Reissig's introductory quartet from "La última carta" reduces a personified landscape in one single, frightening knife stroke. Like the opening shot of Buñuel's *Le Chien andalou,* the sonnet begins:

> Con la quietud de un síncope furtivo,
> desangróse la tarde en la vertiente,
> cual si la hiriera repentinamente
> un aneurisma determinativo . . . [13]

> (With the stillness of a stealthy syncope,
> the afternoon bled into the spring,
> as if suddenly wounded
> by a determinative aneurism . . .)

We have an idea of Lugones as poet—the monster of style, the voracious assimilator whose own style, when not consciously parodic, unconsciously generates its own parody through excess. As trickster of rhyme and master of successive literary identities, we see Lugones first and foremost as stylist. In contrast, the body of criticism concerning Herrera y Reissig's work usually attributes an intimate personal quality to his production of shocking metaphor and wordplay. Where is the difference in gesture? Why does one seem to pound and the other to whisper, even while reworking many of the same materials?

It is the nature of this movement of departure which differentiates much of the poetry of Lugones and Herrera y Reissig. Although they do not overtly destroy the patterns they establish, the seeds of destruction are planted within the very framework of the poetry itself by its subversive movement. Following Roland Barthes' definition, **subtle subversion** does not concern itself with overt denials or oppositions. It is "not directly concerned with destruction, evades the paradigm and seeks some *other* term: a third term, which is not, however, a synthesizing term but an eccentric, extraordinary term."[14] The critical task, then, concerns the identification of this subject in the works of Lugones and Herrera y Reissig during the late stages of *modernismo*. In other words, who speaks? Where is the gesture that directs the poetic process? Considering the body of their works as elements of what Barthes has called the "circular memory of literature" or its "intertext," I would like to focus their works within the movement of *modernismo*, to view this time of production as a fixed scene, a static space frozen in time. The *topos* of the fixed scene was a Parnassian ideal very dear to the *modernistas* themselves, with their preference for the enclosed space or interior garden, the play of light on statues, and the play of sounds on words now frozen in their iconic significance.

The poetic works of both Lugones and Herrera y Reissig share many traits, and instances of poems metaphorizing their own destructive and subversive movements stand as indicators of their *modernista* works as a whole. Lugones highlights poetic fragmentation, and the masked poetic *yo* stands back and directs our gaze. In contrast, Herrera y Reissig introduces a third element apart from the two opposing traditions. This is the movement of shifting perspectives, the unidentifiable movement that creates the sense of loss, the knowledge that our hierarchies are being threatened by invisible forces.

Herrera y Reissig preserves the metaphor even while the movement of operation is similar to that of Lugones. Rather than being destructive, his movement of disclosure is subversive. Subversion does not create the confrontation of polar opposites which invites domination and destruction. With its subtle slant, subversion instead introduces a third element that throws the other two off balance, causing them to collapse. Piling the structure high, layer by layer, the sheer weight of exaggeration and accumulation in Herrera y Reissig's poetry threatens to drag it down, to let it fall. Just at this point, when the bases of credibility are stretched to the limit, we are moved to another plane, quietly and without looking back to the turbulent place we were so involved with. The rapidity of the movement, the total change of scenic space, does not cancel out the other gesture. We are left in suspension, and the space of noncomprehension is the moment of silence, the drop and the fall. When this movement is avoided, however, when the gaze is not removed from the spot, the process of accumulation proceeds to decomposition, the edifice falls down or destroys itself from within like the "gangrena" or putrefaction often present in the sensual imagery of Herrera y Reissig.

HERRERA Y REISSIG'S LITERARY HERITAGE

Herrera y Reissig, like Lugones, saw his age as a crepuscular moment, as a transition period full of confusing signs, extravagant artifice, and distortion. His writings on *fin de siglo* literature, although ostensibly directed at its limitations, give us many insights into his own poetry. His comparisons of the modern decadent style with the *culteranismo* of an earlier epoch, whose excesses had led to satiric reactions and a more sober style, are very revealing. Anticipating the rediscovery of Góngora by the Generation of 1927 in Spain, Herrera y Reissig calls him "este cometa decadentista" ("this decadentist comet") and describes the obscurity of his style as "el marco ebenuz que hizo resaltar la tela chillona de su imaginación, en la que una orgía de colores, sin gradación y sin efecto armónico, causa no sé qué extraño vértigo, y produce la rara embriaguez de una visión que cambia de forma a cada momento, como una serpentina en media de la sombra"[15] ("the ebony frame which emphasized the shrieking fabric of his imagination, in which an orgy of colors, without gradation and without harmonic effect, causes some peculiar vertigo, and produces the strange intoxication of a vision that changes form at each moment, like a serpentine in the midst of shadow"). In characterizing Góngora's difficult and mysterious poetry, Herrera y Reissig uses the same kind of exuberant and textured wording that other critics have seen as marks of his own poetic style:

> Modalidades aderezadas con efectismos, promiscuidad de vocablos de rimbombancia churrigueresca, que saltan a la mente como muñecos elásticos, fraseología fatua, que como un aerostato, más se hincha cuanto más sube de tono; hipérboles gigantes que pasan volando, . . . epítetos que parecen remilgos, frases que son gestos de hipocondríaco.[16]

> (Forms embellished with flashy effects, a promiscuity of words full of Churrigueresque ostentation that leap in the mind like marionettes; a fatuous literary style, that, like a balloon, swells larger and larger as its tone becomes more pompous; giant hyperboles that fly about, . . . epithets that sound affected, phrases that are hypochondriac gestures.)

In the same way that Lugones names Quevedo as his master of an incisive and sparse style, so Herrera y Reissig points to Góngora as his "literary father" in unexpected and densely textured metaphors. Although Herrera y Reissig can hardly be compared to Góngora as a poet of major influence, he can be compared to him in the sense that he exaggerated the literary currents of his day and transformed them. By the excess of his exaggerations he made it impossible for others to continue in the same vein without falling into overt parody or hackneyed repetition.

In the same early essay of 1899, "Conceptos de Crítica," Herrera y Reissig outlines the task of literary criticism. In his reflections on the proper role of the critic, he mediates on his literary heritage. Not surprisingly, many of his judgments of literature echo those of his *modernista* contemporaries. Herrera y Reissig uses a specific organic metaphor, the family analogy, to place the *modernista* writer within a literary heritage, while affirming that his century "es el siglo de las grandes revoluciones artísticas"[17] ("is the century of great artistic revolutions"). Calling eclecticism "esta maternidad sublime" ("this sublime maternity") that has endowed his generation with multiple possibilities of selection, Herrera y Reissig repeats the *modernista* insistence on accumulation and richness in its artistic choices. While condemning "las extravagancias y el esoterismo de los raros" ("the extravagance and esoterism of the strange ones"), he does not refuse the enchantments of the exotic nor the appeal of fashion: "Ser ecléctico es poseer ese refinamiento sibarítico, esa quintaesencia del gusto que constituye la naturaleza intelectual del siglo; es estar a la última moda; ¡es habitar un palacio lujoso del saber!"[18] ("To be eclectic is to possess that sybaritic refinement, that quintessence of taste that constitutes the intellectual nature of the century; it is to be in the latest style; it is to dwell in a luxurious palace of knowledge!"). Herrera y Reissig's choice of images in this critical piece demonstrates the effect of new artistic technologies on the mind of the poet. Looking at the history of literature from the Bible to the present, he describes this procession from the modern technical eye of the camera: "Todos pasan como visiones, en este cinematógrafo lúgubre del tiempo muerto; y los genios se petrifican en mármoles, como las ideas se transforman en religiones"[19] ("They all pass like visions, in this dismal cinematographer of dead time; and geniuses are petrified in marble, just as ideas are transformed into religions"). Herrera's vocabulary from cinematography suggests a more rapid flux of artistic tendencies, a shifting and selection process not given to his realist predecessors, whose craft he describes as static observation—"serio, reflexivo, observador, llevando . . . todos sus instrumentos de anatomía, sus máquinas fotográficas, sus libretas de apuntes, sus útiles de medición, sus bloques y sus pinceles"[20] ("serious, reflective, observant, carrying . . . all his anatomy instruments, his photographic machines, his notebooks, his measuring tools, his blocks and brushes"). Herrera y Reissig reserves his most florid prose for the symbolists, noting here symbolism's exclusivity: "Lo abstruso, lo raro, lo original, . . . que sólo es del gusto de los privilegiados"[21] ("The abstruse, the strange, the original, . . . for which only the privileged have a taste"). Like Lugones and other dissonant *modernistas*, Herrera y Reissig seizes on the contradictory elements of symbolism and considers Baudelaire to be the founder of this movement, as well as the first exemplar of symbolism's many contradictions: "es una flor que se ofrece entre espinas" ("it is a flower offered amid thorns"). What follows in Herrera y Reissig's essay may be taken as a descriptive image for Herrera y Reissig's own thorny poetry:

> Y, en medio de todo esto, une un templo de un lupanar y se acuesta sobre el lodo para mostrarnos sus vicios. Ríe, y se ríe de sus dolores. Sus lágrimas no se ven; se adivinan.[22]

> (And, in the midst of all this, he unites a temple to a brothel and lies down in the mud to show us his vices. He laughs, and he laughs at his pain. His tears cannot be seen; they are sensed.)

Herrera y Reissig's generation in Uruguay, the "Generación del '900" (Generation of 1900), was a brilliant grouping of writers and thinkers that included, among others, Javier de Viana, Carlos Reyles, José Enrique Rodó, Carlos Vaz Ferreira, María Eugenia Vaz Ferreira, Florencio Sánchez, Horacio Quiroga, and Delmira Agustini.[23] According to Emir Rodríguez Monegal, the fundamental shared experience of this group was the impact of *modernismo*, and he cites from Rodó's *El que vendrá* (1896) as evidence of the belief in the expansion of rational consciousness and cultural boundaries: "la imagen ideal del pensamiento no está en la raíz que se soterra sino en la copa desplegada a los aires, y de que las fronteras del mapa son las de la geografía del espíritu, y de que la patria intelectual no es el terruño"[24] ("the ideal image of thought is not in the root which is buried, but in the treetop, unfurled to the breeze, and from which the borders of the map are those of the geography of the spirit, and from which the intellectual homeland is not the land of one's birth"). In his "Conceptos de Crítica," Herrera y Reissig concurs with Rodó in declaring null and void the previous aesthetic theories he finds limiting, such as those that glorify nationalism. He describes the "new" currents as expansive and indefinable: "¿Cuál será el fin de su evolución tan llena de complejidades, de esa verdadera metempsicosis que escapa a la luz de todo análisis y que burla las predicciones de todas las épocas?"[25] ("What will be the end of its evolution, so full of complexities, of that true metempsychosis that escapes the light of all analysis and which deceives the predictions of every epoch?" Like Rodó he uses the organic images of movement and renewal to describe the appearance of the new spirit: "Los siglos le han visto morir para luego renacer glorioso bajo distintas formas; es como un gusano sublime que se enferma mientras le brotan las alas" ("The centuries have seen it die only later to be reborn, glorious, under different forms; it is like a sublime worm that sickens while it sprouts wings"). Rodríguez Monegal attributes to both Rodó and Herrera y Reissig the imposition of their individual wills to create "una jefatura intelectual o poética sobre sus contemporáneos"[26] ("an intellectual or poetic leadership over his contemporaries"). He also points out the curious nature of Herrera y Reissig's fusion of local circumstance with cosmopolitan artistic currents. In a funeral eulogy to Alcides de María, gauchesque poet, Herrera y Reissig gives a portait of himself in the same religious terminology of other *modernista* poets:

> Yo también,—sacerdote del Templo imperecedero de la humanidad que sueña, del más espiritual y gallardo de los templos, del único, incommovible y augusto, de las Cien Torres en éxtasis y de las mil ventanas en expectativa,—cuyo reloj marca la hora azul de la immortalidad y cuyas campanas trascendentales repercuten hasta las estrellas . . . [27]

> (I also,–high priest of the indestructible Temple of dreaming humanity, of the most spiritual and elegant of temples, of the only, inexorable and majestic, with its Hundred Towers in ecstasy and its thousand windows in expectation—whose clock strikes the blue hour of immortality and whose transcendental bells reverberate to the stars.)

Beginning in 1899 Herra y Reissig proclaimed,—from "La Torre de los Panoramas" ("The Tower of Panoramas"), a small third-floor apartment in downtown Montevideo with a view of the port and of the cemetery—his artistic pronouncements to a group of young Uruguayan writers, calling himself the "Imperator." The tower image recalls a favored setting of the romantic gothic novel, which was fitting for Herrera y Reissig's vision of himself as a *poète maudit*. His elevated placement has its parallels in what Angel Rama has called his "fatal desdoblamiento de la personalidad" ("the fatal doubling of his personality"), in which the world of artistic absolutes concedes nothing to mundane humanity.[28] Rama attributes part of Herrera y Reissig's aesthetic stance to the world view he and his contemporaries inherited from positivism. Faced with a desacralization of his society's previously held ethical values, such as the union of good and beauty:

> el poeta descrubre la realidad como un vasto escenario fenoménico donde juegan libremente los sucesos, surgen y se desvanecen, se encadenan mediante leyes físicas o químicas más soñadas que sabidas, eludiendo siempre toda hilación que atraviese un orden moral predeterminado. Es un universo de objetos aislados, y de sensaciones puras y libres, . . . como un laboratorio que se ha liberado definitivamente del bien y del mal y sólo atiende con curiosidad a los efectos.[29]

> (the poet discovers reality as a vast, phenomenal stage where events play freely, appear and disappear, linked through the laws of physics or chemistry, more dreamed of than learned, always eluding any connective process that crosses a predetermined moral order. It is a universe of isolated objects, and of pure and free sensation . . . like a laboratory that has decisively freed itself of the notion of good and evil and only pays attention, with curiosity, to the effects.)

HERRERA Y REISSIG AND THE DISORGANIZATION OF THE CANON

Yuri Lotman, in *The Structure of the Artistic Text*, devotes a chapter to what he calls the "energy of verse."[30] He likens this concept to what Tynjanov calls the "function" of the text. Lotman defines this energy as the

> constant tendency toward collision and conflict, a struggle between different constructive principles. Each principle has an organizing principle within the system it creates, and it functions as a disorganizer outside of that system. Thus word boundaries interfere with the rhythmic ordering of verse; syntactic intonations conflict with rhythmic intonations, and so on. When opposing tendencies coincide, we are not dealing with an absence of conflict but with a particular instance of conflict; the zero expresssion of structural tension.[31]

Lotman explains the changing perceptions in different epochs of this textual "energy." He describes a perception of a text's diminished energy as the triumph of a system:

> [T]he same system (in an isolated synchronic description) which for a given period of time sounded new and original is now perceived as imitative (mostly imitative in relation to itself). What is the point? *The system has triumphed.* What seemed extraordinary has become the ordinary; the anti-system has ceased to offer resistance.[32]

For Lotman, therefore, the synchronic description of a text's structure is insufficient, for the reader must include in his analysis both **internal** and **external** structures "struggling against the system, and must see the text's function in relation to a given system of prohibitions which precede it and lie outside it."[33] Lotman outlines how obligatory restrictions (which can function as content-forming boundaries) can change to optional limitations. In Herrera y Reissig's work we see the "hierarchy of prohibitions" being shaken, leading the way for more radical syntactic and semantic breaks, as in the poetry of Vallejo. Since a great deal of the criticism of Herrera y Reissig's work during his lifetime (for example, criticism by Juan Mas y Pí, Darío, et al.) centered on his eccentricity, on his seeming unconcern for traditional national themes in literature, we may assume that his attraction to the exotic as well as to provocative sound-play was directly perceived as **resistant** or **subversive** to the cultural boundaries of his particular time and place.

DEMATERIALIZATION AND THE FIXED SCENE

The compressed energy and metaphoric fury of Herrera y Reissig's poetry make it one of later *modernismo*'s most striking productions. Allen Phillips notes the suppression of the rules of logic in Herrera y Reissig's surprising metaphors,[34] as in the poem "Alba triste" (*PC*, 317): "Un estremecimiento de Sibilas / epilepsiaba a ratos la ventana" ("A shuddering of Sibyls epilepsed the window at intervals"). At the same time that Phillips observes the almost constant procedure of personification in Herrera y Reissig's poetry, he stresses that the suppression of logic dematerializes the natural world: "En esta desrealización quita materialidad a las cosas; . . . Herrera y Reissig nos invita a contemplar una realidad a veces en el proceso de transformarse, que se esfuma líricamente"[35] ("In this disrealization, he robs things of their material nature; . . . Herrera y Reissig invites us to contemplate a reality, sometimes in the process of being transformed, which fades away lyrically"). In Herrera y Reissig's verse, inert or static, fixed scenes serve as backdrop while the theater occurs on the level of language. As light is reflected and refracted in the visual images, so the linguistic elements reflect back upon themselves, as in "La torre de las Esfinges":

> Las cosas se hacen facsímiles
> de mis alucinaciones
> y son como asociaciones
> simbólicas de facsímiles . . .
>
> (*PC*, 137)
>
> (Things become facsimiles
> of my hallucinations
> and they are like symbolic
> associations of facsimiles . . .)

Gustave Moreau, the favored painter of the decadents and of Spanish American *modernistas* (especially Julián del Casal), is, according to Mario Praz, the painter of inertia's beauty. In contrast to romanticism's furious mixture of voluptousness, blood, action, and eroticism, Moreau paints the same scenes from a different stance.[36] On adopting the iconography favored by

Moreau and other *fin de siglo* painters, many *modernistas* add disquieting or disrupting movements to these stilled, fixed scenes, which turn cultural stereotypes around. The figural use of conventionalized scenes, such as the ornately decorated interior space, reorients the reader to new paths of perception. The *femmes fatales* so often centered in these scenes (Eve, Salomé, Helen of Troy) laugh back at the viewer. A seemingly arbitrary rearrangement of these clichés questions their stability and thus subverts the allegorical meaning of these scenes. Julián del Casal's *Mi museo ideal,* eleven poems based on a series of paintings by Moreau, offers a classic example of the stilled space filled up with luxury goods. Here Casal invites the reader–spectator to become a conspirator in the game of looking. In his ideal museum, the excess of cultural bric-a-brac and stereotypical images is striking. Casal introduces conspiratorial notes in these poems that draw into question their "ideal" aspects. His repainting of the scenes, whose content is drawn from legend and mythology, offers an element unavailable to the viewer of the Moreau canvases. In eight of the poem/paintings, Casal catches the eye of the paintings' subjects in the last tercet, and three are sealed off with an upraised hand, extending the viewer's gaze in an outward swing, flinging out the victory. This swing is an indifferent one, however, and leads the eye outside the painting to another vantage point, perhaps a distanced critical stance. Just as in Casal's "Neurosis," where the "billetes en el cofre" ("bills in the coffer") break the spell of the white enclosure and remind us of the marketplace, so here we find Casal's poetic eye straying away from Moreau's fixed scenes. Though Casal can hardly be called a rebel in his treatment of *modernismo's* fixed scenes (and certainly not to the same extent as Lugones and Herrera y Reissig), his emphasis on the literal aspects of his models' features questions their validity as representations of idealized values.

Herrera y Reissig practices the same type of dislocation. Although he does not overtly point out the deviations from his models as does Lugones, one can see a heightening of the same tactics that Casal so deftly employed. A reading of two poems by Herrera y Reissig can illustrate the subtle complexity of his methods.

The fourth poem of "Tertulia lunática" metaphorizes a type of subtle displacement in Herrera y Reissig's work. With an unexpected change of perspective, moving from the grandeur of infinite space, our gaze is inverted and suddenly reduced to a view through a spider's web:

> El Infinito derrumba
> su interrogación huraña,
> y se suicida, en la extraña vía láctea, el meteoro,
> como un carbunclo de oro
> en una tela de araña.
>
> (*PC*, 141–142)

> (The Infinite demolishes
> its shy interrogation,
> and the meteor commits suicide,
> in the bizarre Milky Way
> like a golden carbuncle
> in a spider's web.)

The poems of this collection reveal, perhaps more effectively than any other group, the rapid and dizzying movement of sound play that subverts the iconic significance not only of words but of accustomed poetic language as well, for example, as in the collection's fifth poem:

> ¡Oh musical y suicida
> tarántula abracadabra
> de mi fanfarria macabra
> y de mi parche suicida! . . .
>
> (*PC*, 142)

> (Oh musical and suicidal
> abracadabra tarantula
> of my macabre fanfare
> and of my suicidal patch! . . .)

Words lose their accustomed role of designation. When the limits of the fixed scene are dissolved, its individual elements begin their own journey into a nonaligned pattern, dispersing in their wake the vestiges of a unified addresser or speaking subject.[37]

In Herrera y Reissig's sonnet "Fiat Lux" (*Los parques aban-donados,* 1906), similar in many ways to Lugones' "La alcoba solitaria" of *Los crepúsculos del jardín,* the metonymical disper-sion and unusual pairings of terms do not produce the same displacement effects as do the "corsé" ("corset") and the discon-certing rhyme scheme in Lugones' similar poem. The reader's gaze is directed outward, threatens to become lost in the "curva abstracta" ("abstract curve") and the "suntuosa línea" ("sumptu-ous line") of the poem's design. The widening gaze, which ex-tends to the "noche estupefacta" ("stupefied night") and the coming dawn with its odd "nimbos grosellas" ("red-currant halos"), returns gently to the erotic scene of the "Venus cur-vilínea" ("curvilinear Venus"): "Y como un huevo, entre el plumón de armiño / que un cisne fecundara, tu desnudo / seno brotó del virginal corpiño . . . " (*PC,* 414) ("And like an egg, amid the ermine plumage / that a swan might fecundate, your naked / breast welled from the virginal bodice . . . "). Rapid, quiet movement relocates the focus, although the air still reso-nates with the possibility of further wanderings. By not shatter-ing the fixed scene, multiple associations are still possible.

EROTICISM AND THE DISSOLUTION OF BOUNDARIES

Most readers, even those accustomed to *fin de siglo* decadent tastes, find the frenzied movement and often macabre eroticism to be the most startling aspects of Herrera y Reissig's verse. The sonnets of "Las Clepsidras" (1909) exhibit an eroticism that goes further than Herrera y Reissig's own models, the poetry of Samain, or that of Lugones' "Los doce gozos" (from *Los cre-púsculos del jardín*). The physicality of erotic union is embodied in the poetic language itself, where alliteration, rhyme, and jolting images remind the reader of language's densely tex-tured physical nature, as in "Oblación abracadabra":

> Lóbrega rosa que tu almizcle efluvias,
> y pitonisa de epilepsias libias,
> ofrendaste a Gonk-Gonk vísceras tibias
> y corazones de panteras nubias.

(*PC,* 480)

(Lugubrious rose, which discharges your musk in effluvium,
and siren of Lybian epilepsies,
you made an offering to Gonk-Gonk of tepid
viscera and Nubian panther hearts.)

Like Lugones, Herrera y Reissig combines classical, biblical, and
liturgical elements in his erotic rites, and he invites a question-
ing of these fixed scenes by placing disruptive images or discor-
dant sounds in his poetry, such as "Gonk-Gonk," or the "mi-
serere de los cocodrilos" ("litany of the crocodiles") which closes
the sonnet "Oblación abracadabra."

The tension between the closure of the sonnet and the way-
ward energy tightly contained within it explodes in poems
such as "Tertulia lunática" (1909), in which excess is heaped
on excess:

¡Oh negra flor de Idealismo!
¡Oh hiena de diplomacia,
con bilis de aristocracia
y lepra azul de idealismo! . . .
Es un cáncer tu erotismo
de absurdidad taciturna,
y florece en mi saturna
fiebre de virus madrastros,
como un cultivo de astros
en la gangrena nocturna.
(*PC,* 142)

(Oh black flower of Idealism!
Oh hyena of diplomacy,
with bile of aristocracy
and blue leprosy of idealism! . . .
Your eroticism is a cancer
of taciturn absurdity,
and it flourishes in my saturn
fever of destructive virus,
like a culture of stars
in the nocturnal gangrene.)

Herrera dissolves constraints of space and time as well as the
borders of intelligible language in his most experimental po-

ems.[38] Dissolution, or the unraveling of the chains of significa-
tion, follows the vertigo of Herrera y Reissig's language itself.
Its combination of eroticism and linguistic play, although uncon-
ventional, is not unexpected given the usual dislocations eroti-
cism creates. According to Georges Bataille, eroticism's move-
ment is always a dissolving and dislocating force, resulting in
discontinuous movement or speech:

> Le passage de l'état normal à celui de désir érotique suppose en
> nous la dissolution relative de l'être constitué dans l'ordre dis-
> continu. Ce terme de dissolution répond à l'expression familière de
> vie *dissolue*, liée à l'activité érotique.[39]

> (The passage from a normal state to that of erotic desire supposes
> in us the relative dissolution of the being constituted by discontin-
> ued order. This term of dissolution responds to the familiar expres-
> sion of *dissolute* life, linked to erotic activity.)

The play of eroticism involves a dissolving of established
forms and a fundamental fascination with death.[40] The mixture
of death, eroticism, and an emphasis on the physical form in its
separate parts, suggested in the work of Herrera y Reissig, is
made explicit in later surrealist writers and artists.[41] Max Ernst's
skeletal, mechanized female forms show the ultimate fetishiza-
tion process implicit in the erociticm of the *modernista* stilled
scenes. Ernst quite literally shows the dismemberment of the
female image, with body parts isolated from their context,
along with a growing dissolution of formal restraints. Herrera y
Reissig's work forecasts this tendency that will be more obvious
in *vanguardista* poetry.

Surrealism's fragmentation is not based on the previous estab-
lishment of a complete image, for it is an association reconstruc-
tion based on contiguity, not continuity. The dissonant voices of
modernismo, especially Lugones and Herrera y Reissig, proceed
along different lines. Offering us first the entire corporal image
(or at least an iconic representation of the physical unity), they
atomize everything received: body, idea, concept, referent, in a
type of metonymy that cancels the initial referent. While union,
harmony, and death itself are to be resolved within the scheme
of Eros, even Rubén Darío reveals the dangerous physicality of

eroticism, as in his portrait of Salomé in "Poema XXIII" of *Cantos de vida y esperanza:*

> Y la cabeza de Juan el Bautista
> ante quien tiemblan los leones,
> cae al hachazo. Sangre llueve.
> Pues la rosa sexual
> al entreabrirse
> conmueve todo lo que existe,
> Con su efluvio carnal
> Y con su enigma espiritual.[42]

> (And the head of John the Baptist
> In whose presence lions tremble,
> falls with the axe blow. It rains blood.
> For the sexual rose
> as it slowly opens
> moves everything that exists,
> With its carnal outpouring
> And with its spiritual enigma.)

In his essay "El caracol y la sirena," Octavio Paz stresses the harmonic balance Darío strikes between the poles of death and eroticism.[43] Yet in retrospect, the more explicit work of Herrera y Reissig—the surrealist works that came later—and the overt threatening quality of eroticism in César Vallejo's poetry make us question and reinterpret the erotic nature in *modernismo's* fixed scenes.

In much *modernista* erotic poetry a scarcely contained violence accompanies scenes of possession. Here the ideas of **dissolution** and **(re)possession** are essential. Visual seizing or possession is possible only if the object to be possessed is expelled from oneself. As Gilles Deleuze describes the expulsion/dissolution process: "One does not truly possess that which is expropriated, placed outside of oneself, doubled, reflected under the gaze, multiplied by possessive spirits."[44]

Raúl Blengio Brito, in his extensive study of Herrera y Reissig's work, finds that Herrera y Reissig does anticipate many of surrealism's reversals, especially in the description of "Desolación absurda" and of "Tertulia lunática." He finds many of these instances to be merely coincidental, however: "Las coincidencias, sin embargo, terminan ahí: en la incorporación de los aportes del subconsciente, en las imágenes que de ella resultan"[45] ("The coincidences, however, end there: in the incorporation of the constributions of the subconscious, in the images that result from it"). He finds that Herrera y Reissig's work is not marked by the disintegration of language, "ni hay huella siquiera de asintaxismo alguna"[46] ("nor is there the slightest trace of any distortion of syntax"). Although Blengio Brito illustrates thoroughly his claims, it is undeniable that Herrera y Reissig's work does indeed anticipate surrealism's reversals in a powerful way. The disintegration, or dissolution, of accustomed stock scenes and mellifluous language are clear indicators of a rupture in poetic language.

TRAITS OF HERRERA Y REISSIG'S WORK

Associated with Herrera y Reissig's fame as a poet are notions of delirium, automatic writing, and autobiographical outpourings, due in part to the intensely personal and anguished tone of much of his production.[47] However, the fact that Herrera y Reissig, like Lugones, was a master stylist in control of a wide array of poetic forms, belies the notions of automatism. In addition recent studies of his revision process, along with existing variants of his poems, confirm the meticulousness of his constructions. Two brief studies by Idea Vilariño, Uruguayan poet and critic, synthesize some of the dominant thematic characteristics of Herrera y Reissig's poetry and briefly categorize his favored techniques.[48] Vilariño notes the poet's spiritual parentage to Baudelaire, his use of "el horror como elemento estético" ("horror as an aesthetic element"), as well as the thematic and stylistic parallels between Herrera y Reissig's *Los parques abandonados* and Paul Valéry's *Le Jeune parc*. Despite Herrera y Reissig's obvious derivations from other writers, Vilariño stresses his variations of received models and notes one of his most important traits, his brevity in adaptation and his inclination toward the theatrical. Strange epithets, pervasive obscurity, ambiguity, the inversion of traditional masculine and feminine roles, a striking use of "prohibited" words, and a "preocupación fonética" ("phonetic preocupation") are other marks of Herrera y Reissig's poetry. Such a list of characteristics points to the works of later poets who will make ambiguity, condensation, and unexpected insertion of the "prohibited" into hallmarks of twentieth-century poetry.

Most critics have noted two divisions in Herrera y Reissig's verse. The first is a tendency toward the hermetic, *culteranista* poetry of decadent themes, including *Los parques abandonados, Los maitines de la noche,* and *Sonetos de Asia,* among others. The second tendency favors the pastoral theme and impressionistic style, as is found in the alexandrine sonnets of *Los éxtasis de la montaña* and in the endecasyllables of *Los parques abandonados.*[49] As will be seen in the following study of selected poems, however, the innovative techniques of Herrera y Reissig are as much present in the more traditional pastoral poetry as in the experimental poems. An important tendency of this second category is an almost photographic realism that disturbs the traditional contours of impressionistic poetry. In this regard, Clara Silva, a Uruguayan poet and critic, has stressed the exotic motivation of much of Herrera y Reissig's production, while noting at the same time the unsettling "exactitud de sus elementos descriptivos del ambiente y su carácter" ("exactitude of his elements describing ambience and its character") in *Los éxtasis de la montaña.*[50]

INDIVIDUAL POEMS AS RESISTANCE AND TRANSGRESSION

In two poems by Herrera y Reissig, "Numen" ("Tertulia lunática") and "Génesis" (*Las clepsidras: Cromos exóticos*), an insistence on formalism coexists with the aggressive intrusion of words from other registers. Many of these poems appear to be abbreviated versions of a more extensive *modernista* staging. In "Numen," the verse "¡Nunca! ¡Jamás! ¡Siempre! ¡Y Antes!" ("Never!" "Ever!" "Always!" "And Before!") could be easily mistaken for a passage from Vallejo's work. Words themselves, here time expressions destined for eternity, take on a sensory nature, like boulders to stumble on, as in Vallejo's work where physicality and metaphysics take on each others' shapes. In Herrera y Reissig's "Numen," abstract words not only acquire a physical nature, but physical signs themselves are overloaded, and the grotesque or monstrous, an element too often overlooked in *modernista* verse, comes to the forefront:

> Carie sórdida y uremia
> felina de blando arrimo,
> intoxícame en tu mimo
> entre dulzuras de uremia . . .
>
> (*PC*, 145)
>
> (Sordid cavity and feline
> uremia of feeble support,
> intoxicate me in your pampering
> amid the sweetness of uremia.)

The selection is not only unpleasant but, given its context, grotesque. Not even "mimo" ("pampering") is fitting with "dulzuras" ("sweetness"). If the focus is on the body, once the site of invitation and pleasure, then the selection process has gone wild. With contexts rearranged, thematic elements have been jolted out of their accustomed boundaries. The introduction of the jargon of modernity, "tu electrosis de té / en la luna de Astarte" ("your electrolysis of tea / on the moon of Astarte"), and its ludicrous, off-key rhyme, even to the repetition of *uremia*, show the working, rhyming band. These elements upset any flow and cause us to notice the blocking of a more conventionally "poetic" hand, while drawing us into the working process of the poem. With no pretense of subtlety, this part of the poem fits into the larger picture. While in general it is a mocking, driving, parodic presentation, its secrets are released at the moments when it drives itself so far away from its paradigms that its own verbal energy and destructive force become the focus.

In the poetry of Lugones and Herrera y Reissig, the destructive and dislocating energies often move toward the feminine image. The relation of this prized image to a series of cultural values can be extended to language in general and to a received poetic idiom, whose misogyny is not always apparent. Roland Barthes reminds us of the transformation process in the representation of the body:

Being analytical, language can come to grips with the body only if it cuts it up; the total body is outside language, only pieces of the body succeed to writing. In order to make a body *seen,* it must either be displaced, refracted through the metonymy of clothing or reduced to one of its parts; now the description becomes visionary, the felicity of the utterance is re-established (perhaps because there exists a fetish vocation of language). . . . Finally, it is this abstract body's theatricality (*perfect body, ravishing body, fit for a painting, etc.*), as though the description of the body had been exhausted by its (implicit) staging: perhaps it is the function of this touch of hysteria which underlies all theater (all lighting) to combat this touch of fetishism contained in the very "cutting" of the written sentence.[51]

Barthes' remarks, with their emphasis on fabrication, cutting up, theatricality, and exhaustion, are suggestive of Herrera y Reissig. It is the gesture in Herrera y Reissig which interests, whether it be a slight, almost unnoticed hand movement or the theatrical and absurd spinning which catches our attention. Movement is always involved with a transgression or a dislodging of the fixed staging, whether it be of the body or of the landscape. It is this movement, not by the speaker but by the one who watches the speaker, that makes us question our footing.

Herrera y Reissig's "Génesis" from *Sonetos de Asia* is like a condensation of Samain-influenced sonnet. The tone is a bit abrupt and almost too quiet—"Proserpina arroja / su sangre al mar. Las horas son eternas" (*PC,* 385) ("Persephone throws / her blood to the sea. The hours are eternal"). In the last tercet, "Brama el Helesponto . . . / Surge un lampo de leche. Y en el cielo / la Vía Láctea escintiló de pronto" (*PC* 386) ("The Hellespont bellows . . . / A flash of milk bursts forth. And the sky / the Milky Way suddenly sparkled"). It could be a list of elements for another kind of more extensive poem, for the "mejillas tiernas" ("tender cheeks") of the stars and "un lúbrico rapto de serpiente" ("the lubricious rape of a serpent") invite more elaborate treatment than they receive here. The rapid change of scenery—"Y en el cielo / la Vía Láctea escintiló de pronto" ("And in the sky / the Milky Way suddenly sparkled")— turns us away, diverts our gaze, even as we are still remembering that "leche" ("milk") is too literal next to "Láctea," and suddenly we are too wise and complicit as readers.

In "Ciles alucinada" of 1902, Herrera y Reissig uses a narrative thread, a pastoral tale, to tie together his *modernista* landscapes. Moving from wider scene to the individual person and back to scenic description, the speaking voice suddenly backs away:

> Un espejo la objetiva. Todo lo que ella ha sentido
> lo contempla en el paisaje, transmigrado y confundido.
>
> Su atención se ratifica de horizonte en horizonte,
> y están llenos de su alma nubes, prados, valle y monte.
>
> (*PC* 348)

> (A mirror objectifies her. All she has felt
> She sees reflected in the landscape, transmigrated and confused.
>
> Her attention is ratified from horizon to horizon,
> and clouds, meadows, valley and hill are filled with her soul.)

In "Le muerte del pastor" from *Las companas solariegas* (1907), the lament for the lost Armando is interrupted by speculations that are too abrupt, or insufficiently expert, as for example, "su corazón va llorando / como un cordero inexperto . . . " (*PC*, 163) ("his heart goes crying / like an inexperienced lamb . . . "). These interruptions take the form of exclamations or questions— "¿Murió su pastor? ¿Es cierto?" (*PC*, 164) "Did his shepherd die?" "Is it true?") or "¿Murió el pastor? ¿Quién lo duda?" ("Did the shepherd die? Without a doubt") and "¿por qué llora? ¿Desde cuándo?" (Why does he cry? How long?"). The presence of diminutives, the repetition of "El perejil y el hinojo, / el romero y el tomillo . . . " (*PC*, 168) ("Parsley and fennel, / rosemary and thyme . . . "), and sprightly rhymes undercut the lament that spreads out "Por el camino violeta" ("along the violet road"). Even the list of questions breaks down with the addition of the lame dog:

> ¿Adónde fue el pastorcillo?
> ¿Adónde irá la pastora?
> ¿Qué será del perro cojo?
>
> (*PC*, 169)

> (Where has the little shepherd gone?

Where will the shepherdess go?
What will become of the lame dog?)

One of Herrera y Reissig's earliest poems, "Los ojos negros" ("Dark Eyes"), begins with an inviting, traditional memory: "De par en par muy abiertos / cual las puertas del amor, / he visto en sueños dos ojos / que me causaron pavor . . . " (*PC*, 265) ("Wide open / like the doors of love, / in dreams I have seen two eyes / that frightened me . . ."). With the stated presence of a first person addresser and the octosyllable form, one is reminded of popular ballads or the poetry of José Martí. Yet Herrera y Reissig includes a range of images—decadent ones—which are largely absent or abbreviated in Martí's verse. Bouncing along on the octosyllable, he dances through all the stock in trade of the night side of exoticism. Delighting in exotic foreign place names, mythological and historical figures (as Lugones does in *Las montañas del oro*), it is hard to feel oneself at the edge of the abyss, drawn to seething forms of darkness and evil, although all of the elements are provided:

> ¡Cuando los estoy mirando
> siento un placer que me duele,
> siento un dolor que me gusta
> y una atracción que me impele! . . .
> >   (*PC*, 273)
>
> (When I am looking at them
> I feel a pleasure that hurts me,
> I feel a pain that pleases me
> and an attraction that incites me! . . .)

The setting is too crowded to feel lost; an entire population of interesting and evil people and places is surging around. One can hardly resist the excitement of recognizing all these figures, their literary and artistic heritage, and submit oneself only to the "dark eyes" where something floats that "es amor y es odio eterno" ("is love and is eternal hate") nor even think much of the "viaje de muerte" (the "voyage of death"). For exactly what happens is that "en su fondo desolado / guiñan noches de Caín" ("in their desolate depths / wink nights of Cain"), and *ennui* and

fear are pushed to the sidelines. Sometimes the journey is even
light-hearted:

> ¡Ojos que hubiera soñado
> el travieso Rabelais,
> que dicen en epigrama
> como bailan un *minué* . . .
> Que en el registro del alma
> tocan, provocando bis,
> un *allegro* de Rossini
> y una sonata de Liszt!
>
>   (*PC*, 274)

> (Eyes that the mischievous Rabelais
> would have dreamed of,
> that speak an epigram
> like they dance a *minuet* . . .
> That play in the register of the soul,
> inciting an encore,
> an *allegro* by Rossini
> and a sonata by Liszt.)

The overloaded signals of danger are played to a lighter tune,
and child's play enters into the dens of iniquity. Even in this
early poem one can see Herrera y Reissig's ostentatious display
of symbols from *modernismo*'s treasures, as well as his playful
mocking. When he returns exclusively to the theme of inviting
eyes in *El collar de Salambó* (1906), a series of five poems, he
quiets the earlier frenzy and reduces the extension of elaborate
machinery almost to a type of poetic shorthand; for example, in
"Ojos de oro" he reduces panoramic perspectives to brief lists—
"India: elefantes, leopardos . . . / Judá: incensarios y cirios . . . "
(*PC*, 465) ("India: elephants, leopards . . . / Judah: censers and
candles . . . "); or in "Ojos negros"—"hay en su noche ener-
vante: Vacío, Caos e Invierno . . . " (*PC*, 465) ("there is in their
enervating night: Emptiness, Chaos and Winter . . . ").

Herrera y Reissig usually inverts the framed, stylized, rural
landscape. Although his innovations do not approach the urban
scenes of the *Lunario sentimental* nor his own pyrotechnics in "La
torre de las esfinges," he does de-allegorize the pastoral roman-
tic landscape. The humdrum nature of the scenes fragments

their possibility as allegorical representation. In "Disfraz senti-
mental" (*Los parques abandonados*) the prosaic intrudes into a
romantic starscape. The azure canopy is "an azul severo de
pizarras" ("a severe chalkboard blue"), and night shelters the
scene "como una tienda" ("like a tent"). Even the floating music,
"con líricas bizarras" ("with bizarre lyrics"), of Chopin is like a
howling torture, and the scene of love is a false one—"Yo te
mentía de un amor ligero" ("I lied to you of a superficial
love")—while his lover's response is given "con unción fingida"
(*PC*, 403) ("with feigned unction"). In *Los parques abandonados*
there is an interpenetration of sounds, both human and animal,
despite the static nature of the scenes. At times this mixture is
almost shocking within the context of such quietness, as in "La
sombra dolorosa," where "El tren lejano" ("the faraway train")
tears the atmosphere with its sounds, "aullando de dolor hacia
la ausencia" (*PC*, 150) ("howling with pain toward absence"). *Los
parques abandonados* does indeed resemble very closely Lugones'
"Los doce gozos" in which eroticism, as well as the settings them-
selves, draws the attention.

LOS ÉXTASIS DE LA MONTAÑA: THE "PROSAIC" SETTING

Just as Ramón López Velarde would later exalt the beauty of
the everyday rhythms of provincial life, in the sonnets of
Herrera y Reissig's *Los éxtasis de la montaña*, the sounds, sights,
and movements of an idealized setting come forth in all their
luminosity. Here the pastoral mode takes another turn, not the
route of the lost Amrando nor of the bewitched shepherdess
Ciles. Some of the scenes are like still-life paintings in their
recreation of the simple beauty of common objects and settings,
as in "La velada"—"La cena ha terminado: legumbres, pan mo-
reno / y uvas aún lujosas de virginal rocío . . . / Rezaron ya . . . "
("The dinner has ended: vegetables, dark bread / and grapes
still luxurious with virginal dew . . . / They have already said
their prayers . . . "). Yet unlike a static painting, Herrera y
Reissig adds household movements as well—"Lux canta, Lidé
corre, Palemón anda en zancos. / Todos ríen. . . . La abuela
demándales sosiego. / *Anfión*, el perro, inclina, junto al anciano

ciego, . . . " (*PC*, 110–111) ("Lux sings, Lidé runs, Palemón
walks on stilts. / They all laugh. . . . The grandmother demands
that they be quiet. / *Anfión*, the dog, lies, next to the old blind
man, . . . ").

In *Los éxtasis de la montaña* (presumably influenced by a trip
Herrera y Reissig made to Minas), Herrera y Reissig gives classi-
cal names to his human subjects and saturates the sonnets' ini-
tial quartets with an overlay of densely textured images and
sounds. The crowning synthesis of the sonnets, the tercets, nev-
ertheless, generally take as their material the most mundane
events and characters from rural life. Though often compared
to Lugones and Samain's work with which they share many
characteristics, Herrera y Reissig's are so different in tone that
they decidedly transform their models. With their settings of
quietness, domestic routine, the small surprises of the day's slow
cycle, and the beatific solemnity imposed by a rural religiosity,
these poems often contrast sharply with *Los parques abandonados*.
"La granja" well exemplifies the lighter tone of the volume's
eroticism, where the image of the seducer Don Juan is usurped
by the rooster—"Can pulida elegancia de Tenorio en desplante,
/ un Aramís erótico, fanfarrón galante, / el gallo erige. . . . ¡Oh
huerto de la dicha sin fiebre!" (*PC*, 128) ("With the polished
elagance of Tenorio in an impudent remark, / an erotic Aramis,
a braggart and galant, / the rooster crows. . . . Oh garden of
delight without fever!"). These "Eglogánimas" (or "Églogas de
ánima" ["Eclogues of the spirit"]) also contrast with the early *Los
peregrinos de piedra* by their obvious attention to the more intri-
cately elaborated nature of their settings. Rather than rhapso-
dize to his poetic masters, as he does in the final verses of "El
laurel rosa" ("¡A Sully Prudhomme!, / y Homero y Hugo y
Verlaine . . . " [*PC*, 107] ["To Sully Prudhomme!, / and Homer
and Hugo and Verlaine . . . "]), here Herrera y Reissig declares
his artistic independence by establishing the immediate locality
and circumstances as a fitting scene for polished sonnets in the
manner of Góngora, as filtered through a late nineteenth-
century poetic eye via Samain, Lugones, and Laforgue. Mythi-
cal figures are transposed onto domesticated animals, yet the
scene is no less splendid, for the quartets of the poems prepare
for their entrance with ornately wrought settings and richly

textured metaphors. The entrance of the mundane is rarely used for shock effect, as is evident in the harmonies of "La misa cándida":

> ¡Jardín de rosa angélico, la tierra guipuzcoana!
> Edén que un Fra Doménico soñara en acuarelas . . .
> Los hombres tienen rostros vírgenes de manzana,
> y son las frescas mozas óleos de antiguas telas.
>
> (*PC*, 124)

> (Angelic garden of the rose, land of Guizpuzcoan!
> Eden that a Fra Doménico might dream in watercolors . . .
> The men have virgin, apple faces,
> and the fresh young maidens are like paintings from old
>   canvases.)

"La misa cándida" (1907) shows Herrera y Reissig's delight in sound and color, the complex interplay of sounds, colors, and memories painting an unexpected landscape. With no pretense at naturalness, the "Edén" presented is one that Fra Doménico might have painted. The Baudelairian "bosque de sonidos," "forest of sounds," is here a veritable explosion of sounds:

> Y estimula el buen ocio un trin-trin de campana,
> un pum-pum de timbales y un fron-fron de vihuelas
>
> ¡Oh campo siempre niño! ¡Oh patria de alma proba!
> Como una vírgen mística de tramonto, se arroba . . .
> Aves, mar, bosques: todo ruge, solloza y trina
>
> (*PC*, 124)

> (And the good idleness stimulates a ding-ding of the bell,
> a pum-pum of the kettledrum and throm-throm of vihuelas.
>
> Oh ever-youthful field! Oh homeland of tested soul!
> Like a mystical virgin of the north wind, it is enraptured . . .
> Birds, sea, forests: everything roars, sobs and trills)

In *Los éxtasis de la montaña* animals are rarely used for comic effect. In "La siesta" their movement merely completes the scene beneath "Un cielo sin rigores" ("a sky without severity"): "Y el asno vagabundo que ha entrado en la vereda / huye, soltando coces, de los perros vecinos" (*PC*, 110) ("And the vagabond ass that has entered the lane / flees, bucking, from the nearby dogs"). In this series of alexandrine sonnets the most dominant force is silence, but not the spectral quiet of *Los parques abandonados* nor the foreboding of suspense. Here life moves beneath the stillness of decades of custom amidst the always towering presence of rural religiosity, where routine noises echo like thunder, as in the following selections:

> Cae un silencio austero . . . Del charco que se nimba
> estalla una gangosa balada de marimba.
> Los lagos se amortiguan con espectrales lampos,
> > "La vuelta de los campos" (*PC*, 112)

> (An austere silence falls . . . From the haloed pond
> erupts a twanging marimba ballad.
> The lakes are softened with ghostly flashes of light,)

> Oscurece. Una mística Majestad unge el dedo
> pensative en los labios de la noche sin miedo . . .
> No llega un solo eco, de lo que al mundo asombra,
> > "La huerta" (*PC*, 113)

> (It grows dark, A mystical Majesty anoints
> its pensive finger on the lips of the fearless night . . .
> Not a single echo can be heard, of what astonishes the world.)

> Acá y allá maniobra después con un plumero,
> mientras, por una puerta que da a la sacristía,
> irrumpe la gloriosa turba del gallinero.
> > "La iglesia" (*PC*, 114)

> (Here and there she maneuvers later with a feather duster,
> while, through the door which leads to the sacristy,
> the glorious mob of the henhouse erupts.)

Herrera y Reissig establishes silence's reign in the quartets to make even more vivid the occasional burst of movement and sound in the tercets where "irrumpe la gloriosa turba del gallinero," in the midst of the "beato silencio" ("blessed silence") of the stately church, with its "decoro / de terciopelo lívido y de esmalte incoloro" ("decorum / of livid velvet and of colorless enamel") ("La iglesia," *PC*, 113–114). Such silences prepare for the sounds of the opening grain, as if it were flesh—"Salpica, se abre, humea, como la carne herida, / bajo el fecundo tajo, la palpitante gleba . . . " ("El Angelus," *PC*, 116) ("Spatters, opens, smolders like wounded flesh, / beneath the fecund cut, the palpitating clod . . . "). In the midst of this silence, "en medio de una dulce paz embelesadora" ("amid a sweet, enchanting peace"), one can hear background noises more clearly, like the swish of the barber's razor interspersed with his chatter, the "folletín de la aldea" ("La dicha," *PC*, 121) (the "village newspaper serial").

"Dominus vobiscum" is as far from Parnassian sunsets as is Vallejo's work. The placid, indeed boring, Sunday scene opens with a yawn: "Bosteza el buen domingo . . . " (*PC*, 450) ("the good Sunday yawns . . . "). The chattering of the toads next to the fountain in the hub of an unremarkable village is the scene where the slight action occurs. On this scene, on which "el cielo inclina un gesto de bendición cristiana" ("the sky bends in a gesture of Christ-like benediction"), intrude two tourists, "muñecos rubios" ("blond dolls"), in "un fogoso automóvil" ("a spirited automobile"). Technology—the car, "su lente" ("its lens"), "el zootécnico" ("the zoo technician")—moves in like an affront. Herrera y Reissig ends the sonnet with a gesture named in the poem itself, "en un gesto salvaje" ("in a savage gesture"), and we, voyeuristic and embarrassed readers, are caught looking at two boys with their fingers in their noses. Tourists mark the difference; their foreignness and their barbarity contrast with the overly placid town fountain. This is surely not the reverence for the foreign by which *modernismo* is so often characterized. There is no clear duality here. The town is hardly picturesque, although it is placid. The ragpicker, the toads, the shadows of the gloomy seminary hardly present a picture of provincial felicity. Yet the gesture from the outside is indeed intrusive. The equipment, the ugly physical gesture, and the triviality of tourists and classification experts—"el zootécnico, profesor de lombrices" ("the zoo technician, professor of earthworms")—are not in praise of the coming modern world.

With the juxtaposition of Symbolist ornamentation and the simple, rustic setting, Herrera y Reissig prepares for the entry of a different poetry, a current that will mark much of the poetry written after *modernismo*. Like Lugones' "Emoción aldeana" these poems show the way to include the rhythms and colors of everyday circumstance usually without overt caricature or the explicit nationalism of the gauchesque poets. One has only to look at Vallejo's *Los heraldos negros*, the poetry of the Mexican Ramón López Velarde, the poems of Gabriela Mistral, Banchs, or even many elements of Borges' first poems of the wonders of the suburbs of Buenos Aires to understand the rich inheritance poets such as Herrera y Reissig bequeathed to succeeding poets. One can see clearly here a type of exaltation of the local setting which would find its maximum expression in the poetry of Ramón López Velarde, whose "La suave patria" from his *El son del corazón* is a national anthem to be sung *sotto voce*, a poem that changed the notion of a national epic as a grandiloquent march: "Diré con una épica sordina: / la patria es impecable y diamantina"[52] ("I will say with a muted epic: / the homeland is impeccable and glittering"). López Velarde was to include in his epic not only the heroic voices but the "risas y gritos de muchachas / y pájaros de oficio carpintero"[53] ("laughter and shouts of girls and woodpeckers").

7
Modernismo's Legacy in Three Poets: Vallejo, López Velarde, and Storni

Many modern readers, except for those who treat *fin de siglo* poetry as period pieces, find little interest in *modernismo*. Yet there is a way to view this poetic production other than as a historical relic or as a series of ornaments to be brushed aside in the dedication to newer, sparser styles. The very elements of staging, theatricality, and pictorial intensity which make *modernismo* seem distant offer us a point of entrance into another way of viewing *modernismo*'s creations. Unlike José Enrique Rodó's "reino interior," the richly decorated scenes of *modernismo* are designed with a twist. Their purpose is not to offer us a soul's rest but to intensify our consciousness of the artisan and the artist's tools, the poems' scaffolding, and the endless permutations of design. While Rodó's "reino interior" of *Ariel* asks us to still our thoughts, most *modernista* techniques ask us to notice what could be called the consumerism of this art.[1] Its poets are collectors, connoisseurs, magicians, who invite us into their decorated and stylized scenes or interiors and ask us to suspend our sense of everyday reality. Their tricks and feats are not all innocent sensuous plays of light and color, despite the emphasis on staging and pictorial qualities. Within the clearly bounded scenes (framed like a picture in a museum) there moves a wayward energy, a distancing effect that calls to the spectator who also knows the rules of the game.[2] Because they are working with highly conventionalized forms (just as the Pre-Raphaelites asked their viewers to see the long heritage of medieval and romantic painting in their canvases), they make the trained observer notice the flattening out of perspectives, the not-complete figure, the jarring element of decor that calls us away from a total im-

mersion. What creates this wayward energy, this note of violence
that often disturbs the placid scenes? Is it a willful toying with
the "bourgeois" reader, the one whom Rubén Darío so dis-
dained? Is it a subtle rejection of the oppressive yet enchanting
heritage of European influence? It is clear that the *modernistas*
made a peculiar reading of their European precursors. Does
their slavish imitation contain the seeds of a subtle subversion of
such a transposition?

Although more recent poets clearly use their work to decry
the surfeit and debris of mass production and the artificial impe-
tus to consume, the *modernistas'* questioning of their world's
values is perhaps less apparent to us as modern readers. In "Los
nueve monstruos" from *Poemas humanos,* Vallejo writes:

> El dolor nos agarra, hermanos hombres,
> por detrás, de perfil,
> y nos aloca en los cinemas,
> nos clava en los gramófonos,
> nos desclava en los lechos, cae perpendicularmente
> a nuestros boletos, a nuestras cartas;
> y es muy grave sufrir, puede uno orar. . . . [3]

> (Pain grabs us, my brothers,
> from behind, in profile,
> and drives us crazy in the cinemas,
> nails us up in the gramophones,
> pries us loose in bed, falls perpendicularly
> to our tickets, to our letters;
> it is very painful to suffer, one can pray. . . .)

Here, we understand quite clearly that this suffering is en-
twined with the world of objects, with a disaster made out of an
excess of useless goods that are badly distributed. Clearly there
is no refuge in the machines created to amuse us, to make us
forget the hungers of both the body and the soul.

Vallejo's prose poem "Aquí no vive nadie" not only suggests
possibilities for a reading of his poems, but the house of which
he speaks could be used as a metaphor for the habitable spaces
of poetry itself: "Una casa viene al mundo, no cuando la acaban
de edificar, sino cuando empiezan a habitarla" (*CV,* 200) ("A
house comes into the world, not when they finish building it,

but when they begin to live in it"). Such a comparison can be extended to speak of the overwrought mansions of *modernismo:*

> Todos han partido de la casa, en realidad, pero todos se han quedado en verdad. . . . Lo que continúa en la casa es el órgano, el agente en gerundio y en círculo. Los pasos se han ido, los besos, los perdones, los crímenes. Lo que continúa en la casa es el pie, los labios, los ojos, el corazón, las negaciones y las afirmaciones, el bien y el mal, se han dispersado. Lo que continúa en la casa, es el sujeto del acto. (*CV*, 200)

> (All have actually left the house, but all truly have remained. . . . What continues in the house is the organ, the gerundial and circular agent. The steps have gone, the kisses, the pardons, the crimes. What stays on in the house is the foot, the lips, the eyes, the hearts; the negations and affirmations, the good and the evil have scattered. What stays on in the house is the subject of the act.)

How can we define this "subject of the act"? I choose here to use Vallejo's term—"the organ, the gerundial and circular agent," and by extension its absence, the beckoning, empty spaces in modern poetry that tell us that something has been taken away.

Like the house in Vallejo's poem, the house of *modernismo* finds few inhabitants today. Its elegant contours, its interiors draped in rich fabrics and populated by mysterious and seductive females, its gardens enlivened by strange animals such as peacocks and swans, find parallels in the architecture of the poems themselves. Ornately wrought of the finest poetic materials of antiquity and from contemporary European fashion, these poems appear to invite the entrance of only those schooled in the intricacies of poetic value judgment. Yet *modernista* poets, like newcomers to aristocracy, insert strange and contradictory elements in their constructions. Though they leave the foundations intact, they rearrange color schemes, substitute chickens for peacocks, and even at times point out that they are clearly imitating others' work, as one would leave a manufacturer's tag on a piece of furniture.

What links the poetry of Leopoldo Lugones and Julio Herrera y Reissig to later poets is their explicit revelation of the physical nature of the objects (animate and inanimate) they present. Lugones and Herrera y Reissig insistently push forth the palpable presence of their erotic subjects, minutely paint landscape and domestic scenes, have their pastoral animals bray out of turn, and show the fraying threads of the sumptuous damask furnishings. At the same time that they reveal the tangible nature of stylized scenes, they are lifting off the covers from the grinding gears beneath the poetic machinery. The clanking of the rhyme, the heavily laden lines of *esdrújulos,* and the top-heavy towers of extended metaphors stand out like a show of fabricated goods in the spirit of the industrial expositions favored in the late nineteenth century. In this display of stylish wares, strange worlds are brought closer together. Amid the shawls from India, the chinoiserie, the porcelain from France, stand the machines of a faster-paced type of production. The gentle bestiaries of *modernismo*—swans, doves, fawns, peacocks, owls—find their new substitutes to be of a different nature. Sheep and cows stand alongside railroad tracks, and the "cubo de ranas" ("bucket of frogs") spills over Lugones' festival scene while a dog madly howls over an unromanticized lunar cityscape.

In the following sections the selected works of three poets, César Vallejo (Peru), Ramón López Velarde (Mexico), and Alfonsina Storni (Argentina), illustrate important rewritings of *modernismo*'s landscapes and embodied values. These studies will examine the heritage of *modernismo* in the twentieth century. They do not pretend to be comprehensive. Instead the focus is on aspects of the poets' works that reveal the continuity and enduring presence of a poetic tradition.

CÉSAR VALLEJO

César Vallejo's first book of poetry, *Los heraldos negros* (1918), shows *modernismo*'s influence, with the special imprint of Darío, Lugones, and Herrera y Reissig.[4] Less apparent is *modernismo*'s presence in Vallejo's later works, *Trilce* and *Poemas humanos.* Vallejo was drawn to the experimental aspects of *modernismo,* its fascination with writing as a nontransparent medium and its elaborate sound systems. Unlike the *modernistas* in general, however, Vallejo introduces a social consciousness that makes the reader look past the elaborate linguistic and scenic displacements in his poetry. His peculiar combining of a prosaic and conversational tone with exalted language, a broken allegorical framework, and palpable eroticism reappears in all three collections. Mythical figures, allegorized words ("Vida, Hembra, Miedo" ["Life, Female, Fear"]), once emptied of meaning by endless repetition in contexts of ornamentality and preciosity, are shocked into signification by the abruptness of their presence in new contexts, especially in *Los heraldos negros* and *Trilce*.

Many of the poems from the section "Nostalgias imperiales" of *Los heraldos negros* are reminiscent of the sonnets of *Los éxtasis de la montaña*, where Herrera y Reissig creates pastoral scenes and adds symbolist and decadent images. In "Nostalgias imperiales" Vallejo includes concrete elements from his own local setting, the Inca heritage of the Andes. The first three sonnets of "Terceto Autóctono" present bucolic scenes interrupted by specific details pointing out the harsh realities of rural life. The first sonnet begins, "El puño labrador se aterciopela" ("The peasant fist becomes like velvet"), and the "nostalgias" and "raras estampas seculares" ("odd secular engravings") repeat some of *modernismo*'s iconography. In all three poems, however, the idealized and distant past is now not a classical golden age but a lost indigenous heritage, contrasted with the indignities of daily poverty as in the third sonnet:

> Madrugada. La chicha al fin revienta
> en sollozos, lujurias, pugilatos;
> entre olores de urea y pimienta
> traza un ebrio al andar mil garabatos.
>
> (CV, 53)
>
> (Dawn. Finally the chicha bursts
> into tears, lust and heated controversy
> amid the smell of urea and pepper
> the drunk traces a thousand scribbles as he walks.)

Here the local situation cannot be harmonized with the sonnet's closing melodies, where the river "anda borracho y canta y llora / prehistorias de agua, tiempos viejos" (*CV*, 53) ("runs drunk and sings and cries / prehistories of water, old times").

Vallejo's departures from the works of Herrera y Reissig and other *modernistas* show the extent of his changes. Vallejo weaves the subversive effect of dislocating Herrera y Ressig's and Lugones' poetic world into a larger landscape. The sights, smells, and sounds of rural existence are further naturalized, taking their place in the tapestry of an enlarging poetic surface. Phrases from the "Truenos" section of "Aldeana" such as "Sangra su despedida el sol poniente" ("The sun bleeds its farewell") "el ámbar otoñal," ("the autumnal amber"), and "el tiempo con sus garras torna ojosa" ("time with its claws returns full of eyes") let us know that the landscapes of *modernismo* are still in memory. Yet the same sun spilling its glory over a rustic, not a magical, house, the distant echo of "el dulce yaraví de una guitarra" ("the sweet yaraví of a guitar") and the sad voice "de un indio" ("of an Indian"), show a new fusion of *modernismo*'s exotic strains with the more local tone of *mundonovismo*. In fusing these two currents, Vallejo then departs from both of them.

"La voz del espejo," also from "Truenos," surely asks us to remember the works of Rubén Darío, who viewed life as procession, change, and delight as well as pain: "Así pasa la vida, como raro espejismo. / ¡La rosa azul que alumbra y da el ser al cardo!" (*CV*, 65) ("So life passes, like a strange mirage. / The blue rose that illuminates and gives being to the thistle!". Though its conversational tone is ironic, its faltering notes revive what has become a deadened image:

> Así pasa la vida,
> con cánticos aleves de agostada bacante.
> Yo voy todo azorado, adelante . . . adelante,
> rezongando mi marcha funeral.
>
> (CV, 65)

> (And so life goes by,
> With treacherous songs of the withered bacchante.
> I go on . . . and on, totally bewildered,
> grumbling my funeral march.)

The fearful march pushes onward with "adelante . . . adelante" ("on . . . and on"), and in Vallejo's treatment of the scene, with its "sórdido abejeo de un hervor mercurial" ("sordid droning of a mercurial fervor"), the procession has lost its magical colorful qualities. Its troubling "olvidados crepúsculos" ("forgotten twi-

lights") cause not just a tightening of the throat but put a "cruz
en la boca" (a "cross in the mouth"), a betrayal of faith's prom-
ises. The orchestra (of Sphinxes and forgotten twilights) brings
forth memories of earlier poetic visions of life's journey, but the
exhaustion of the fund of imagery from which he must draw
for poetic expression has become "el manzano seco de la
muerta Illusión" ("the withered apple tree of dead Illusion"). In
"Retablo" (also from the section "Truenos") Vallejo refers di-
rectly to Darío, and in the encounter in "la nave sagrada" ("the
sacred ship") with "la dulce Musa" ("the sweet Muse"), the vi-
sions that appear are swathed in the cherished dress of *modern-
ismo* (*CV*, 78). Yet again the exhaustion of these images, as well
as the values and sensations they are to embody, are seen by
eyes that have lost faith in these powers:

> Como ánimas que buscan entierros de oro absurdo,
> aquellos arciprestes vagos del corazón,
> se internan, y aparecen . . . y, hablándonos de lejos,
> nos lloran el suicidio monótono de Dios!
>
> (*CV*, 78)

> (Like souls in search of burials of absurd gold,
> those vague archpriests of the heart,
> confine themselves and reappear . . . and, speaking to us from
>   far off,
> they cry to us the monotonous suicide of God.)

"La cena miserable" brings the anguish home to the most
elemental sensations, to childhood hunger and tears. The sight
of food is more powerful than abstract formulations of the
resurrection scene—"al borde de una mañana eterna, desayuna-
dos todos" (*CV*, 74) ("on the edge of an eternal morning, every-
one finished with breakfast")—and is a spectacle more lumi-
nous than any array of fantasmic lights. The dark night of the
soul is to be hungry with no supper and be obligated to suffer
the special presence of a drunken man, whose distance threat-
ens, "como negra cuchara / de amarga esencia humana, la
tumba" ("like a black knife / of bitter human essence, the
tomb"). The scene of abandonment as well as the joy of reunifi-
cation are seen through the child's eyes: "con la amargura de un

niño / que a media noche, llora de hambre, desvelado"'" ("with
the bitterness of a child / who in the middle of the night, cries of
hunger, unable to sleep"). The vale of tears is one of desolation
and hunger, and the concept of injustice is a simple one—to be
in a place "a donde / yo nunca dije que me trajeran." ("where I
never told them to take me"). The alternation of these elemen-
tal scenes with traces of more highly wrought, traditional im-
ages makes the novelty of Vallejo's work even more apparent.
Working with the remnants of the poetic system he inherited,
he goes many steps farther than his discordant predecessors in
shocking these patterns out of their accustomed contexts, forc-
ing the reader to see not only the loss of power of these images
but also the devaluing of the ideologies that shaped them. The
realities of a world of economic and political violence make
more turbulent a personal crisis of faith.[5]

Vallejo often frames his poems within the setting of the domes-
tic household, the lovers' encounter, or the prison of the body, as
well as within the world's real prisons. Enclosure, through the
child's eyes, is protection, security, maternal presence: every-
thing that fragments this enclosure, that slips in surreptitiously,
is likened to the presence of fear. The fixed focus constantly
disappears; the eye ranges without transition from the apoca-
lypse to the fly on the wall. Such a passage through space, time,
and intellectual struggles is disturbing and frightening. Familiar
contours, even the reassuring frames of poetic tradition, have
been broken. On the most elementary levels of delight and suffer-
ing, Vallejo returns to the bliss and terror of childhood, from
memories of maternal protection to crying in the night.

One of Vallejo's more optimistic poems "Enereida," repeats
the idea of resurrection and completion as the satisfaction of
childlike hunger. The father, returned by the cycle of time to
the innocence of childlike clarity, and the "caravanas" of "La
voz del espejo" here find another context:

> Día eterno es éste, día ingenuo, infante,
> coral, oracional;
> se corona el tiempo de palomas,
> y el futuro se puebla
> de caravanas de inmortales rosas.
>
> (*CV*, 95)

> (Eternal is this day, ingenuous, infant day,
> choral, prayerful
> time is crowned with doves,
> and the future is populated
> by caravans of immortal roses.)

The emphasis on the family scene and childhood longings is a focus not often seen in *modernista* poetry, except in the works of José Martí and José Asunción Silva. Like William Butler Yeats, Vallejo goes to the "rag and bone shop of the heart" and to everyday needs to find expression for power and sorrow. More powerful images of plentitude and loss are difficult to imagine than those of childhood abandonment, hunger, or happy reunion. So total are the extremes, so common to every human being, that the memory of these images resonates throughout his entire work, even in his most difficult poems.

The female is a powerful and often anguished presence in Vallejo's early poetry. From "el femenino en mi alma" ("the feminine in my soul") to the distant and inaccessible "Eva" ("Eve"), Vallejo shifts from pleasure to pain and destablizes the dichotomy of male and female. He combines the feminine image of Christian tradition with the mother of his childhood and the legendary *femme fatale*. In "Los pasos lejanos" the mother's portrait receives lavish verbal treatment in a sparsely described physical setting:

> Y mi madre pasea allá an los huertos,
> saboreando un sabor ya sin sabor.
> Está ahora tan suave,
> tan ala, tan salida, tan amor.
>
>   (*CV*, 92)
>
> (And my mother strolls over there in the orchards,
> savoring a taste already tastless.
> Now she is so gentle,
> Such wing, such leaving, such love.)

He takes *modernismo's femme fatale* and expands her to a towering life enigma, whose violence and power are protean, as in "Pagana":

¿:La vida? Hembra proteica. Contemplarla asustada
escaparse en sus velos, infiel, falsa Judith;
verla desde la herida, y asirla en la mirada,
incrustando un capricho de cera en un rubí.

(*CV*, 79)

(Life? Protean female. To contemplate her terrified
escaping in her veils, unfaithful, false Judith;
to see her from the wound, and seize her in a gaze
incrusting a wax whim on a ruby.)

Religious language gives powerful emblems of human needs,
and Vallejo materializes their iconic value, even pluralizing Ma-
ría and humanizing God in "Los dados eternos":

Dios mío, estoy llorando el ser que vivo;
me pesa haber tomádote tu pan;
pero este pobre barro pensativo
no es costra fermentada en tu costado:
tú no tienes Marías que se van!

(*CV*, 80)

(Dear God, I'm weeping the being that I am;
I regret having taken your bread;
but this poor thinking clay
is not a fermented scab in your side:
you don't have Marias who leave you!)

As *Trilce* will make more explicit, desire and fulfillment are
dangerous and dislocating experiences, as expressed in the fear
of the female in "Desnudo en barro": "La tumba es todavía /
un sexo de mujer que atrae al hombre" (*CV*, 71) ("The tomb is still /
a woman's sex which attracts man"). Using religious, literary,
and childhood visions of the female, Vallejo combines these
areas of experience into a single, perplexing plane of daily ques-
tioning, desire, anguish, and hope.

TRILCE

In *Trilce* Vallejo so physicalizes the abstract that the usual poetic
markers, the ways of mapping meaning, are completely turned

around: streets bleed, spiritual revelations are like the opening of a wound, the leap of faith is the anguished push through the needle's eye, philosophy has black wings, and "Es de madera mi paciencia, sorda vegetal" ("My patience is wooden, mute, vegetal"). Death itself oozes white blood, earliness "lacerates like an explanation," light is comsumptive, shade fat. Spiritual pain creates bonds like family ties, and God is like the horse who stamps outside the door:

> Dios en la paz foránea,
> estornuda, cual llamando también, el bruto;
> husmea, golpeando el empedrado. Luego duda
> relincha,
> orejea a viva oreja.
>
> (LXI, *CV*, 164)

> (God in alien peace,
> the animal sneezes, as if also calling, the brute;
> sniffs, pounding the stone pavement. Then hesitates
> neighs
> pricks up his live ears.)

It is not just on a thematic level that Vallejo physicalizes abstract elements. Language itself shows itself to be part of the body of existence. Like the allegorical body of the communion supper (an important element in *Los heraldos negros*), words are broken apart and syntactical elements become interchangeable. In *Trilce* XXXVI, changing lexical and grammatical functions accompany changes in allegorical meanings. Just as physical impossibilities are stated as fact—"Amoniácase casi el cuarto ángulo del círculo. / ¡Hembra se continúa el macho, a raíz / de probables senos, y precisamente / a raíz de cuanto no florece!" (*CV*, 138) ("The fourth angle of the circle turns to ammonia. / The male remains female, at the root / of probable breasts, and precisely at the root of what doesn't flourish!")—so language shows itself to be reversible. In the same poem there are "aunes que gatean" ("yets that creep on all fours") and other adverbs that begin to take on verbal action: "todaviiza / perenne imperfección" ("it alreadys / perennial imperfection"). Following *modernista* experiments of verse construction, with overloaded rhyme and alliterative patterns, Vallejo extends much farther the attention to language itself and, most importantly, to its limitations. In *Trilce* LV, which begins "Samain diría el aire es quieto y de una contenida tristeza" ("Samain would say the air is still and has a contained sadness"), Vallejo continues by rejecting any such containment, either of the physical scene itself or of the language to express it:

> Vallejo dice hoy la Muerte está soldando cada lindero a cada hebra de cabello perdido, desde la cubeta de un frontal, donde hay algas, toronjiles que cantan divinos almácigos en guardia, y versos antisépticos sin dueño.
>
> (*CV*, 157)

> (Vallejo says today death is welding each boundary to each
> strand of lost hair, from the cask of a frontal, where
> there are algae, lemon balms that sing divine seedbeds on
>   guard,
> and antiseptic verses with no owner.)

The framing landscape of Parnassian scenes can in no way contain the dispersal of either nature or poetry, nor reflect the simultaneity of time:

> El miércoles, con uñas destronadas se abre las propias uñas
> de alcanfor, e instila por polvorientos
> harneros, ecos, páginas vueltas, sarros,
> zumbidos de moscas
> cuando hay muerto, y pena clara esponjosa y cierta esperanza.
>
> (*CV*, 157)

> (Wednesday, with its dethroned fingernails opens its own
>   nails
> of camphor, and pours drop by drop through the dusty
> sieves, echoes, turned pages, crusts,
> the buzzing of flies
> when there is a corpse present, and clear and spongy sorrow
>   and a certain hope.)

Vallejo makes palpable the contained erotic violence of *modernismo* by showing explicitly its fetishistic nature.[6] Just as he draws attention to the breakdown of language, the dispersal of its building blocks, he extends the parceling out of the feminine image, as in *Trilce* XIII where the clichés of *modernista* erotic scenes are absent:

> Pienso en tu sexo.
> Simplificado el corazón, pienso en tu sexo,
> ante el hijar maduro del día.
> Palpo el botón de dicha, está en sazón.
> Y muere un sentimiento antiguo
> degenerado en seso.
>
> (CV, 113)
>
> (I think about your sex.
> My heart simplified, I think of your sex,
> Before the ripe flank of the day.
> I grope at the button of bliss, it is at its ripest
> And an old sentiment dies
> degenerated into brain.)

By dismantling *modernismo*'s erotic scenes, Vallejo destroys the kind of perspectivism that allows their containment in bejeweled interiors and formal gardens. The human body itself becomes the landscape, and physical boundaries no longer mark separate entities, as in *Trilce* XLVII:

> Ciliado arrecife donde nací,
> según refieren cronicones y pliegos
> de labios familiares historiados
> en segunda gracia.
>
> (CV, 149)
>
> (Ciliated reef where I was born,
> according to the brief chronicles and documents
> recited from the lips of family
> in second grace.)

And as landscapes merge into bodies and into time, language shows its part in the transformation; in *Trilce* IX it loses its written boundaries:

> Vusco volvvver de golpe el golpe.
> Sus dos hojas anchas, su válvula
> que se abre en suculenta recepción,
> de multiplicando a multiplicador,

su condición excelente para el placer,
todo avía verdad.

(I want to pusssh back thrust for thrust.
Her two wide-spreading leaves, her valve
opening in succulent reception,
from multiplicand to multiplier,
her excellent condition for pleasure,
everything still waz true.)

POEMAS HUMANOS

In *Poemas humanos* the dispersal of human existence grows and
threatens to break down all symmetries. Vallejo breaks apart
and reassembles stereotypes such as the Paris of legend, the
decorated and alluring body, and the framed theatrical scene.
Poemas humanos, which includes poems written over a period of
many years, reflects Vallejo's growing political commitment. In
this collection he reorganizes and reshapes his broken language
to incorporate a recognizable, social universe, where the ex-
change between *tú* and *yo* is not a reversible play of signifiers.
Like Pablo Neruda's "Walking Around" from *Residencia en la
tierra,* Vallejo's "Considerando en frío, imparcialmente" details
the emptiness and terror of everyday existence:

> Considerando en frío, imparcialmente,
> que el hombre es triste, tose y, sin embargo,
> se complace en su pecho colorado;
> que lo único que hace es componerse
> de días;
> que es lóbrego mamífero y se peina . . .
>
> (CV, 249)

> (Considering coldly, impartially,
> that man is sad, coughs and, in spite of it all,
> takes pleasure within his ruddy chest;
> that the only thing he does is to compose himself
> with days;
> that he is a gloomy mammal and combs his hair . . .)

Ironically cataloguing the insufficiency of existence, the poem
nevertheless ends with a recognition that reestablishes a logic of

existence, a relationship with the other that cancels out the previous parceling into separate parts:

> le hago una seña,
> viene,
> y le doy un abrazo, emocionado.
> ¡Qué más da! Emocionado . . . Emocionado . . .
> > > > (*CV*, 250)
>
> (I make him a sign,
> he comes,
> and I embrace him, moved
> What more can you do! Moved . . . Moved . . .)

However tenuous and ironic the poem's final lines may be, they illustrate the recurring summation gesture in many selections from *Poemas humanos*, a reframing of a scene whose boundaries have been dissolved.

Vallejo brings forth the physical nature of language by showing the generation of his metonymies. Substantiation, the process by which all things become united, is forever frustrated in his poems. The impossible journey to fulfillment is like the push through the needle's eye in *Trilce* XXXVI: "Pugnamos ensartarnos por un ojo de aguja" (*CV*, 138) ("We fight to thread ourselves through the needle's eye"). The endless proliferation of signifiers, in the end, cannot put into any meaningful order the chaos that lies beneath the surface. Like the body that betrays the mind's directions, language is resistant to intention. In the same poem from *Trilce*, Venus de Milo's absent arm reminds him that his little finger is superflous and that the "brazos plenarios / de la existencia" ("full arms / of existence") are perennially imperfect. Time also disintegrates like bodies in *Trilce* XXVI:

> Nudo alvino deshecho, una pierna por allí,
> más allá todavía la otra,
> > > desgajadas,
> > > > péndulas.
> Deshecho nudo de lácteas glándulas
> de la sinamayera,
> bueno para alpacas brillantes,

para abrigo de pluma inservible
¡más piernas los brazos que piernas!

(*CV*, 126)

(Alvine knot, untied; a leg over there,
way over there another,
                disjointed,
                    hanging.
Dissolved knot of lacteal glands
of the woman cloth seller,
good for bright alpacas,
for an overcoat of useless feathers
the arms more legs than legs!)

In his fascination with time and numbers, the reversibility of language, and the shapelessness of human existence, Vallejo shows the indeterminacy of all organizing systems. Time, physical space, bodies, numerical systems, and the body of language take on each others' shapes.

In "Los nueve monstruos" the listing of objects, recited like a biblical chant, is not an expression of the absurdity of the world's objects, bodies, and acts. It is tied to a call to action, a call to recognize pain's relationship to surrounding circumstance. The oxymoronic structure, so favored by Vallejo, is here not an arbitrary construction:

Jamás, hombres humanos,
hubo tanto dolor en el pecho, en la solapa, en la cartera,
en el vaso, en la carnicería, en la aritmética!
Jamás tanto cariño doloroso,
jamás tan cerca arremetió lo lejos,
jamás el fuego nunca
jugó mejor su rol de frío muerto!
Jamás, señor ministro de salud, fue la salud
más mortal

(*CV*, 242)

(Never, human men,
was there so much pain in the heart, in the lapels, in the wallet,
in the glass, in the butcher shop, in the arithmetic!
Never so much painful affection

never did distance assault so close,
never, the fire never
acted better its role of cold death!
Never, Mr. Minister of Health, was health
more mortal)

Making explicit the relationship between presence and absence, cause and effect, Vallejo also makes explicit language's metonymic power. He again uses food symbolically to represent the interconnection between loss and possession, need and plenitude:

> Y también de resultas
> del sufrimiento, estoy triste
> hasta la cabeza, y más triste hasta el tobillo,
> de ver al pan, crucificado, al nabo,
> ensangrentado,
> llorando, a la cebolla,
> al cereal, en general, harina,
> a la sal, hecha polvo, al agua, huyendo,
> al vino, un ecce-homo,
> tan pálida a la nieve, al sol tan ardio!
>
> (CV, 244)

> (And also from the effects
> of suffering, I am sad
> up to my head, and sadder down to my ankles,
> to see the bread, crucified, the turnip,
> bloodied,
> crying, the onion,
> the cereal, in general, flour,
> the salt, turned to dust, the water, fleeing,
> the wine, a behold-man,
> the snow so palid, the sun so burning!)

The use of the personal *a* with inanimate objects, along with the "pan crucificado" ("crucified bread"), suggests what will become explicit with "un ecce-homo" ("a behold-man"). Vallejo plays with sound resemblances ("hecha polvo" and "ecce-homo" ["turned to dust" and "behold-man"]) to suggest the finality of human existence. The same elemental symbols function in "Intensidad y altura" to express lack of power in writing:

> Quiero escribir, pero me sale espuma,
> quiero decir mucho y me atollo;
> no hay cifra hablada que no sea suma,
> no hay pirámide escrita, sin cogollo.
>
> .   .   .   .
>
> Vámonos, pues, por eso, a comer yerba,
> carne de llanto, fruta de gemido,
> nuestra alma melancólica en conserva.
>
> (*CV*, 261)
>
> (I want to write but all I get is foam,
> I want to say so much, and I bog down;
> there is no cipher spoken that isn't a sum,
> there is no pyramid written without a core.
>
> .   .   .   .
>
> Let's go there, and feed on grass,
> sob meat, groan fruit,
> our melancholy soul canned.)

The absurdity of the rhyme's direction, like speech's foaming babble, points up language's insufficiency.

Vallejo, like the *modernistas,* pushes forward the artificiality of his medium, poetic language, and shows its limits. His theater of language is nevertheless one of constant dispersal and renewal. Carrying to extremes the reversal of roles and the subversive entrance of the absurd, Vallejo shifts the viewer's vantage point completely. As Roberto Fernández Retamar has stated, "[E]n Vallejo, la poesía no surge del calco, sino de una situación vital, *y por lo tanto histórica,* irrespirable" ("In Vallejo, poetry doesn't come out of tracing an old pattern, but out of a vital, *and therefore historical,* situation not fit to be breathed")[7] Vallejo opens up new habitable spaces for poetry by reinserting a historical referent. By completely exposing the fabricated nature and fleetingness of language, he regains the freedom to reestablish a new chain of signification, to reorder the surface of language in reference to its context. The vital situation is indeed historical, and Vallejo reveals language's shape within the body of history.

RAMÓN LÓPEZ VELARDE

Ramón López Velarde, best known as a poet of the Mexican Revolution, reshaped *modernismo*'s canon to write poetry with a distinctly local and personal stamp. Octavio Paz has described the essential themes of López Velarde's work as provincial life and eroticism, while noting also the influences of Laforgue and Lugones on the amalgam of the provincial theme with eroticism.[8] Pablo Neruda calls the force of López Velarde's poetry, "el líquido erotismo" ("the liquid eroticism") that circulates deeply throughout all his work, and names López Velarde as *modernismo*'s final master:

En la gran trilogía del modernismo, es Ramón López Velarde el maestro final, el que pone el punto sin coma. Una época rumorosa ha terminado. Sus grandes hermanos, el caudaloso Rubén y el lunático Herrera y Reissig, han abierto las puertas de una América anticuada, han hecho circular el aire libre. . . . Pero esta revolución no es completa si no consideramos este arcángel final que dio a la poesía americana un sabor y una fragrancia que durará para siempre. Sus breves páginas alcanzan, de algún modo sutil, la eternidad de la poesía.[9]

(In the great trilogy of *Modernismo,* Ramón López Velarde is the last master, the one who closes an entire period. A noisy epoch has come to an end. His two great brothers, the opulent Rubén and the lunatic Herrera y Reissig, have opened the doors of an antiquated America; they have brought a breath of fresh air. . . . But his revolution would not be complete if we didn't consider this last archangel who gave to American poetry a flavor and a fragrance that will last forever. His few pages achieve in some subtle way, the eternity of poetry.)

According to Neruda, López Velarde captures the scenes of his poetic heritage in a sidelong glance, "como si alguna vez hubiera visto la escena de soslayo y hubiera conservado fielmente una visión oblicua, una luz torcida que da a toda su creación tal inesperada claridad" ("as if at some time he had glimpsed the scene out of the corner of his eye and had faithfully conserved an oblique vision, a twisted light that gives to his whole creation such unexpected clarity")[10] The question of perspective is crucial in understanding López Velarde's relationship to his *modern-*

ista predecessors. Abbreviating *modernismo*'s stylized descriptions, he clearly sets forth the contrast between the old and new worlds, identifying his personal voice with the unsettling pendulum swing between two worlds, as in "El son del corazón":

> Yo soy el suspirante cristianismo
> al hojear las bienaventuranzas
> de la virgen que fue mi catecismo.
>
> Y la nueva delicia que acomoda
> sus hipnotismos de color de tango
> al figurín y al precio de la moda.
>
> La redondez de la Creación atrueno
> cortejando a las hembras y a las cosas
> con un clamor pagano y nazareno.
>
> ¡Oh, Psiquis, oh mi alma: suena a son
> moderno, a son de selva, a son de orgía
> y a son mariano, el son del corazón![11]
>
> (I am sighing Christianity
> as I leaf through the beatitudes
> of the virgin which was my catechism.
>
> And the new delight arranges
> its tango-colored hypnotisms
> on the dummy model and at the price of fashion.
>
> I thunder out the roundness of Creation
> courting females and courting things
> with a pagan and Nazarene clamor.
>
> Oh Psyche, oh my soul: play a modern
> tune, a tune of the forest, a tune of orgy,
> and a Marian tune, the tune of the heart.)

López Velarde wrote three books of poetry: *La sangre devota* (1916), *Zozobra* (1919), and *El son del corazón* (published posthumously in 1932), as well as many essays. Profoundly influenced in his early poetry by Lugones, he integrated the legacies of Baudelaire and Laforgue, filtered through the eyes of a Mexican provincial reality and years of harsh revolution. Xavier Villarrutia also finds López Velarde's poetic antecedents in Luis Carlos López and Julio Herrera y Reissig.[12]

In his essays, López Velarde devotes special attention to Leopoldo Lugones, Enrique González Martínez, and José Juan Tablada. In defending Tablada's spare experimental verse against its critics, he writes what could be his own *art poétique;*

> Ciertamente, la Poesía es un ropaje; pero ante todo, es una sustancia. Ora celestes éteres becquerianos, ora tabacos de pecado. La quiebra del Parnaso constitió en pretender suplantar las esencias desiguales de la vida del hombre con una vestidura fementida. Para los actos transcendentales—sueño, baño o amor—nos desnudamos.[13]

> (Certainly Poetry is a dress; but above all, it is a substance. Whether celestial Becquerian ethers, or tobaccos of sin. The shattering of Parnassus came about by trying to supplant the unequal essences of man's existence with a dress that didn't quite fit. For all transcendental acts—sleeping, bathing, or love-making—we undress ourselves.)

For López Velarde, there are no objects that enter into poetic language in a totally innocent state. Even childhood or virginity form their own codes. Following Lugones and Herrera y Reissig, López Velarde chooses the provincial, the quiet side of Mexico, as the range of the unmarked, the space still undefiled by a weighted, cosmopolitan scheme of values. In his literary critisism, López Velarde is always clear about his contextual scheme of values:

> El hecho próspero consiste en que se ha conquistado el decoro de los temas con el hallazgo de lo que yo llamaría el *criollismo.* No lo criollo de hamaca, de siesta tropical. . . . Eso queda en devaneo. No; trátase de lo criollo neto, expresión absurda étnicamente, pero adecuada para contener el sentido artístico de la cuestión que someramente voy fijando, como un prendido de alfileres. Trátase de lo que no cabe ni en lo hispano ficticio ni en lo aborigen de pega. Trátase de lo criollo neto: las calles por cuyo arroyo se propaga la hierba; . . . las anilinas de la botica que irradian rojas y verdes y enorgullecen a los paseantes nocturnos de la plaza. . . .[14]

(The happy deed consists of the fact that the propriety of themes has been conquered by the discovery of what I would call *criollismo.* But not the *criollismo* that relies heavily on visions of hammocks and tropical siestas. . . . That ends up becoming total nonsense. No, I'm talking about the genuine *criollo,* an absurd expression in ethnic

terms, but quite appropriate in expressing the artistic meaning of
the matter that I'm trying briefly, and somewhat loosely, to estab-
lish. It deals basically with the elements that don't fit within what is
considered false Hispanism or patched-up indigenous characteris-
tics. It deals with what is genuinely *criollo:* the streets with their
water courses full of grass; . . . the anilines of the drug stores radiat-
ing red and green, filling the nocturnal stroller of the plaza with
pride. . . .)

For López Velarde, the child, the native past, the woman, and
the elderly may participate in this special world.

Deeply marked by the devastation of the Mexican Revolution,
the move from quiet provincial life to the city ("ojerosa y
pintada" ["hollow-eyed and painted"], as he describes it in "La
suave patria"), and by a tormented religiosity, López Velarde
shows the distance between the two worlds. City/country, purity/
transgression, and tranquillity/violence are the thematic opposi-
tions he draws in his portraits. On a technical level, one can see
other contrasts in his verse construction. His poems show traces
of conversational prose and parenthetical, densely wrought syn-
tax. Like Lugones, López Velarde often departs from fixed me-
ter and, unlike Lugones, leaves behind rhyme. He moves be-
tween fixed meters and *versolibrismo* and experiments with subtle
rhymes, internal assonance, and alliteration. Like Lugones and
Herrera y Reissig (as well as Vallejo) he sets side by side the
modernista paradigm with a prosaic detail, often mixed with a
nostalgic religiosity, as in "El son del corazón":

> Una música íntima no cesa
> porque transida en un abrazo de oro
> la Caridad con el Amor se besa.
>
> ¿Oyes el diapasón del corazón?
> Oye en su nota múltiple el estrépito
> de los que fueron y de los que son.
> <div align="right">(<i>SV</i>, 233)</div>

> (An intimate music doesn't cease,
> because fainting in a golden embrace
> Charity and Love kiss.
>
> Do you hear the diapason of the heart?

Hear in its multiple note the deafening sound
of those who were and those who are.)

López Velarde's verses are rarely as explicit as these, however. Elliptical expressions, hyperbaton, and syntactical breaks make comprehension difficult. His poetry resists overt signification, and the language of dreams or the ramblings of childhood memory make their own logic, as they do in Vallejo's poetry. This is why "El retorno maléfico" is such a threatening poem. Its silences and ambivalences are the response of a village that does not know how to speak to an intrusive attack by forces which partake in other dialogues, those of revolution and politics. Like the prostitution in the city, the mutilation of the town at the hands of an enemy from without leaves it mute. The town can no more marshal itself against physical devastation that it can call forth a discourse to describe it.

Like Vallejo's house in "Aquí no vive nadi," where only sounds and gestures of past lives resonate, the return to the village in "El retorno maléfico" is an impossible one: "Mejor será no regresar al pueblo, / al edén subvertido que se calla / en la mutilación de la metralla" (*LV*, 174) ("It will be better not to return to the village / to the subverted Eden / hushed in the machine gun's mutilation"). The return of the prodigal son to the "edén subvertido" ("subverted Eden") removes all blame from the village itself and attributes its destruction to an outside force, a tangible one that comes in the shape of military violence. The elliptical questioning of a destroyed past echoes in the complexity of the poem's sound patterns. For example, the repetition of sounds takes on the effect of an incantation: "un cubo de cuero, / goteando su gota categórica / como un estribillo plañidero" ("a leather bucket, / dripping its categorical drop / like a mournful refrain"), "el lloro de recientes recentales / por la ubérrima ubre prohibida / de la vaca" ("the crying of recent calves / for the plentiful forbidden udder / of the cow"), and "el amor amoroso / de las parejas pares" ("the amorous love / of the even-numbered couples"). The most prosaic elements are those that receive the most "poetic" treatment, either by latinate construction ("ubérrima ubre" ["plentiful udder"]) or by the distance between terms of the metaphor ("muchachas / frescas y

humildes, como humildes coles" ["young girls / fresh and hum-
ble, like humble cabbages"]). The Edenic, timeless atmosphere
so lovingly detailed contrasts with the tomblike entrance of the
village. The town's present, broken state—locked, closed, and
sealed off as if by death—must be left alone, unentered. Its
evocation must respond to "una íntima tristeza reaccionaria"
("an intimate, reactionary sadness") which closes off any possi-
ble entrance. This last verse reestablishes an intellectual dis-
tance, combining the personal and political into a present that
cannot return.

The oscillation between extremes and the impossibility of
resolution mark López Velarde's poetry. Like "Dos péndulos
distantes / que oscilan paralelos" ("Two distant pendulums /
that oscillate parallel"), the dualities are never to be resolved.
Erotic love and death are intimately connected in "Hermana
hazme llorar." Fuensanta, his love of the province, is the em-
blem for the woman left behind, and she embodies the longing
for purity and innocence of the past:[15]

> Fuensanta:
> dame todas las lágrimas del mar
> Mis ojos están secos y yo sufro
> unas inmensas ganas de llorar.
>
> .   .   .   .
>
> Hazme llorar, hermana,
> y la piedad cristiana
> de tu mano inconsútil
> enjúgueme los llantos con que llore
> el tiempo amargo de mi vida inútil.
>
> > (*LV*, 89)
>
> (Fuensanta:
> give me all the tears of the sea.
> My eyes are dry and I feel
> an overpowering need to cry.
>
> .   .   .   .
>
> Sister, make me cry,
> and let the Christian mercy
> of your seamless hand
> wipe the tears with which I lament
> the bitter time of my useless life.)

The figure of Fuensanta always evokes the communion with the past and with wholeness, and contrasts with later loves.

"Mi prima Águeda" from *La sangre devota* highlights the memories of childhood, and the poem's parenthetical condensations show only fragments of the *femme fatale* in the transformation into her rustic counterpart: "Águeda era / (luto, pupilas verdes y mejillas / rubicundas) un cesto policromo / de manzanas y uvas / en el ébano de un armario añoso" (*LV*, 59) ("Águeda was / [black dress, green pupils, and rosy / cheeks] a polychrome basket / of apples and grapes / in the ebony of an old armoire"). Seen through the child's eyes—"Yo era rapaz / y concocía la *o* por lo redondo" ("I was a young boy / and I knew the *o* by its roundness")—Águeda represents the inaccessible distance and beauty of female power. However, the trappings of her power are the most common traits of everyday village dress, "con un contradictorio / prestigio de almidón y de temible / luto ceremonioso" ("with a contradictory / prestige of starch and of fearsome, / ceremonious mourning dress"). In this poem the mixture of colors, sounds, and bewitching movement—"me iba embelesando un quebradizo / sonar intermitente de vajilla / y el timbre caricioso / de la voz de mi prima" ("I was becoming enchanted by the brittle / intermittent sound of silver on porcelain / and the caressing tone / of my cousin's voice")—is no less complex than *modernismo*'s compositions, but the effect is one of simplicity. Taking his direction from Lugones and Herrera y Reissig, López Velarde transforms interior landscapes and the idealized female figure within contexts of provincial life and a child's experiences.

In López Velarde's "Mi corazón se amerita," the last strophe could be read as a commentary on Herrera y Reissig's *Tertulia lunática:*

> Así extirparé el cáncer de mi fatiga dura,
> seré impasible por el Este y el Oeste,
> asistiré con dura sonrisa depravada
> a las ineptitudes de la inepta cultura
> y habrá en mi corazón la llama que le preste
> el incendio sinfónico de la esfera celeste.
>
> (*LV*, 156)

(And so I will destroy the cancer of my harsh fatigue,
I will become impassive from East to West,
I will respond with a harsh, depraved smile
to all the ineptitude of the inept culture
and there will be in my heart the flame lent by
the symphonic fire of the celestial sphere.)

The element of pose, the Baudelairian disdain, the emphasis on hardness and ugliness, is turned around by an equally exaggerated proclamation of faith: "el incendio sinfónico de la esfera celeste" ("the symphonic fire of the celestial sphere"). It honors the pendulum's swinging back and forth, and by plainly placing side by side two extremes of now-familiar phrasing, as if they were pieces unto themselves, he acknowledges the reality of both theatrical modes.

"Te honro en el espanto . . . ," from *Zozobra*, is a tribute to death, as well as a collection of all the usual images that fill up "una perdida alcoba / de nigromante" ("the lost bedroom / of a necromancer"). As the *yo* binds together the memory of a woman, reclaiming her from death's funerary fetishes, the eroticism and lightness return in a strangly playful image of a game:

> mis besos te recorren en devotas hileras
> encima de un sacrílego manto de calaveras
> como sobre una erótica ficha de dominó.
> (*LV*, 214)

> (my kisses travel your body in devout rows
> above the sacrilegious cloak of skulls
> as if over an erotic domino chip.)

Here López Velarde takes *modernismo*'s fetishistic attraction to rare objects and clearly shows their elaboration, and thus destroys their power as objects "bewitched".[16]

In "Suave patria" López Velarde celebrates the grandeur of Mexico's simple, rustic life, as well as its glorious indigenous past. In this long poem, divided into "Proemio," "Primer acto," "Intermedio: Cuauhtémoc," and "Segundo acto" ("Preface," "First Act" "Intermezzo: Cuauhtémoc," and "Second Act"), Mexico's daily life is pictured against its enormous expanses as well as its turbulent history. In the "Proemio," the narrator states his purpose, "Para cortar a la epopeya un gajo" ("To cut a branch from the epic"). Rejecting the grandiloquence of past national epics, "Diré con una epíca sordina: / la patria es impecable y diamantina" (*LV*, 264) ("I will say with a muted epic: / the homeland is impeccable and glittering"). As in "Mi prima Águeda," López Velarde shows the astonishing beauty of the mundane in the "Primer acto":

> Patria: tu mutilado territorio
> se viste de percal y de abalorio.
>
> Suave Patria: tu casa todavía
> es tan grande, que el tren va por la vía
> como aguinaldo de juguetería.
>
> (LV, 265)
>
> (Homeland: your mutilated territory
> dresses in calico and glass beads.
>
> Gentle Country: your house is
> still so vast that the train runs along its track
> Like a Christmas present in a toyshop.)

Here the train is not *modernismo*'s mythological monster; it is a toy dwarfed by natural and human splendors. In the "Segundo acto," López Velarde continues his exaltation of the commonplace:

> Suave Patria: te amo no cual mito,
> sino por tu verdad de pan bendito,
> como a niña que asoma por la reja
> con la blusa corrida hasta la oreja
> y la falda bajada hasta el huesito.
>
> (LV, 268)
>
> (Gentle Country: I love you not as a legend,
> but for the truth of your blessed bread,
> as I love a young girl appearing at the railing
> with her blouse reaching her ear
> and her skirt down to her ankle.)

Like Vallejo's evocation of childhood scenes, there is a reverence for elemental satisfactions and a reduction of the grandiose to the commonplace. López Velarde's portrait of Mexico is a kaleidoscope of past and present. Even though his experiments in lexical and syntactical distortion in no way approach Vallejo's innovations, his expansion of content boundaries has been an important source for later poets.

In López Velarde's work the heritage of his *modernista* predecessors is clearly apparent, and he pays tribute to them as well in his literary criticism.[17] But like many of his generation, López Velarde will transform the provincial setting and the dynamics of eroticism with his apparent "simplicity." In this way he closes the *modernista* chapter and paves the way for another generation of Mexican poets. In his swings between the pull of a provincial past that can no longer be recaptured and the attraction of cosmopolitan temptations, López Velarde does not parody his poetic models as does Lugones. Leaving the paradigms to coexist side by side, he shows their incongruity with a fleeting sidelong gesture. As Neruda describes his practice:

> Como si alguna vez hubiera visto la escena de soslayo y hubiera conservado fielmente una visión oblicua, una luz torcida que da a toda su creación tal inesperada claridad.[18]

> (As if at some time he had glimpsed the scene out of the corner of his eye and had faithfully conserved an oblique vision, a twisted light that gives his whole creation such unexpected clarity.)

With no need of twisting the swan's neck, a gesture enacted previously by Enrique González Martínez, López Velarde changes the perspectives in viewing many of *modernismo*'s favored scenes. He redecorates their interiors, sees them with the rapt wonder of a child, and changes their profusion of harmonies to sing to "el son del corazón."

ALFONSINA STORNI: NEW VISIONS OF THE CITY AND THE BODY OF POETRY

The poetry of Alfonsina Storni, especially that part which is most often presented in anthologies, reads like an inventory of the concerns of nonconformist women, with its rage at male expectations, the seeming impossibility of equality in love, and dissatisfaction at the traditional roles imposed on women. It is as if the female voice in her poetry speaks from (and against) the vision of the woman embodied in a male discourse. The earth, the sea, the female body, and love are seen in terms of passion, despair, and yearning for fulfillment on an ideal plane. These are the traits that have helped make Alfonsina Storni one of Latin America's best-known poets, make her poetry accessible to a large audience, and serve almost as "thesis" poems to illustrate the plight of the woman. Yet the real ringing of independence, the move to refocus these issues and to develop another kind of voice in her poetry, is the voice less often heard.

Though Storni is better known for her erotic verse and the death poems, there is a side less recognized, the sharp-edged hand of humor and the quick eye that notes the contours of the cityscape and of the body. Her ironies, concise and cutting, move in the shortened phrase, interrupting the flow of what start out to be rapturous love poems. *Mascarilla y trébol* (1938) and many of the selections from her uncollected poems show the growing distance from the earlier *modernista*-influenced poetry. Here I shall discuss Storni's reinscription of the erotic in another series of gestures and body heraldry, to show its representation leaves the symbolic order of her previous poetry and takes on a coherence sufficient unto itself, seemingly distanced from the external determinations of desire.

In the introduction to *Mascarilla y trébol* Storni describes the development process of "estos antisonetos de postura literaria" ("these anti-sonnets of literary posture"), stressing the spontaneous nature of their creation, "la exaltación de aquel micromundo" ("the exaltation of that microworld"). Yet viewing her poetic production in its entirety (and within its literary context), it is clear that the later concision and apparent spontaneity are the results of a long process of adaptation and disavowals of a poetic language that can no longer serve her purpose.

Some of the poetry of *Mascarilla y trébol* is stunning by its lack of attachment to old wounds. Though it does not leave the sea as the deep site of spiritual ferment and holds to the body as the testing ground of the spirit, the changing focus allows for the incorporation of elements outside the personal sphere. The doleful *yo* of the earlier poems (often associated with the blessing and curse of writing) moves from the position of the body observed, shifting to watch from the sidelines with a sharp eye. It is the decentering process, or off-center stance, which allows perspectives to be arranged. The insistent framing voice gives way to the fleeting glimpse and to the rearrangement of visual hierarchies. And ultimately it moves to a new constitution of the self. The poem "A Eros" with its trivialization of the all-powerful god, its "coro asustado de sirenas" ("frightened chorus of sirens"), and gesture of dismissal at its close, signals this new treatment of a landscape that once pulsated with response to personal emotions. Its staginess and theatricality will be unmasked, just as the cityscape will be examined from all angles, as if its voracity and coldness were an object of observation rather than a mirror of personal interiority.

In one of her early poems, "Tú me quieres blanca" from *El dulce daño* (1918), Storni formulates an insolent answer to the romantic–*modernista* aesthetic from the victim's point of view, but still responds as the object viewed, the one observed:

> Tú me quieres alba,
> Me quieres de espumas,
> Me quieres de nácar.
> Que sea azucena
> Sobre todas, casta.
> De perfume tenue
> Corola cerrada.[19]

> (You want me white,
> You want me to be foam,
> You want me to be mother-of pearl.
> To be a delicate lily
> Above all others, chaste.
> With subdued perfume
> closed corolla.)

The *tú* she addresses is the full possessor, not only of the vision that frames her intact and immobile, but of a different, more structured kind of physical existence:

> Tú que el esqueleto
> Conservas intacto

No sé todavía
Por cuáles milagros,

Me pretendes blanca
(Dios te lo perdone)
Me pretendes casta
(Dios te lo perdone)
¡Me pretendes alba!

(AS, 108)

(You who keep
your skeleton intact
I still don't know
by what strange miracles,

You expect me to be white
(God forgive you)
You expect me to be chaste
(God forgive you)
You expect me to be snow white!)

It is the change from being the observed, as in this poem, to being the observer that marks a transformation in Storni's later poetry. Moving from the position of only responding to the conditions of formulaic notions of viewing woman's eroticism, she turns to become the observer. And it is no surprise that many of the preoccupations with love, always elusive and disturbing, and the guilt of passion are transformed. Just as the Medusa image has been the representation of a theme of diabolical fascination, of entrapment incarnated in the figure of the woman who seduces and turns men into stone, it has also served as an entrapment for women attempting to write within male discourse.[20] The powers of attraction, the perils of bewitchment by the female nature, are assumed as a burdensome sin from which to expiate themselves.

In "Women in Space and Time" Claudine Herrmann points out the respective values accorded to the idea of a void, or vacuum, by men and women over the centuries, and relates it to a presence or absence of grammar: "Women, who for centuries have been *cut off* from space, subjected to time without any means of recuperating it through action, have written poetry, uniquely, much longer than men. . . . However, as soon as woman conceives of space as a function of rapprochement rather than in terms of its separating function, she becomes an intrepid traveler."[21] And in her later poems we see Storni moving to new landscapes, to the close-up microscopic focus that unbinds the body from its previous settings.

In Storni's change of stance, the alterations occur not only on the thematic level. There is a perceptible difference in the visual perspectives that frame, or leave unframed, these poems. Just as landscape painting created expectations for Parnassian and *modernista* poetry, so previous poetry prepares us for a landscape in which to speak of the body. Storni's early precursors were the *modernistas*. Favoring exotic interior settings or blue-tinged seascapes and landscapes, the *modernistas* often fitted these interiors or landscapes as a setting for a close-up focus on the female body. This focus, with its distortion of perspectives, seeks to freeze the finality of the erotic body, rendering it static. In general, this plenitude is seen as a treasure of physicality, often implying robbed or stolen treasure. *Modernista* poets insist on showing the physicality of the referent, pushing it to the forefront and accentuating as well as the physical nature of the words themselves. In the case of the feminine icon, the litany of these parts and the bodily dismemberment underscore the traditional fetishization of the erotic image of the woman. The body of the woman is used by poets like a Parnassian sunset, a canvas on which to cut, decorate, and engrave its images.

Storni begins the process of taking the body outside the gilded cage and initiates a restoration process by turning it over to a less rarefied setting. In "Trío" from *Poesías inéditas*, "la pobre literata" ("the poor woman of letters") recounts an interior tragedy within the beauty of a domestic setting:

> Olor a pan del horno
> Olor a pan del horno . . .
> Y yo quieta y opaca.
> Casero. Movimiento.
>
> (*AS*, 529)

> (The smell of bread from the oven
> The smell of bread from the oven . . .

And I motionless and opaque.
Homelike. Movement.)

The scenes of the house, with its smells and sounds, describe an inner setting far removed from the earlier cosmic imagery.

The sonnet "Gran cuadro" (*Mascarilla y trébol*) exemplifies the process Storni uses to dismantle the formulas of her predecessors. The idea of a painting is significant—its static imagery, iconographic possibilities ("la luna," "un cuervo herido" ["the moon," "a wounded crow"]) pretend to be self-contained, bordered, finished. As with so many *modernista* landscapes and interiors, the stylized setting is meant to evoke an air of impassibility, refinement, and suggestive eroticism. But just as many *modernistas* intrude upon the exotic enclosures with disconcerting objects and voices, so Storni shows the overt movement of the disturbing hand:

> No; no era un cuadro aún para pintores
> de mucho fuste, pero entré en la tela
> y ágil movió la muerte sus pinceles.
>
> (*AS*, 376)
>
> (No; it wasn't a picture even meant for painters
> of great substance, but I penetrated the canvas
> and death, agile, moved his brushes.)

The same process of stripping down the enchantments of Eros—in "A Eros": "destripé tu vientre / y examiné sus ruedas engañosas" (*AS*, 359) ("I disemboweled you / and examined your deceitful wheels")—is repeated with other stock poetic scenes. The series of cityscapes, "Río de la Plata en negro y ocre," "Río de la Plata en gris áureo," and "Río de la Plata en arena pálido," disclose the underside of a city whose cavernous mouth opens to receive and discharge its wares:

> La niebla había comido su horizonte
> y sus altas columnas agrisadas
> se echaban hacia el mar y parapetos
> eran sobre la atlántica marea.
>
> Se estaba anclado allí, ferruginoso,

viendo venir sus padres desde el norte;
dos pumas verdes que por monte y piedra
saltaban desde el trópico a roerlo.

                                        (*AS*, 360)

(The fog had devoured its horizon
and its tall, greyish pillars
cast themselves into the sea and were
ramparts over the Atlantic tide.

It remained anchored there, ferruginous
seeing its forefathers come from the north;
two green panthers that jumped from the tropics
through the hills and rocks to gnaw at it.)

The devouring mouth, while metonymically referring us back to the moon, is detached from a personal and individual expression.

Poems such as "Una oreja," "Un lápiz," and "Una gallina" use the grand scope of vision to celebrate small, concrete, and earthy elements. Prefiguring Neruda's *Odas elementales,* they document the magic power of everyday objects. The heavily laden vocabulary of *modernismo,* once used to adorn the picture of the *femme fatale* and the sumptuous interior setting, performs its magic now on a close-up of a bodily part, the ear, in "Una oreja" from *Mascarilla y trébol:*

Pequeño foso de irisadas cuencas
y marfiles ya muertos, con estrías
de contraluces; misteriosa valva
vuelta caverna en las alturas tristes

del cuello humano; rósea caracola
traída zumbadora de los mares;
punzada de envolventes laberintos
donde el crimen esconde sus acechos.

                                        (*AS*, 389)

(Small well of irridescent valleys
and long dead ivories with black-lighted
grooves; mysterious valve
turned into a cavern on the sad height

of the human neck, rosy conch
brought buzzing from the sea;

punctured by enveloping labyrinths
where crime hides its ambushes.)

In "La oreja," the luxuriant, erotic nature of the ear's description stands even more independently in its self-sustaining eroticism. Here mystery and crime are deeply buried in the curving richness of the body. As some critics have suggested, the mention of crime may refer to the notion of inherited characteristics, of an "ear type" associated with the born criminal.[22] More suggestively, however, it may also refer to Cassandra's gift of unheeded prophecy. Licked on the ear by a serpent while sleeping, Cassandra was given the blessing and curse of prophecy, condemned to decipher the songs of birds and the voices of the air.[23] Nonetheless, most powerful is its evocation of the female—mysterious, prone to crime, and linked to the sea. The poem lingers in the erotic intricacy of such mystery. An interesting comparison can be made between this poem and the title poem of *Mundo de siete pozos,* where the description of the ear mixes graphic and abstract elements:

> pozos de sonidos,
> caracoles de nácar donde resuena
> la palabra expresada
> y la no expresa;
> tubos colocados a derecha e izquierda
> para que el mar no calle nunca,
> y el ala mecánica de los mundos
> rumorosa sea.
>
> (AS, 286)

> (wells full of sounds,
> mother-of-pearl spiral shells where
> the uttered and unuttered word
> resounds;
> tubes arranged to the right and to the left
> to keep the sea from ever turning silent,
> to keep the mechanical wing of the worlds
> full of sound.)

The section is framed within a more extensive examination of the head ("el mundo de siete puertas" ["the world of seven doors"]), and parts of the body are also framed in landscape terms—"planetas," "bosque," "mansas aguas," "pozos," "montaña," "cráter," "praderas rosadas," "calles de seda" ("planets," "forest," "smooth waters," "wells," "mountain," "crater," "rose-colored meadows," "silken valleys"). At the end, its summing-up comes as a landscape vision:

> Y riela
> sobre la comba de la frente,
> desierto blanco,
> a luz lejana de una luna muerta . . .
>
> (*AS*, 287)

> (And it flickers
> over the curve of the forehead,
> white desert,
> the distant light of the dead moon . . .)

Rather than seeing this lunarlike landscape as a bleak, disturbing vision of the human form, it can be seen as an early reorientation of the landscape as frame of the human figure. Like contemporary art photography's deliberately perverse framing with its cut-off limbs, crazy horizons, and the photographer's shadows and footprints which litter the frames of extraterrestial photographs,[24] so Storni points the function of the poet not just as a meditative seeker but as a cooly calculating fabricator. She becomes a knowing and stalking voyager through new landscapes of the body.

"Flor en una mano" from *Mascarilla y trébol* registers this same dispersal of bodily parts, inscribed in its own logical universe. The delicate flower rests in a hand, "blanda, casi dormida" ("soft, almost sleeping"). The hand, like the flower, has five petals. "Cuán gemelos sus pálidos perfiles!" (*AS*, 379) ("How twin their palid profiles!". The identification of woman–flower is displaced and the flower's vulnerability, as opposed to the hand, resides in its lack of bones:

> Y ésta ungulada, presta a la rapiña,
> con lacres de Satán aleccionada
> en viejas artes negras sabedoras.
>
> (*AS*, 379)

(And this ungulate, ready for pillage,
With sealing wax from Satan and instructed
in ancient, knowing, black arts.)

Its microscopic context deprives us of the symbolic framing we might be eager to assume. The reading eye can not make clear identity pictures from so small a context. The flower in other poems takes on new dimensions, as in "Mar de pantalla" where the flower and the hand transform the enduring images of the sea and the mystic flower, revealing not only the trickery of the cinema but of the changing place of these images in poetry:

> Se escapa el mar que el celuloide arrolla
> y en los dedos te queda, fulgurante,
> una mística flor, técnica y fría.
>
> (AS, 388)
>
> (The sea, which the celluloid rolls up, escapes
> and in your fingers remains, resplendent,
> a mystical flower, technical and cold.)

Storni turns around poetic icons, strips them of an accustomed mystery, and delivers them back to wander in unfamiliar territories.

In her earlier poetry, Storni continues the fetishization of the female body in line with many of her predecessors, and this fetishization is like the detached sign of a more encompassing ideology. The duality of the jeweled cage, its inhabitant "blanca y casta" ("white and chaste"), or its inversion, the Medusa-like Salomé or *femme fatale,* created a subterranean ferment in Storni's earlier poetry. But with changes in perspective of time and distance, like those of cinema and photography, these poems decentralize the bodily focus, opening up stunning and unsettling vistas. Rather than reading these poems as a last mournful cry of bleakness and despair at the world's disjointedness, they may be read as a voyage outward from the bodily cage, voyages that create temporal and spatial innovations in Storni's poetic landscape.

CONCLUSION

The practices and cherished ideals of *modernismo* have provoked passionate commentary, including voices of enthusiastic acclaim and equally scornful derision. Rarely has a literary movement in Spanish America been the object of so much discussion, and few literary models have stamped themselves to firmly in literary consciousness. In effect, a Spanish American writes always against the backdrop of the inescapable scenic and textual surfaces of the *modernista* legacy. Considering that *modernismo* claims, to a large extent, to be a nonreferential practice (especially in regard to daily social and political realities), the vehemence of its defenders and detractors is especially notable. For beneath the presumed absence of external conflict in *modernista* poetry, readers have sensed its turbulence, signaled by its extraordinary feats of verbal construction and exaggerated exoticism.

Although Rubén Darío is the undisputed master of the movement, many later poets have found the complex, sometimes troubling, poetic experiments of Leopoldo Lugones to signal openings for a renewed poetic practice. His ever-changing combinations of technical prowess, disturbing and often violent eroticism, and the inclusion of daily life (both urban and rural) inspired others to break new poetic ground. Contradictions and conflicts only hinted at in other *modernistas* come to the fore in Lugones' works. In his poetry the clash of Parnassian sculptural forms and their representation in a newly energized Spanish American language, an older European value system transplanted in an American ground where a renewed consciousness of *americanismo* was beginning to take shape, and the reflection of a rapidly shifting social-class dynamic, give a problematic legacy for later poets. Lugones accentuates the speed, energy, and resistance of such changes in his early poetic works, extreme in his innovation and in his resistance as well.

In *Las montañas del oro* Lugones pairs grotesque physicality and sublime transcendence with experimental verse forms, including praise of scientific and technological advances within an ostensibly Dantesque journey. In *Los crepúsculos de jardín* the overwrought twilight scenes of erotic display stand in contrast to other poems and lead to a parody of many of *modernismo*'s most cherished tenets. In *Lunario sentimental* he deals a resounding blow to *modernista* practices and, at the same time, opens the way for the representation of urban speech, the depiction of the unglamorous middle class, and declares that experimentation with metaphor is to be the motor of poetic practice. Yet here Lugones most clearly reveals the tension between the poetry he espouses and the nostalgia for the past. Just as he rips apart in his verses the dangerous and beautiful sirens, symbolic of a world of mystery and beauty, he tempers the prosaic quality of his new poetry with an extraordinary lyricism and ambiguity. In twisting the swan's elegant neck, he makes palpable its extraordinary power. It is this hesitation, a footing poised between two worlds, that gives a special poignancy and power to the volume. Though many of these changes in his work seem inexplicable, a reading of his early prose and literary criticism forecasts these poetic changes, and predicts as well his renunciation of his own innovations.

Although Lugones does not continue on the paths he marked out, except on rare occasions, other poets perceived the energy released in his fracturing of *modernismo*. Uruguay's Julio Herrera y Reissig, like his compatriot Delmira Agustini, is a recognizable *modernista* poet, straining its poetic practices with the almost frenetic energy of his amazing constructions. Herrera y Reissig makes explicit the violent, troubled eroticism and physicality that lurked so close to the surface in Lugones' poetry. Within conventional landscapes he inserts characters and descriptive detail that draw his readers away from these scenes, forcing them to confront the ludicrous nature of much *modernista* scene painting. Like Lugones, he fervently believed in the necessity of metaphoric renewal and experimentation, and he extended such experiments to sound patterns themselves, veering off at times into the incomprehensibility that would mark much *vanguardista* poetry.

Three later poets—Ramón López Velarde, César Vallejo, and Alfonsina Storni—inherit the contradictions of *modernismo*. Given the individual nature of their works, marked by distinct nationalities, by gender, and by differing levels of political involvement, it would be foolish to declare them mere continuers of the vestiges of an earlier poetic tradition. Yet the resonance of *modernista* language and tenets reappears in their poetry in extraordinary patterns. In their works they make clear *modernismo's* contradictions, its focus on eroticism, and its profound striving to forge a new poetic language to represent a changed world.

Ramón López Velarde's work hauntingly evokes the battle between carnal and spiritual attractions and portrays a provincial Mexico mutilated by war. His national poem, "Suave patria," has changed the nature of patriotic verse. Clearly linked to the mysteries of *modernismo,* he creates extraordinary combinations of provincial life, urban sorrows, and an acute sense of being Mexican in an era of upheaval. Without the type of parody so evident in the works of Lugones and Herrera y Reissig, he builds his poetic universes with unexpected twists, combining *modernista* exoticism with the echoes of popular and liturgical language, and an aching awareness of the massive encroaching changes that will transform a previous way of life.

No other poet of the twentieth century has so revitalized poetic language in Spanish as César Vallejo. Aware as no other of the radical discontinuities between an inherited poetic tradition and its insufficiencies for expressing his own visions, Vallejo shows only the leftover fragments of a *modernista* tradition. It is precisely this character of inherited language as deadened, almost unintelligible artifact that creates many of Vallejo's most powerful ironies. Although his first volume, *Los heraldos negros,* is often labeled *"modernista-*influenced," his subsequent verse speaks equally powerfully of this tradition in disarray. Joining artifacts of this fading poetic language to raw physicality, family nostalgia, and juxtaposing its luxuries to scenes of hunger and to calls for social and political change, he strikes a discordant note that few subsequent poets have been able to ignore. If for the *modernistas,* Europe was the nostalgic focus of longing and beauty, for Vallejo the scenes of Andean childhood and American legacy contrast with an impoverished and desperate European present. He erases the myths that bound Latin Americans to a mythic European homeland and, with the gaps in his language and anguished ironies, he asks for a radically new poetic practice.

Alfonsina Storni, so often seen in isolation from any poetic tradition other than a narrowly defined feminine one, explicitly calls into question the place of the body, specifically, the female body, in *modernista* and *postmodernista* poetry. In her reversal of the typical subject–object relationship, the viewed female critically returns the voyeuristic gaze. Her poetry, when read in contrast to that of her immediate predecessors, incorporates their emphasis on eroticism and physical detail. With its unmistakable female stance, her poetry dismantles and subverts this poetic discourse as surely as Vallejo disrupts its sonority and luxury. If the female body at center stage is the focus of many *modernista* scenes, in Storni's work the viewer or reader shifts position to occupy the center, thus rearranging all other relationships. Her poetry carries to an inevitable, ironic conclusion the vision so apparent in Lugones' and Herrera y Reissig's work.

While López Velarde, Vallejo, and Storni are clear in their dismantling of *modernismo*'s stock scenes and impossible, elaborate settings, they are also clear in their rejection of its detachment from current American realities. Yet they are also inheritors of the uneasy ironies of poets such as Lugones and Herrera y Reissig, who began *modernismo*'s dismantling from within. These two late *modernistas,* with the hollow brilliance of their elaborate poetic language and their harsh evaluations of a more technological and egalitarian world, give an unhesitant and seething portrayal of a poetry in the making. In their works, the physical or mechanical apsects of poetic construction rise to the surface in dazzling bits and pieces, while the unity of the poem begins to dissolve. Each stream of images that begins to achieve coherence is quickly dismantled, and no single edifice or body is seen in its totality, framed by an appropriate setting. Over and over again we are drawn away from the picture to notice the craftsman who modifies details, as well as the ironic observer who makes his sideways remarks. Our willingness to suspend disbelief, so necessary for *modernista* poetry, is constantly tested by this intrusive activity. The body and the city take on this sense of artifice in the dissonant *modernistas.* And as these elements are divided and detached, traditional notions of perspective lose ground. Through their radical experiments in poetic language, and their dissonance within their epoch, they surreptitiously dismantle the language of *modernism.* In their experiments, ironies, discordance, and ambiguities, later poets will find the legacy from which they will construct new poetic languages.

Notes

INTRODUCTION

1. "The concept of simplicity as an esthetic value comes with the following stage (i.e., after "ornamentality") and is invariably connected with the rejection of ornamentality. Perception of artistic simplicity is possible only against a background of "ornamental" art whose memory is present in the consciousness of the viewer–listener. . . . Consequently, simplicity is structurally a much more complex phenomenon than ornamentality," Yuri Lotman, *Analysis of the Poetic Text*, ed. and trans. D. Barton Johnson (Ann Arbor, Mich.: Ardis Press, 1976), 26.

1. THE TRADITION OF *MODERNISMO*

1. José Lezama Lima, *La expresión americana* (La Habana: Instituto Nacional de la Cultura, 1957), 74.
2. Lezama Lima, *La expresión*, 78.
3. Roland Barthes, *Writing Degree Zero and Elements of Semiology*, trans. Annette Lavers and Colin Smith (Boston: Beacon Press, 1967), 48–49.
4. Walter Benjamin discusses the concept of "aura" and the "mystical" role of the artist and the movement of "l'art pour l'art" in "The Work of Art in the Age of Mechanical Reproduction," in *Illuminations*, trans. Harry Zohn (New York: Schocken Books, 1973), 224.
5. Severo Sarduy, *Escrito sobre un cuerpo* (Buenos Aires: Editorial Sudamericana, 1969), 94.
6. For a discussion of the concept of *fetish* used in this sense, see Jean Baudrillard, *For a Critique of the Political Economy of the Sign*, trans. Charles Levin (St. Louis, Mo.: Telos Press, 1981), 92.
7. Julia Kristeva, "D'une identité l'autre," *Polylogues* (Paris: Editions du Seuil, 1977), 165–169.
8. These poets will be studied in the final chapter.
9. Octavio Paz, *Cuadrivio* (México: Joaquín Mortiz, 1969), 36.
10. Paz, *Cuadrivio*, 13.
11. Octavio Paz, *Los hijos del limo* (Barcelona: Seix Barral, 1981), 138.
12. Paz, *Los hijos del limo*, 202.
13. Nancy Morejón, the contemporary Cuban poet, gives an example of this rejection of *modernista* thematics in "Desilusión para Rubén

Darío," in *Nueva poesía cubana,* ed. José Agustín Goytisolo (Barcelona: Ediciones Península, 1972). Her poem echoes, from a woman's point of view, the famous swan song of *modernismo,* "Tuércele el cuello al cisne" (1911) by Enrique González Martínez. She writes:

> Pero es que hay otro pavo real no tuyo
> que yo desgarro sobre el patio de mi casa imaginaria
>
> al que retuerzo el cuello casi con pena,
> a quien creo tan azul, tan azul como el azul del cielo.
>   (p. 202)
>
> (But there is another peacock, not yours,
> I tear apart in the patio of my imaginary house
> whose neck I wring almost with grief,
> so blue, so blue, it appears, like the blue of the sky.)

14. On the "automatization" of literary forms, see J. Tynianov, "De l'évolution littéraire," *Théorie de la littérature,* ed., and trans. Tzvetan Todorov (Paris: Editions du Seuil, 1965), 125.

15. Sarduy, *Barroco* (Buenos Aires: Sudamericana, 1974), 51.

16. For a discussion of the role of the reader, see Wolfgang Iser, *The Implied Reader* (Baltimore, Md.: The Johns Hopkins University Press, 1974) and *Reading: A Theory of Aesthetic Response* (Baltimore: The Johns Hopkins University Press, 1978).

17. Jorge Luis Borges, "Acotación del árbol en la lírica," *Proa* 10 (1925): 58–59.

18. Jorge Luis Borges, "Herrera y Reissig," *Inicial* (Buenos Aires) 1 (1924): 31–34.

19. In regard to *El romancero* by Lugones, Borges once again speaks disparagingly of the sculptural and pictorial side of his predecessors: "Los parnasianos (malos carpinteros y joyeros metidos a poetas) hablan de sonetos perfectos, pero no los he visto en ningún lugar." ("The Parnassians [bad carpenters and jewellers turned into poets] speak of perfect sonnets, but I haven't seen them anywhere.]) Jorge Luis Borges, "Leopoldo Lugones, romancero," *Inicial* (Buenos Aires) 2 (1926): 207–209.

20. Borges, "Herrera y Reissig," 31.

21. Borges, "Herrera y Reissig," 31.

22. Renato Poggioli, *The Theory of the Avant-Garde,* trans. Gerald Fitzgerald (Cambridge, Mass.: Harvard University Press, 1968), originally *Teoria dell'arte d'avanguardia* (Società editrice il mulino, 1962), 178–179.

23. "Relation de communication entre un émetteur et un récep-

teur, fondée sur le chiffrement et le déchiffrement, donc sur la mise en oeuvre d'un code, ou d'une compétence génératrice, l'échange linguistique est aussi en échange économique, qui s'établit dans un certain rapport de force symbolique entre un producteur, pourvu d'un certain capital linguistique, et un consommateur (ou un marché), et qui est propre a procurer un certain profit matériel ou symbolique. Autrement dit, les discours ne sont pas seulement (ou seulement par exception) des destinés à être compris, déchiffrés; ce sont aussi des *signes de richesse* destinés à être évalués, appréciés et des *signes d'autorité*, destinés à être crus et obéis. En dehors même des usages littéraires— et spécialement poétiques—du language, il est rare que, dans l'existence ordinaire, la langue fonctionne comme pur instrument de communication: la recherche de la maximisation du rendement in-formatif n'est que par exception la fin exclusive de la production linguistique et l'usage purement instrumental du langage qu'elle implique entre ordinairement en contradiction avec la recherche, souvent inconsciente, du profit symbolique." ("Linguistic exchange— a relation of communication between an emitter and a receiver, based on the coding and decoding, thus on the application of a code, of a generative competence—is also an economic exchange. It is estab-lished in a relation of symbolic force between a producer, supplied with a certain linguistic capital, and a consumer (or a market), and it can obtain a certain material or symbolic benefit. In other words, discourses are not (or only by exception) signs destined to be under-stood, decoded; they are also *signs of richness* destined to be evaluated, appreciated, and *signs of authority*, destined to be believed and obeyed. Besides the literary—and especially poetic—uses of language, it is rare, in ordinary life, that language functions as a pure instrument of communication: the search for the maximization of informative yield is only exceptionally the exclusive aim of linguistic production, and the purely instrumental use of language it (the production) implies usually enters into contradiction with the often unconscious search of symbolic benefit.") Pierre Bourdieu, "La formation des prix et l'antici-pation des profits," *Ce que parler veut dire: L'économie des échanges lin-guistiques* (Paris: Fayard, 1982), 59–60.

24. Several studies have played an important role in establishing the concept of *modernismo* in recent decades. A partial listing includes: Luis Monguió, "Sobre la caracterización del modernismo," *Revista Iberoamericana* 7 (1943): 69–79; Federico de Onís, "Sobre el concepto del modernismo," *La Torre* 1 (1953): 95–103; Ivan Schulman, *Génesis del modernismo: Martí, Nájera, Silva, Casal* (México: El Colegio de Méx-ico, Washington University Press, 1966); and I. Schulman, "Re-

flexiones en torno a la definición del modernismo," *Cuadernos Americanos* 25 (1966): 211–240.

25. José Emilio Pacheco, *Antología del modernismo (1994–1921),* 2 vols. (México: Universidad Nacional Autónoma de México, 1970), 1: xiii.

26. Michael Foucault, "What Is an Author?" *Textual Strategies: Perspectives in Post-Structuralist Criticism,* ed. Josue V. Harari (Ithaca, N.Y.: Cornell University Press, 1979), 141–160.

27. In *Contradicciones del modernismo* (México: El Colegio de México, 1978) (especially chap. 6, "Ruptura y reconciliación"), Noé Jitrik specifies the necessity of returning to *modernismo* if today's reader is to understand the literary position of the twentieth century (see especially p. 103). Here in his discussion of *modernismo,* he notes the conflicting claims made for its "commitment" to literary and social realities: "Problema todavía vigente en el que nadan múltiples conceptos no aclarados y se entrelazan equívocos sin fin; sin embargo, hay una necesidad de volver, a él, es como si a través de su esclarecimiento algo del secreto de un proceso de constitución de la cultura latinoamericana se esclareciera. Por de pronto, muchos piensan o sostienen que sin el modernismo no habría literatura de vanguardia, otros lo siguen enjuiciando como el gran traidor de esta historia, como si deliberadamente hubiera querido sustituir un proceso más legitimo que no se sabe bien cual es o cual hubiera podido ser. En todo caso, más acotadamente, protesis o solución genial, es necesario volver a pensar sus términos, su empresa, lo que puede significar en una historia que no es la de la literatura, con su mundo de valores y de exaltaciones ajustadas a necesidades de exaltación social, sino de la escritura latinoamericana, escena particular de la producción social, con su dramática por descubrir, con sus palpitaciones por reconocer" (104–105). ("A still valid problem is that not-very-clear, multiple concepts swim around, and endless mistaken ideas are interwoven. Nonetheless, there is a need to return to it; it is as if by way of its clarification, something secret of the constituting process of Spanish American culture might be cleared up. Meanwhile, many think or maintain that without *modernismo* there would be no literature of the avant-garde; others continue to judge it as the great traitor of this history, as if it had deliberately wanted to substitute a more legitimate process about which one cannot easily say what it is or what it could have been. In any case, more concretely, whether prothesis or inspired solution, it is necessary to think again about its terms, its enterprise, what it is able to signify in a history that isn't that of literature, with its world of values and passion adjusted to the needs of social exaltation, but of

Latin American writing, specific scene of social production, with its drama still to be discovered, with its heartbeat still to be recognized.")

28. In *Historia contemporánea de América Latina* (Madrid: Alianza, 1970), Tulio Halperín Donghi summarizes the economic changes in late nineteenth-century Latin America along with the accompanying realignment of social structure: "En 1880–años más, años menos–el avance en casi toda Hispanoamérica de una economía primaria y exportadora significa la sustitución finalmente consumada del pacto colonial impuesto por las metrópolis ibéricas por uno nuevo. A partir de entonces se va a continuar la marcha por el camino ya decididamente tomado. El crecimiento será aún más rápido que antes, pero estará acompañado de crisis de intensidad creciente: desde las primeras etapas de su afirmación, el orden neocolonial parece revelar a través de ellas los límites de sus logros; si no puede decirse que nace viejo— por el contrario, el vigor de su avance no tiene par en el pasado latinoamericano—nace por lo menos con los signos ya visibles de un agotamiento que llegará muy pronto. . . . Estos ejemplos, sin duda extremos, revelan, sin embargo, una tendencia más general: el debilitamiento de las clases altas terratenientes, pese a sus apoyos en estructuras políticas, comerciales y financieras locales, frente a los emisarios de las economías metropolitanas. Ese debilitamiento va acompañado de otro proceso, de intensidad variable según las regiones, por el cual las clases altas ven surgir a su lado las clases medias—predominantemente urbanas—cada vez máz exigentes, y en algunas zonas aún más limitadas deben enfrentar también las exigencias de sectores de trabajadores incorporados a formas de actividad económica modernizadas. Este último proceso . . . tiene su correlato político en un comienzo de democratización: mientras en México ésta se da revolucionariamente, en Argentina, Uruguay y Chile se manifiesta a través del acceso al poder de nuevos sectores mediante el sufragio universal" (280–282). ("Around 1880, the advance in almost all of Spanish America of a primary economy of exportation signified the finally concluded substitution of the colonial past, imposed by the Iberian metropolises, by a new one. Since then, the march has continued along that decidedly taken path. Growth would be even more rapid than before, but it would be accompanied by an intellectual crisis of growing intensity: from the first stages of its affirmation, the neocolonial order seemed to reveal, by means of these stages, the limits of its achievements; one cannot say that it was born old; on the contrary, the vigor of its advance has no equal in the history of Spanish America—it was born, at least, with the already visible signs of a rapidly arriving exhaustion. . . . These examples, doubtless extreme

ones, reveal nonetheless a more general tendency: the weakening of the landowning classes, in spite of their supports in local political, commercial and financial structures, in the face of the emissaries of the metropolitan economies. This weakening was accompanied by another process, varying in intensity according to region, by which the upper classes saw the rise of the middle classes—predominantly urban—growing more demanding. And in some more limited areas they had to face as well the demands of sectors of workers incorporated by modernized economic activity. This last process. . . . has its political correlate in a beginning of democratization: while in Mexico this is revolutionary, in Argentina, Uruguay and Chile it is manifested through access to the power of new sectors by universal suffrage.")

29. Halperín Donghi, *Historia,* summarizes the shifting of centers of power to the metropolis toward the end of the nineteenth century: "Al mismo tiempo que se afirma, el nuevo pacto colonial comienza a modificarse en favor de las metrópolis. La distribución de tareas entre ellas y las clases altas locales (que había comenzado por asignar a estas últimas en casi todos los casos la producción primaria y a las primeras la comercialización) aún allí donde se mantiene adquiere un sentido nuevo gracias a la organización cada vez menos libre de los mercados, facilitada por las tranformaciones técnicas pero vinculada sobre todo con la de las estructuras financieras. . . . La misma complejidad creciente de las actividades vinculadas con transporte y comercialización multiplica la presencia de esa economía en el área latinoamericana: no sólo los ferrocarriles, también frigoríficos, silos de cereales e ingenios de azúcar pasan a ser, en medida variable según las regiones, enclaves de la economía metropolitana en tierras marginales; en particular son las metrópolis de presencia más reciente las que se lanzan más agresivamente a la conquista de las economías dependientes, que culmina en la de la tierra" (281). ("At the same time it was affirmed, the new colonial pact began to be modified in favor of the metropolises. The distribution of functions between them and the local upper classes [which had begun in almost all cases by assigning primary commercialization to the metropolises], even there where it was maintained it acquired a new meaning thanks to the organization— ever less free—of the markets, facilitated by technical transformations but linked above all with financial structures. . . . The same growing complexity of the activities linked with transport and commercialization multiplied the presence of that economy in the Latin American area: not only railroads, but meat processors, grain silos, sugar refineries, came to be, in different degrees depending on the area, enclaves of the metropolitan economy in the marginal areas; in particular it was the

metropolises of most recent presence who launched most aggressively the conquest of the dependent economies, which culminated in the conquest of the land.")

30. Manuel González Prada. "Discurso en el Politeama," *Textos: una antología general* (México: SEP/UNAM, 1982), 47.

31. See also González Prada's essay on the artist as worker in "El intelectual y el obrero," in *Textos*, 191–198.

32. Walter Benjamin, "The Work of Art in the Age of Mechanical Reproduction," *Illuminations*, trans. Harry Zohn (New York: Schocken Books, 1973), 224; Michel Foucault, *Les mots et les choses* (Paris: Gallimard, 1966), 313.

33. Angel Rama, *Rubén Darío y el modernismo* (Caracas: Ediciones de la Biblioteca de la Universidad Central de Venezuela, 1970); Noé Jitrik, *Contradicciones del modernismo* (México: Colegio de México, 1978) and *Producción literaria y producción social* (Buenos Aires: Sudamericana, 1975); and Françoise Perus, *Literatura y sociedad en América Latina* (México: Siglo XXI, 1976), who counters part of Rama's analysis while focusing on economic and class divisions.

34. Paz, *Los hijos del limo* and *Cuadrivio*.

35. Rama, *Rubén Darío*, 52.

36. Rama, *Rubén Darío*, 53.

37. Roberto J. Payró, *La Revista Nacional* (Buenos Aires) 2 (1894): 341–342.

38. Rubén Darío, "Introducción a *Nosotros* por Roberto J. Payró," *Escritos inéditos de Rubén Darío*, ed. E. K. Mapes (New York: Instituto de las Españas en los Estados Unidos, 1938) (first published in *La Nación* [Buenos Aires], 1 May 1897), 100–101.

39. See Jitrik, *Contradicciones del modernismo*, for a study of *production* in Darío's poetics.

40. Paul Groussac, *La Biblioteca* 1 (1896): 5.

41. Severo Cascarrabias, "La propiedad literaria," *Buenos Aires* 2, (1894): 358–359.

42. Quoted in "Prólogo," *Antología de los poetas modernistas mexicanos (1884–1921)*, ed. José Emilio Pacheco (México: UNAM, 1970), 1 xlvi.

43. Jean Franco has commented on the exaltation of taste and its self-generating parody in *modernista* writing, placing it in the context of a dependent culture. Although the notion of a common bond between artists of all nations and social classes can be formulated by stressing their attack on bourgeois culture, there is a gap between the writer of the metropolis and the writer of the dependent culture: "A subtle gap is disclosed when the Spanish American writer . . . assiduously cultivates the manners and values of the metropolis and his

metropolitan peers, which often takes the form of explicit allusion to or exaggeration of that which can be understated (because obvious) in the primary culture. I am thinking here of the tendency of the Modernist, Rubén Darío, to dwell on cultural references, classical allusions and even luxury commodities for their own sake, implying a certain celebration of 'taste' whose canons the metropolis would take for granted. . . . Thus *Modernism* comes to imply not only a literary renewal under the influence of France but a certain exaltation of taste which the very notion of taste implies and which turns taste into a virtue extending into the moral realm itself." "Criticism and Literature within the Context of a Dependent Culture," *Occasional Papers* 15 (New York: Ibero-American Language and Area Center, New York University), 8.

44. Paz, *Cuadrivio*, 9.

45. José Martí, "El poema de Niágara," *Obras* (México: Editorial Porrúa, 1973), 174–175.

46. José Enrique Rodó, "Rubén Darío (Carta al Sr. Eugenio Díaz Romero)," *El Mercurio de America* 1 (1899): 81–93. For a study of Darío's "adaptation" of this text for use as a prologue see Sylvia Molloy's "Ser/Decir: Tácticas de un autorretrato," *Essays on Hispanic Literature in Honor of Edmund L. King*, ed. S. Molloy and L. Fernández Cifuentes (London: Tamesis Books, 1983), 187–199.

47. In discussing the poetry of "art for art's sake," Roman Jakobson has commented on the stress on the reality of the linguistic signs themselves, rather than on their representational value: "Qu'est-ce que la poésie?" in *Questions du Poétique* (Paris: Editions du Seuil, 1973) 122–125. In an era of inflation of linguistic signs, or modes of writing, a cult of language is aroused to restore confidence in it as a separate reality, rather than as a range of styles, all equally valid and therefore diminished in importance. The inflation of linguistic signs is seen as a corollary to the equally inflated diversification of objects, trades, or modes of behavior. The creation of a cult value of poetic language is an attempt to ward off its devalorization. Jakobson's observations may be applied with relevance to the attitudes of the *modernistas*. Because of their placement in a sphere lacking power and influence, they chose to exalt their isolation.

48. Roberto González Echevarría, "Modernidad, modernismo y nueva narrativa: el recurso del método," *Revista Interamericana de Bibliografía* 30 (1980): 157.

49. See n. 32, chap. 1, concerning Walter Benjamin's work.

50. See chap. 3 for the discussion of technology and eroticism in Lugones' *Las montañas del oro, (The Mountains of Gold)*.

51. The impact of growing technologies on North American literature in particular is examined by Leo Marx in *The Machine in the Garden* (New York: Oxford University Press, 1976). Juan Cano Ballesta discusses this topic in Spanish literature in *Literatura y tecnología: las letras españolas ante la revolución industrial* (Madrid: Orígenes, 1981).

52. See Saúl Yurkiévich, *Celebración del modernismo* (Barcelona: Tusquets Editor, 1976).

53. Aníbal González, "La escritura modernista y la filología," *Cuadernos Americanos* 40 (1981): 99–106. Using Octavio Paz' work as a point of departure, González discusses Paz' insistence on the critical tendency as *modernismo*'s most definite characteristic. González calls attention to the work of Renan, whose *L'avenir de la science* (1890), along with earlier works (*Vie de Jesus* [1863] and *Histoire générale et systeme comparé des langues sémitiques* [1855], was influential not only in contributing to the intellectual climate that formed the movement of naturalism but which infiltrated spheres even farther removed from the scientific realm. Philology, according to Renan, is "la *science exacte* des choses de l'esprit. Elle est aux sciences de l'humanité ce que la physique et la chimie sont a la science philosophique des corps" ("the *exact science* of the things of the spirit. It is to the human sciences what physics and chemistry are to the philosophic science of the body") (*L'avenir de la science: Pensées de 1848* [Paris: Calmann-Levy, 1890], 143, quoted in González, "La escritura," 96). González (101) also cites such examples of decadence, e.g., J. L. Huysmans' *A rebours* (1883), as an evasion of a direct confrontation with science in literature. The problematics of this proliferation of scientific information and theories have parallels in the proliferation of -*isms* toward the end of the century—Parnassianism, symbolism, naturalism, impressionism—indicating the urgency of self-definition for the science of "literature."

54. For a detailed review of the magazines of the epoch at the height of *modernismo,* see Boyd Carter, "El modernismo en las revistas literarias," *Chasqui* 8 (1979): 5–18; see also his more extensive study *Las Revistas Literarias de Hispanoamérica* (México: Ediciones de Andrea, 1959).

55. "Nuestros propósitos," *Revista de América* (facsimile edition) (Carbondale, Ill.: Latin American Institute, Southern Illinois University, 1970), 63, first published in 1 (August 1894).

56. *Revista de América,* 128 (first published in 3 [October 1894]: 58).

57. In "Martí y su 'Amor de cuidad grande': notas hacia la poética de *Versos libres*," in *Isla a su vuelo fugitiva* (Madrid: José Porrúa Turanzas, 1983), 27–42, González Echevarría singles out *Versos Libres* as the para-

dox of *modernista* poetry: "mientras que la poesía modernista—que
había hecho del mundo artificial de la ciudad, pletórico de productos
'finos' de la industria incipiente, manufacturados a base de materias
primas importadas por el creciente colonialismo, una segunda natur-
aleza—ostentaba el lustre de su perfección" ("while *modernista* poetry—
that had made a second nature of the artificial world of the city, over-
flowing with 'fine' products of an incipient industry, manufactured
with raw materials imported by a growing colonialism—showed off the
polish of its perfection") (30). With its "movimiento de contracción y
expanión," "El poema ['Amor de ciudad grande'] dramatiza de su
modo su propia meditación sobre un vacío que pronto se ve poblado
por su propio lenguaje. Temáticamente, la cuidad representa ese
lenguaje. El vacío antes del poema es el mundo anterior a la caída: la
ciudad, es el mundo post-edénico, babélico" (with its "movement of
contraction and expansion . . . the poem ['Amor de ciudad grande']
dramatizes in its way its own meditation of a vacuum that soon is filled
with its own language. Thematically, the city represents that language.
The vacuum facing the poem is the world before the fall; the city is the
post-Edenic, Babelic world") (11). González Echevarría accords this
poem a central place in the formation of the modern aesthetic.
"Reintegrar esos fragmentos de tiempo y palabra que pueblan el pres-
ente es la aventura de la poesía post-moderna—proferir el lenguaje de
la 'tierra baldía'—y a ello es a lo que apunta el poema de Martí" ("Reinte-
grating those fragments of time and words that populate the present is
the adventure of postmodern poetry—to utter the language of the
'waste land'—and that is what Martí's poem points to") (12).

   58. This discussion on the concepts of organic unity and "Genius"
draws to a large extent from the following studies: M. H. Abrams, *The
Mirror and the Lamp: Romantic Theory and the Critical Tradition* (New
York: Oxford University Press, 1953); Harold Bloom, ed., *Romanti-
cism and Consciousness: Essays in Criticism* (New York: W. W. Norton and
Co., 1970); Hugo Friedrich, *The Structure of Modern Poetry*, trans. Joa-
chim Neugroschel (Evanston, Ill.: Northwestern University Press,
1974); Northrop Frye, ed., *Romanticism Reconsidered* (New York: Co-
lumbia University Press, 1963); Octavio Paz, *Los hijos del limo*; and
Mario Praz, *The Romantic Agony*, trans. Angus Davidson, 2d ed. (Lon-
don: Oxford University Press, 1978).

   59. Emilio Carilla offers the most complete discussion of the diffu-
sion of romanticism in Latin America in *El romanticismo en la América
hispánica* (Madrid: Gredos, 1958).

   60. "The Concept of Romanticism," *Concepts of Criticism* (New
Haven: Yale University Press, 1971), 174.

   61. A good overview is presented by Hugo D. Barbagelata in "Vic-

tor Hugo y la América latina," *Revista Nacional* 56 (October 1952): 104–119.

62. See Suzanne Nash, *"Les Contemplations" of Victor Hugo: An Allegory of the Creative Process.* (Princeton, N.J. Princeton University Press, 1976), especially chap. 1.

63. *Concepts,* 167.

64. Julia Kristeva, *La révolution du langage poétique* (Paris: Editions du Seuil, 1974), 429.

65. Kristeva, *Révolution,* 437–438.

66. Groussac, "Boletín bibliográfico—*Los raros* de Rubén Darío," *La Biblioteca* 1 (1896): 480.

67. Lezama Lima, *La expresión americana,* 52.

68. Max Henríquez-Ureña, *Breve historia del modernismo* (México: Fondo de Cultura Económica, 1954), gives a detailed account of the influences and innovations of all the major *modernista* poets.

69. For a complete discussion of this aspect of Casal's work, see Robert Jay Glickman, *The Poetry of Julián del Casal: A Critical Edition,* 3 vols. (Gainesville, Fla.: The University Presses of Florida, 1978), 2: 178–217.

70. Amado Nervo, "El modernismo," *Obras completas,* ed. Francisco González Guerrero and Alfonso Méndez Plancarte, 2 vols. (Madrid: Aguilar, 1955–1956), 2: 397–398.

71. Edgar Allan Poe, "The Poetic Principle," *The Complete Poetry and Selected Criticism of Edgar Allan Poe,* ed. Allen Tate (New York: New American Library, 1968), 161.

72. Much romantic poetry is based on this parallel system of the inner journey as expressed through outward forms. According to Georges Poulet, this duality forms the conceptual base for the romantic hero: "Ainsi le héros romantique . . . débouchant par-delà la monisme sensualiste, fait l'experience de la dualité fondamentale de l'esprit centre et de la realité-péripherie" (135). "Le retrait de l'être en soi-même, loin de la nature extérieure, devient le principe même d'un nouveau retour vers la nature et, par conséquent, d'un nouvel épanouissement de l'être hors du centre où il s'est revigoré" ("Thus the romantic hero . . . emerging beyond the sensualist monism, experiences the fundamental duality of the spiritual center and peripheral reality" (135). "His retreat into himself, far from exterior nature, becomes the very principle of a new return to nature and, consequently, of a new expansion of the self outside the center where he has been renewed") (138). *Les métamorphoses du cercle* (Paris: Librairie Plon, 1961), 135–138.

73. Charles Baudelaire, "Théophile Gautier," *Oeuvres complètes* (Paris: Editions Gallimard, 1961), 690.

74. Stéphane Mallarmé, *Variations sur un sujet: Oeuvres complètes* (Paris: Gallimard, 1945), 368.

75. Rubén Darío, "Dilucidaciones," *El canto errante: poesías completas* (Madrid: Aguilar, 1968), 700.

76. Darío, "Dilucidaciones," 699.

77. *Las primeras letras de Leopoldo Lugones* (facsimile edition of his first literary works) (Buenos Aires: Ediciones Centurión, 1963), 68, first published in 1897, hereafter cited in text as *PL* with date of original publication.

2. LUGONES: POETRY, IDEOLOGY, HISTORY

1. In regard to the study of signifying systems in general, A. J. Greimas has treated the problem of perception as the ordering principle on which to base a study of the radical discontinuity of analogical systems. "La seule façon d'aborder le problème de la signification consiste à affirmer l'existence de discontinuités, sur le plan de la perception, et celle d'écarts différentiels (ainsi Lévi-Strauss), créateurs de signification sans se préoccuper de la nature des différences perçues." ("The only way of approaching the problem of signification consists of affirming the existence of discontinuities in the perception plane, and of differential distances [thus Lévi-Strauss], these being creators of signification, without worrying about the nature of perceived difference." *Sémantique structurale* (Paris: Larousse, 1966), 18.

Using this statement as a point of departure, it is thus possible to speak of adaptations of systems of iconography in a historical sense, keeping in mind that these systems of reference do not remain constant, nor does the idea of "borrowing" patterns of frameworks of imagery imply that their reception and transposition involves a faithful rendering of the total content. Following the lead taken by Greimas, Umberto Eco has stressed the primary importance of studying foremost the pattern of perception, rather than the referential link of the sign to its object: "le rapport code–message ne regarde pas la nature du signe iconique, *mais la mécanique elle-même de la perception, qui, à la limite, peut-être considérée comme un fait de communication,* comme un processus qui s'engendre seulement quand, par rapport à un apprentissage, on a conféré une signification à des stimuli déterminés et pas à d'autres" ("the code–message relationship doesn't concern the nature of the iconic sign, *but rather the very mechanism of perception, which, in the end, can be considered as a fact of communication,* as a process only engendered when, in relation to an apprenticeship, a signification has been granted to certain stimuli, but not to others"). "Sémiologie des messages visuels," *Communications* 15 (1970): 14.

2. Roberto F. Guisti, "Leopoldo Lugones: a propósito de *Lunario sentimental*," *Nosotros* 3 (Jul.–Aug. 1909): 290.

3. Giusti, "Leopoldo Lugones," 294.

4. Amado Nervo, "Leopoldo Lugones," *Obras completas*, 2 vols., ed. Francisco González Guerrero and Alfonso Méndez Plancarte (Madrid: Aguilar, 1955–1956), 2: 289.

5. Rubén Darío, "Un poeta socialista," *Escritos inéditos de Rubén Darío*, ed. E. K. Mapes (New York: Instituto de las Españas, 1938), 102–103.

6. Ezequiel Martínez Estrada, *Leopoldo Lugones: retrato sin tocar* (Buenos Aires: Emecé, 1968), 113.

7. Rámon López Velarde, "La corona y el cetro de Lugones," *Obras completas* (México: Fondo de Cultura Económica, 1952), 478.

8. López Velarde, "La corona," 479.

9. López Velarde, "La corona," 478.

10. See the discussion of López Velarde's work in the final chapter.

11. Carlos Altamirano and Beatriz Sarlo, "Vanguardia y criollismo: la aventura de 'Martín Fierro,' " *Ensayos argentinos: De Sarmiento a la vanguardia* (Buenos Aires: Centro Editor, 1983), 137–138.

12. See the discussion of Storni's work in the final chapter.

13. Alfonsina Storni, "Alrededor de la muerte de Lugones," *Nosotros* (Número extraordinario dedicado a Leopoldo Lugones), 2 (May–Jul. 1938): 118–121.

14. Storni, "Alrededor de la muerte," 220.

15. Leopoldo Marechal, "Filípica a Lugones y a otras especies de anteayer," in *El periódico "Martín Fierro,"* ed. Adolfo Prieto (Buenos Aires: Editorial Galerna, 1968), 65.

16. Walter Benjamin, "The Work of Art," 249.

17. Jorge Luis Borges, with Betina Edelberg, *Leopoldo Lugones* (Buenos Aires: Editorial Troquel, 1955), 30.

18. Jorge Luis Borges, "La adjetivación," in *El tamaño de mi esperanza* (Buenos Aires: Editorial Proa, 1926), 55.

19. Jorge Luis Borges, "Palabrería para versos," in *El tamaño de mi esperanza* (Buenos Aires: Editorial Proa, 1926), 45, 47.

20. "Una encuesta a *Nosotros*," in *La revista "Nosotros,"* ed. Noemí Ulla (Buenos Aires: Editorial Galerna, 1969), 241–338.

21. Julio Noé, rev. of *El payador* (first published in 1916), in *La revista "Nosotros,"* ed. Noemí Ulla, 136.

22. Borges, "Leopoldo Lugones," *Inter-American Review of Bibliography* 13 (1963): 145.

23. Borges, with Edelberg, *Leopoldo Lugones,* 97.

24. Borges, with Edelberg, *Leopoldo Lugones,* 31.

25. Borges, "Prólogo," *Antología poética argentina* (Buenos Aires: Sudamericana, 1941), 8. See also the discussion of Lugones' influence on the *ultraístas* in Pedro Luis Barcia, "Lugones y el ultraísmo," *Estudios literarios* (La Plata: Universidad Nacional de la Plata, Facultad de Humanidades y Ciencias de la Educación, 1966), 149–193.

26. Jorge Luis Borges, "Prólogo," *Indice de la nueva poesía americana,* ed. Alberto Hidalgo et al. (Buenos Aires: Sociedad de Publicaciones El Inca, 1926), 15.

27. López Velarde, "La corona . . . , 479.

28. Harold Bloom, *The Anxiety of Influence* (New York: Oxford University Press, 1973), offers a persuasive view of precursor influence.

29. In this preface Darío responds to those who accuse him of imitating foreign models: "Yo no tengo literatura 'mía'—como lo ha manifestado una magistral autoridad—para marcar el rumbo de los demás: mi literatura es *mía* en mí; quien siga servilmente mis huellas perderá su tesoro personal y, paje o esclavo, no podrá ocultar sello o librea. Wagner, a Augusta Holmes, su discípula, dijo un día: 'Lo primero, no imitar a nadie, y sobre todo, a mí.' Gran decir." ("I didn't make 'my' literature–as a masterful critic has shown–to mark out the path for others: my literature is 'mine' within myself; whoever servilely follows my traces will lose his personal treasure and, page or slave, cannot hide its seal or livery. Wagner said one day to Augusta Holmes, his disciple: 'First don't imitate anyone, and above all, me.' A great statement.") "Palabras liminares," *Prosas profanas,* in Poesías completas (Madrid: Aguilar, 1968), 545.

30. See bibliography for references, especially, Bischoff, Canedo, and Dardo Cúneo.

31. For example, "El pañuelo" was published in *El Tiempo,* 24 Aug. 1897, and later included in *Los crepúsculos del jardín* (1905). Among other poems later included in this volume were "El Buque," "La vejez de Anacreonte," "Hortus deliciarum," all published in *El Mercurio de América* in 1899, while the poems of "Ramillete" were also published in 1899 in *Buenos Aires.* As early as 1897 "Taburete para máscaras," included in *Lunario sentimental* (1909), was published in *El Tiempo.*

32. Pierina Lidia Moreau examines some of the early journalism in *Leopoldo Lugones y el simbolismo* (Buenos Aires: Ediciones "La Reja," 1972). Alfredo Canedo studies the early journalistic works in a study of Lugones' political activities and writings in *Aspectos del pensamiento político de Leopoldo Lugones* (Buenos Aires: Ediciones Marcos, 1974).

33. See chap. 2, n. 31.

34. In *Las contradicciones del modernismo* Noé Jitrik calls for a reeval-

uation of *modernismo* and for a clarification of its relation to parallel systems of production. His questioning of the evolution of *modernismo* as a social phenomenon could well be applied to the particular case of Lugones: "¿[P]or qué, desde ese comienzo combativo, pasa a convertirse, al cabo de cierto tiempo, en el código poético más oficial y académico, como si hubiera llegado a la universalidad y la estuviera definiendo de modo tal por sus rasgos que la cultura no puede que rendirse totalmente?" (107). ("Why does it [*modernismo*] abandon its initial, combative stance to become, after a certain time, the most official and academic poetic code, as if it had achieved universality and, by definition of its characteristics, culture should completely surrender to it?")

35. Robert Mario Scari, "La formación literaria de Lugones," dissertation, University of California, Berkeley, 1963, 27.

36. *El Payador y antología de poesía y prosa*, ed. Guillermo Ara (Caracas: Ayacucho, 1979), 15.

37. Octavio Electro Corvalán, "La madurez de Leopoldo Lugones," dissertation, Yale University, 1971, 4.

38. Domingo F. Sarmiento, *Obras* (Reimpresión Paris: Belín Hermanos, 1909), 1: 318, cited in Boyd G. Carter, *Las revistas literarias de Hispanoamérica* (México: Ediciones de Andrea, 1959).

39. Barthes, *Writing Degree Zero*, 20.

40. *La Montaña*, 1 (June 1897): 4.

41. As has been noted, these ideas are common currency in Lugones' time. However, his reference to "el concepto idealista" and his frequent references to Remy de Gourmont suggest that the following passages from "L'idéalisme" may have been an influence on Lugones' thinking: "L'art est libre de toute la liberté de la conscience; il est son propre juge et son propre esthète. . . . L'Art (que je considère ici comme une des *Facultés* de l'âme individuelle) est donc de même que l'individu lui-même: anormal, illogique et incompréhensible." ("Art is free with all freedom of conscience; it is its own judge and its own aesthete. . . . Art [which I consider here as one of the *Faculties* of the individual spirit] is then one with the individual himself: abnormal, illogical and incomprehensible.") Remy de Gourmont, *Le chemin de velours* (Paris: Mercure de France, 1911), 228–229.

42. Frederic Jameson, *Marxism and Form* (Princeton, N.J.: Princeton University Press, 1971), 85.

3. LUGONES AS *MODERNISTA* POET

1. As Northrop Frye has noted, the totalizing impulse in romantic poetry is "akin to romance, with its effort to maintain a self-consistent

idealized world without the intrusions of realism or irony." The perspective is important for an understanding of individual images and their organization in Lugones' work. Northrop Frye, "The Drunken Boat: The Revolutionary Element in Romanticism," *Romanticism Reconsidered*, ed. N. Frye (New York: Columbia University Press, 1963), 11.

2. Paz, *Cuadrivio*, 14.

3. Noé Jitrik, *Leopold Lugones: mito nacional* (Buenos Aires: Editorial Palestra, 1960), 12.

4. Jitrik, *Leopoldo Lugones*, 12.

5. Jitrik, *Leopold Lugones*, 43.

6. Amado Nervo, "Leopoldo Lugones," 2: 390.

7. Rubén Darío, "Leopoldo Lugones," *Semblanzas: obras completas,* 5 vols., ed. M. Sanmiguel Raimúndez (Madrid: Afrodisio Aguado, 1950), 2: 993.

8. Darío, "Leopoldo Lugones," 2: 992–993.

9. Leopoldo Lugones, *Obras poéticas completas,* ed. Pedro Miguel Obligado, 3d ed. (Madrid: Aguilar, 1959), 99, hereafter cited in text as *OPC* with page number.

10. See chap. 1, n. 72, and Georges Poulet, *Les métamorphoses du cercle,* 135–138.

11. In his discussion of Ludwig Binswanger's work on imagination, Paul DeMan uses the category of the "upward fall," the involuntary swing produced by the desire for transcendence, to describe the search for poetic self-knowledge. *Blindness and Insight* (New York: Oxford University Press, 1971), 48–49.

12. See also Juan José Hernández, "Leopoldo Lugones: la luna doncella en su poesía erótica," *Cuadernos Hispanoamericanos* 371 (1981): 266–280.

13. The history of the presentation of the *femme fatale* in romantic and postromantic literature is outlined by Mario Praz in chap. 4, "La belle dame sans merci," of *Romantic Agony,* trans. Angus Davidson, 2d ed. (London: Oxford University Press, 1978), 197–300.

14. "Ainsi, le couple *jour/nuit* n'oppose pas deux contraires à parts égales, car la nuit est beaucoup plus le contraire du jour que le jour n'est le contraire de la nuit. En vérité, la nuit n'est que *l'autre* du jour, ou encore, comme on l'a dit d'un mot brutal et décisif, son *envers.* Et cela, bien sûr, est sans réciproque. Aussi la valorisation poétique de la nuit est-elle presque toujours sentie comme une reaction, comme une contrevalorisation. . . . C'est que la préference accordée à la nuit n'est pas, comme elle le prétend, un choix licite et sanctionné (sanctifié) par l'adhésion divine, mais au contraire un choix coupable, un parti pris

de l'interdit, une transgression." ("Thus, the pair day/night does not oppose two equal opposites, for night is much more the opposite of day than day is the opposite of night. Truly, night is only day's other, or rather, as has been said in a brutal and decisive word, its inverse. And that, certainly, is without reciprocal. Thus, the poetic valorization of the night is almost always felt as a reaction, as a countervalorization. . . . The preference accorded to the night is not, as it pretends to be, a licit choice sanctioned [sanctified] by divine adherence, but, on the contrary, a culpable choice, a decision to do the forbidden, a transgression.") Gérard Genette, *Figures II* (Paris: Editions du Seuil, 1969), 106–107.

15. Saúl Yurkiévich, *Celebración del modernismo* (Barcelona: Editorial Tusquets, 1976), 49–74.

LOS CREPÚSCULOS DEL JARDÍN: SUBVERSION, IRONY, PARODY

1. See n. 14 in chap. 1.
2. In *Esthétique et théorie du roman,* trans. Daria Oliver (Paris: Editions Gallimard, 1978), Mikhail Bakhtine discusses the difficulties in establishing the *intentionality* of a parodic discourse: "Dès lors dans certains cas, il est fort difficile de décider de ce qui apparaît à l'auteur comme un élément déjà canonisé du langage littéraire, et de ce qui donne encore le sentiment d'un plurilinguisme. Plus l'oeuvre analysée se trouve éloignée de notre conscience moderne, plus cette difficulté est sérieuse" (229). ("Thus, in certain cases, it is extremely difficult to distinguish between what appeared to the author as an already canonized element of literary language and what again gives the sense of plurilingualism. The more distant the work being analyzed is from our modern consciousness, the more difficult this problem becomes.")
3. Roland Barthes, in his definition or irony and parody in *S/Z* (Paris: Editions de Seuil, 1970), speaks of irony as a trope that respects the paternity of the text, whereas the multivalent text transgresses the boundaries of literary property: "Car la multivalence (démentie par l'ironie) est une transgression de la propriété. Il s'agit de traverser le mur de la voix pour atteindre l'écriture: celle-ci refuse toute designation de propriété et par conséquent ne peut jamais être *ironique;* ou du moins son ironie n'est jamais sûre (incertitude qui marque quelques grands textes: Sade, Fourier, Flaubert)" (52). ("For the multivalence [denied by irony] is a transgression of property. It is a matter of scaling the wall of the voice in order to reach writing: the latter refuses all designations as property and consequently can never be *ironic,* or at

least its irony is never certain [a lack of certainty which marks some great texts: Sade, Fourier, Flaubert].")

4. For a discussion of the automatization of literary forms in relation to their social or literary series, see J. Tynianov, "De l'évolution littéraire," *Théorie de la littérature* (Paris: Editions du Seuil, 1965), 125.

5. Charles Baudelaire, "Le Peintre de la vie moderne." *Oeuvres complètes* (Paris: Editions Gallimard, 1961), 1167.

6. Gilles Deleuze, *Logique du Sens* (Paris: Editions de Minuit, 1969), 332.

7. Albert Samain, *Au Jardin de l'infante* (Buenos Aires: Viau, 1944), 45.

8. Robert M. Scari, *"Los crepúsculos del jardín* de Leopoldo Lugones," *Revista Iberoamericana* 25 (1964): 105–121.

9. Samain, *Au Jardin,* 61.

10. Samain, *Au Jardin,* 102.

11. Samain, *Au Jardin,* 135.

12. Leopoldo Lugones, "Prólogo," *Castalia bárbara y otros poemas,* by Ricardo Jaimes Freyre (México: Cultura, 1920), ix–x.

13. Lugones, "Prólogo," *Castalia,* xiii–xiv.

14. Lugones, "Prólogo," *Castalia,* xiv.

15. Lugones, "Prólogo," *Castalia,* xix.

16. Lugones, "Prólogo," Castalia, vii.

17. Such poets reject a vision of seduction, implicit in much *modernista* poetry, which has been described by critics such as Jean Baudrillard. The body's static role in the seduction play is commented on by Baudrillard in *De la séduction* (Paris: Editions Galilée, 1979): "Ainsi dans la séduction, la femme est sans corps propre, et sans désir propre. Mais qu'est-ce que le corps, es qu'est-ce que le désir? Elle n'y croit pas, et elle en joue. N'ayant pas de corps propre, elle se fait apparence pure, construction artificielle où vient se prendre le désir de l'autre. Toute la séduction consiste à laisser croire à l'autre qu'il est et reste le sujet du désir, sans se prendre elle-même à ce piège. . . . Pour la séduction, le désir n'est pas une fin, c'est un enjeu hypotétique" (119). ("Thus in seduction, the woman is lacking her own body, and her own desire. But what is the body, and what is desire? She doesn't believe in it, and plays a game. Not having her own body, she becomes pure appearance, an artificial construction where the other places his desire. All seduction consists in letting the other believe that he is and continues to be the subject of desire, without herself falling into the trap. . . . For seduction, desire is not an end in itself; it is a hypothetical gamble.")

18. Deleuze, *Logique du Sens,* 166.

5. *LUNARIO SENTIMENTAL* AND THE DESTRUCTION OF *MODERNISMO*

1. Paz, *Cuadrivio*, 36.
2. Baudelaire, *Oeuvres*, 989–990.
3. Baudelaire, *Oeuvres*, 683.
4. Baudelaire, *Oeuvres*, 1179.
5. For a detailed examination of Lugones' adaptations from Laforgue's poetry, see the following studies: Marie-Josèphe Faurie, "Imagination créatrice—Lugones ou le ruisellement des images," *Le Modernisme hispanoaméricain et ses sources francaises* (Paris: Institut d'Études Hispaniques, 1966), 221–240. Allen W. Phillips, "Notas sobre una afinidad poética: Jules Laforgue y el Lugones del *Lunario sentimental*," *Estudios y notas sobre literatura hispanoamericana* (México: Editorial Cultura, 1965), 53–72; and Raquel Halty Ferguson, *Laforgue y Lugones: dos poetas de la luna* (London: Tamesis, 1981).
6. Warren Ramsey presents a complete study of the life, work, and influence of Laforgue in *Jules Laforgue and the Ironic Inheritance* (New York: Oxford University Press, 1953).
7. Jules Laforgue, "Étonnement," *Poésies complètes* (Paris: Editions Gallimard et Librairie Générale Francaise, 1970), 452.
8. Laforgue, *Poésies*, 127–128:

> L'Inconscient, c'est l'Eden-Levant que tout saigne;
> Si la Terre ne veut sécher, qu'elle s'y baigne!
> C'est la grand Nounou où nous nous aimerions
> A la grâce des divines sélections.
> C'est le Tout-Vrai, l'Omniversel Ombdelliforme
> Mancenilier, sous qui, mes bébés, faut qu'on dorme!

> (The unconscious, it is the Eden-East that all bleeds;
> If the Earth doesn't want to dry herself, let her bathe there!
> It is the great Nanny where we would love each other
> at the hands of divine selection.
> It is the Whole Truth, the Omniversal Ombdelliform
> Manchineel tree, under which, my babes, one must sleep!)

9. Walter Benjamin, *Charles Baudelaire: A Lyric Poet in the Era of High Capitalism* (London: New Left Books, 1973).
10. Borges, with Edelberg, *Leopoldo Lugones*, 78.
11. For discussions of the trope of irony see José Ferrater Mora, "De la ironía a la admiración," *Cuestiones disputadas: ensayos de filosofía* (Madrid: Revista de Occidente, 1955), 27–103; and Hayden White, "The Historical Imagination between Mataphor and Irony," *Metahistory* (Baltimore: Johns Hopkins University Press, 1973), 45–80.

12. Baudelaire, *Oeuvres*, 981.

13. Carlos Navarro, "La visión del mundo en el *Lunario sentimental*," *Revista Iberoamericana* 30 (1964): 133–152.

14. Gérard Genette treats the structure of metonymy in "Métonymie Chez Proust," *Figures III* (Paris: Seuil, 1977), 42–43.

15. The process of exaggeration which will be used to achieve this sensation of emptiness is prefigured in the *Los crepúsculos del jardín*, especially in the "Loas de nuestra servidumbre." What an image should suggest is explicitly stated along with the image itself, as in "Canto del amor y de la noche":

> La luna, histerizando celestes albores,
> Aparece, estañada por la bruma,
> Tras cipreses agudos como apagadores.
> En esbozo harto zurdo
> Que transparenta monstruosos reveses,
> Resbalan con desnivel absurdo
> Aquella luna y aquellos cipreses.
> Y la vislumbre tibia,
> Sugiriendo congojas de almas crédulas
> Arde como una lúgubre lascivia
> Cual pálido alcohol en nuestras médulas.
> *(OPC, 171)*

> (The moon, exciting celestial dawns,
> Appears, galvanized by the mist,
> Behind cypresses sharp like extinguishers.
> In a clumsy sketch
> Which shows monstrous revisions,
> That moon, those cypresses,
> slip with absurd unevenness.
> And the lukewarm glimmer,
> Suggesting the anguish of credulous souls
> Burns with a dismal lewdness
> Like pale alcohol in our medulas.)

or in "Canto de la tarde y de la muerte":

> Y, a cada paso,
> En la ilusoria monstruosidad de un mueble.
> En los tapices de marchito raso,
> Sentíamos la inminencia del caso
> Que hacía peligrar tu ser endeble.
> *(OPC, 176)*

(And, with each step,
In the illusory monstrosity of a piece of furniture,
In the upholsteries of withered satin,
We perceived the imminence of the event
That endangered your frail being.)

6. THE FRENZY OF *MODERNISMO:* HERRERA Y REISSIG

1. Julio Herrera y Reissig, "El círculo de la muerte," *Páginas escogidas* (Barcelona: Casa Editorial Maucci, 1919), 245, n. 1.

2. Yuri Lotman, *Analysis of the Poetic Text*, ed. and trans. D. Barton Johnson (Ann Arbor, Mich.: Ardis Press, 1976), 26.

3. Federico García Lorca, "Presentación de Pablo Neruda en la Facultad de Filosofía y Letras de Madrid," *Obras completas*, 2 vols., ed. Arturo del Hoyo (Madrid: Aguilar, 1974), 1: 1184.

4. Arturo Torres Rioseco, *Precursores del modernismo: Casal, Guitiérrez Nájera, Martí, Silva* (Madrid: Calpe, 1925), 10.

5. Torres Rioseco, *Precursores*, 10.

6. Quoted in C. Sabat Ercasty and Manuel de Castro, "Opiniones sobre Julio Herrera y Reissig," *Antología lírica de Herrera y Reissig* (Santiago: Ercilla, 1939), 41.

7. In Sabat Ercasty and de Castro, "Opiniones," 42.

8. In Sabat Ercasty and de Castro, "Opiniones," 41.

9. In Sabat Ercasty and de Castro, "Opiniones," 19.

10. Oscar Hahn, "Herrera y Reissig o el discreto encanto de lo 'cursi,' " *Texto Crítico* 5 (1979): 261–266.

11. Severo Sarduy, *Escrito*, 51.

12. For a discussion of the influence of Samain, Lugones, and the plagiarism polemic concerning the origin of these poems, see: Roberto Leviller, "Herrera y Reissig y Lugones," *Hommage a Ernest Martinenche* (Paris: Editions D'Artry, 1939), 262–270; Víctor Pérez Petit, "El pleito Lugones—Herrera y Reissig," *Nosotros* 2 (1938): 227–244; and Guillermo de Torre, *La aventura y el orden* (Buenos Aires: Losada, 1948), 89–97.

13. Julio Herrera y Reissig, *Poesías completas y páginas en prosa*, ed. Roberto Bula Píriz (Madrid: Aguilar, 1961), 156, hereafter cited in text as *PC* with page number.

14. Roland Barthes, *The Pleasure of the Text*, trans. Richard Miller (New York: Hill & Wang, 1975), 55.

15. Julio Herrera y Reissig, "Conceptos de crítica," *Prosas: Crítica, cuentos, comentarios* (Montevideo: Máximo García, 1918), 40.

16. Herrera y Reissig, *Prosas*, 46.

17. Herrera y Reissig, *Prosas*, 28.
18. Herrera y Reissig, *Prosas*, 30.
19. Herrera y Reissig, *Prosas*, 32–33.
20. Herrera y Reissig, *Prosas*, 33–34.
21. Herrera y Reissig, *Prosas*, 34.
22. Herrera y Reissig, *Prosas*, 35.
23. Emir Rodríquez Monegal, "La Generación del 900," *Número* 2 (1950): 43.
24. José Enrique Rodó, cited in Rodríguez Monegal, 49–50.
25. Herrera y Reissig, *Prosas*, 34.
26. Rodríguez Monegal, 53.
27. Julio Herrera y Reissig, *Obras completas* (Madrid: Aguilar, 1961), 827.
28. Angel Rama, "La estética de Julio Herrera y Reissig: el travestido de la muerte," *Revista de la Facultad de Humanidades de Puerto Rico* (Río Piedras), Sobretiro, 26, quoted in Rogelio Mirza, *Herrera y Reissig: Antología, estudio crítico, y notas* (Montevideo: Arca, 1975), 30.
29. Rama, cited in Mirza, *Herrera y Reissig*, 31.
30. Yuri Lotman, *The Structure of the Artistic Text*, trans. Ronald Vroon, Michigan Slavic Contributions 7 (Ann Arbor, Mich.: University of Michigan Press,1977), 190. (See also n. 47 on Roman Jakobson in chap. 1).
31. Lotman, *Structure*, 193.
32. Lotman, *Structure*, 194.
33. Lotman, *Structure*, 194.
34. Allen W. Phillips, "La metáfora en la obra de Julio Herrera y Reissig," *Revista Iberoamericana* 16 (1950): 31–48.
35. Phillips, "La metáfora," 40.
36. Mario Praz, *The Romantic Agony*, 2d ed. (London: Oxford University Press, 1978), 303, quoted in Lily Litvak, *Erotismo fin de siglo* (Barcelona: Antoni Bosch, 1979), 98.
37. See n. 65, chap. 1, on the subject (Julia Kristeva).
38. W. J. T. Mitchell reminds us of the kind of spatial mapping that readers use to guide themselves through a fictional or poetic text in which history or narrative continuity are replaced by features of simultaneity and discontinuity: "The traditional comparisons of space and time to body and soul seem worth keeping in mind, for it expresses in a concise way the main elements of our experience of both modalities. Space is the body of time, the form or image that gives us an intuition of something that is not directly perceivable but which permeates all that we apprehend. Time is the soul of space, the invisible entity which animates the field of our experience" (227–278). W. J. T. Mitch-

ell, "Spatial Form in Literature: Toward a General Theory," *The Language of Images,* ed. W. J. T. Mitchell (Chicago: University of Chicago Press, 1980), 271–299.

39. Georges Bataille, *L'Erotisme* (Paris: Editions de Minuit, 1957), 24.

40. Bataille, *L'Erotisme,* 25.

41. For a discussion of eroticism within the surrealist movement, see Xavière Gauthier, *Surréalisme et sexualité* (Paris: Gallimard, 1971).

42. Darío, *Poesías completas,* 673.

43. Paz, *Cuadrivio,* 11–65.

44. Deleuze, *Logique du Sens,* 328.

45. Raúl Blengio Brito, *Herrera y Reissig: del romanticismo a la vanguardia* (Montevideo: Universidad de la República, División Publicaciones y Ediciones, 1978), 150.

46. Blengio Brito, *Herrera y Reissig,* 151.

47. For a review of the legends about Herrera y Reissig and biographical studies on him, see "El País de los jueves extraordinario en homenaje a Julio Herrera y Reissig," ed. Arturo Sergio Visca, Special Supplement to *El País* (Montevideo) June 5, 12, 18, 1975.

48. "Julio Herrera y Reissig: seis años de poesía," *Número* (Montevideo) 2 (1950): 118–161; and "La Torre de las esfinges como tarea," *Número* 2 (1950): 601–609.

49. See Mirza, *Herrera y Reissig,* 22–23. Among other studies named in the bibliography, see two short essays: Ana Victoria Mondada, "Introducción," *Poesía de Julio Herrera y Reissig* (México: Porrúa, 1977), ix–xxv; and Angel Luis Morales, "Julio Herrera y Reissig," *Introduccíon a la literatura hispanoamericana* (Río Piedras, P.R.: Editorial Edil, 1974), 312–320.

50. Clara Silva, "Realidad idealizada," *El país de los jueves extraordinario,* 19.

51. Roland Barthes, *Sade, Fourier, Loyola,* trans. Richard Miller (New York: Hill and Wang, 1976), 127–128.

52. Ramón López Velarde, *Poesías completas y el minutero* (México: Editorial Porrúa, 1971), 264.

53. López Velarde, *Poesías,* 265.

7. *MODERNISMO'S* LEGACY IN THREE POETS: VALLEJO, LÓPEZ VELARDE, AND STORNI

1. Carlos Blanco-Aguinaga offers a reading of "consumerism" in *modernista* aesthetics in "Crítica marxista y poesía: Lectura de un poema de Julián del Casal," *The Analysis of Hispanic Texts: Current*

Trends in Methodology, ed. Mary Ann Beck et al. (New York: Bilingual Press, 1976), 191–205.

2. For a discussion of the role of the spectator in the visual arts, see John Berger, *Ways of Seeing* (London: British Broadcasting Corporation and Penguin Books, 1978); and Roland Barthes, *Images, Music, Text,* trans. Stephen Heath (New York: Hill & Wang, 1977).

3. César Vallejo, *Obras completas,* 3 vols. (Lima: Mosca Azul Editores, 1973–1974), vol. 3, *Obra poética completa,* 243 (hereafter referred to in text as *CV* with page number).

4. For a discussion of the influence of Leopoldo Lugones and Julio Herrera y Reissig in the work of Vallejo, see the following: André Coyné, *César Vallejo* (Buenos Aires: Ediciones Nueva Visión, 1968), 51; Luis Monguió, *César Vallejo: vida y obra* (New York: Hispanic Institute, 1952), 49–50; and Saúl Yurkiévich, *Fundadores de la nueva poesía latinoamericana: Vallejo, Huidobro, Borges, Neruda, Paz* (Barcelona: Barral Editores, 1971), 16.

5. For a discussion of these factors in Vallejo's work, see Jean Franco, *César Vallejo: The Dialectics of Poetry and Silence* (Cambridge: Cambridge University Press, 1976).

6. For a discussion of the concept of *fetish* used in this sense, see n. 1, chap. 1; Baudrillard, *For a Critique,* 92; and Benjamin, *Charles Baudelaire,* 104–105, 166.

7. Roberto Fernández Retamar, "Prólogo," *César Vallejo: obras poéticas completas* (La Habana: Casa de las Américas, 1965), xii.

8. Paz, "El camino de la pasión (Ramón López Velarde)," *Cuadrivio,* 67–130.

9. Pablo Neruda, "Ramón López Velarde," *Para nacer he nacido* (Barcelona: Editorial Bruguera, 1978), 185–186.

10. Neruda, "Ramón López Velarde," 185.

11. Ramón López Velarde, *Poesías completas y el minutero* (México: Editorial Porrúa, 1971), 234, hereafter cited in text as *LV* with page number.

12. Xavier Villarrutia, "La poesía de Ramón López Velarde," *El león y la virgen* (México: Ediciones de La UNAM, 1942), xxii.

13. Ramón López Velarde, "José Juan Tablada," *Obras,* ed. José Luis Martínez (México: Fondo de Cultura Económica, 1971), 507–508.

14. López Velarde, *Obras,* 476.

15. A discussion of the presence of Fuensanta in López Velarde's work is found in Otto Olivera, "El ideal femenino en la obra de López Velarde," in *Honor of Boyd G. Carter,* ed. Catherine Vera and G. Mc-

Murray (Laramie, Wyo.: The University of Wyoming Press, 1981), 77–83.

16. See chap. 1, n. 7, on Baudrillard.

17. López Velarde, *Obras,* 449–512.

18. Neruda, "Ramón López Velarde," 185.

19. Alfonsina Storni, *Obras completas* (Buenos Aires: Sociedad Editora Latinoamericana, 1976), 1: 108 (hereafter cited in text as *AS* with page number).

20. John Freccero examines the Medusa image in Dante's allegory as a basis for a discussion of a poetics of reification versus transcendence in "Medusa: The Letter and the Spirit," *Yearbook of Italian Studies* (Florence: A Publication of Italian Cultural Institute, 1972), 1–18.

21. Claudine Herrmann, from *Les Voleuses de langue,* trans. M. R. Schuster, in *New French Feminisms: An Anthology,* ed. Elaine Marks and Isabelle de Courtivon (Amherst, Mass.: University of Massachusetts Press, 1980), 170, 171.

22. Rachel Phillips, *Alfonsina Storni: From Poetress to Poet* (London: Tamesis, 1975), 118, n. 36. Here Phillips cites other critics' objections to the obscurity of Storni's reference.

23. In "Exámenes" from *Analecta del reloj,* José Lezama Lima explores the Cassandra myth "a fin de aislar el devaneo que provoca experiencias en la poesía" ("in order to isolate the delirium that provokes experiences in poetry"), from which follows a series of questionings about the origins of poetry. Although not in reference to any work by Storni, Lezama's questionings evoke possibilities that can be significant in a study of the transformations in her work, for example: "El sueño aprovechada también por la sierpe, aprovechado allí donde mejor testifica, calmándose en un oída que se la brinda como espiral, inalcanzable sucesivo que devora en cuanto testifica y aguarda esa lenta destrucción de lo sagrado" ("The dream also used by the serpent, used where it best testifies, sounding in an ear that is offered to it like an unreachable, successive spiral that devours as soon as it testifies and awaits that slow destruction of the sacred). Lezama Lima, *Obras completas,* 2: 214–227.

24. Susan Sontag, *On Photography* (New York: Farrar, Strauss and Giroux, 1977).

Bibliography

REFERENCES ON SPANISH AMERICAN LITERATURE

Abril, Xavier. *César Vallejo o la teoría poética*. Madrid: Taurus, 1962.

———. *Exégesis Trílcica*. Lima: Editorial Gráfica Labor, 1980.

Alegría, Fernando. *Walt Whitman en Hispanoamérica*. México: Colección Studium, 1954.

Altamirano, Carlos, and Beatriz Sarlo. *Ensayos argentinos: de Sarmiento a la vanguardia*. Buenos Aires: Centro Editor, 1983.

Andrade, Olegario V. *Obras poéticas*. Buenos Aires: Academia Argentina de Letras, 1943.

Ara, Guillermo, *Leopoldo Lugones*. Buenos Aires: Editorial Mandrágora, 1958.

———. *Leopoldo Lugones: uno y múltiple*. Buenos Aires: Ediciones Maru, 1947.

Arrieta, Rafael Alberto. *Introducción al modernismo literario*. Buenos Aires: Editorial Columba, 1956.

Ashhurst, Anna W. "El simbolismo en *Las montañas del oro.*" *Revista Iberoamericana* 57 (1964): 93–104.

Asturrizaga, Juan Espejo. *César Vallejo: itinerario del hombre, 1892–1923*. Lima: Editorial Juan Mejía Baca, 1965.

Baciu, Stefan. *Antología de la poesía surrealista latinoamericana*. México: Joaquín Mortiz, 1974.

Banchs, Enrique. *Obra poética (1907–1955)*. Buenos Aires: Academia Argentina de Letras, 1973.

Barbagelata, Hugo D. "Victor Hugo y la América latina." *Revista Nacional* (Montevideo) 55 (1952): 104–119.

Barcia, Pedro Luis. "Lugones y el ultraísmo." *Estudios literarios*. La Plata: Universidad Nacional de la Plata, Facultad de Humanidades y Ciencias de la Educación, 1966. 149–193.

Beltrán Guerrero, Luis. *Modernismo y modernistas*. Caracas: Academia Nacional de la Historia, 1978.

Bischoff, Efraín V. *Aquel rebelde Leopoldo Lugones (sus primeros 22 años: 1874–1896)*. Córdoba: Junta Provincial de Historia de Córdoba, 1981.

Blanco-Aguinaga, Carlos. "Critica marxista y poesía: lectura de un poema de Julián del Casal." *The Analysis of Hispanic Texts: Current*

Trends in Methodology, ed. Mary Ann Beck, et al. New York: Bilingual Press, 1976.

Blengio Brito, Raul. *Aproximación a la poesía de Herrera.* Montevideo: La Casa del Estudiante, 1967.

Boneo, Martín Alberto. *Poesía argentina: ensayos.* Buenos Aires: Instituto Amigos del Libro Argentino, 1968.

Borges, Jorge Luis. "Herrera y Reissig." *Inquisiciones.* Buenos Aires: Editorial Proa, 1925. 139–145.

———. *Leopoldo Lugones.* Buenos Aires: Ediciones Troquel, 1955.

———. "Leopoldo Lugones." *Revista Interamericana de Bibliografía* 13, 2 (1963): 137–146.

———. Prólogo. *Antología poética argentina.* Comp. Jorge Luis Borges, Silvina Ocampo, y Adolfo Bioy Casares. Buenos Aires: Editorial Sudamericana, 1941. 7–11.

———. *El tamaño de mi esperanza.* Buenos Aires: Editorial Proa, 1926.

Brotherston, Gordon. *Latin American Poetry: Origins and Presence.* Cambridge, Eng.: Cambridge University Press, 1975.

Bula Píriz, Roberto, ed. Estudio preliminar. *Poesías completas y páginas en prosa.* By Julio Herrera y Reissig. Madrid: Aguilar, 1951. 13–90.

Cambours-Ocampo, Arturo. *Lugones: el escritor y su lenguaje.* Buenos Aires: Ediciones Theoría, 1957.

Canedo, Alfredo. *Aspectos del pensamiento político de Leopoldo Lugones.* Buenos Aires: Ediciones Marcos, 1974.

Cano Ballesta, Juan. *Literatura y tecnología: las letras españolas ante la Revolución Industrial.* Madrid: Orígenes, 1981.

Cansinos Assens, Rafael. "Herrera y Reissig." *Poetas y prosistas del novecientos.* Madrid: Editorial América, 1919. 114–139.

Capdevila, Arturo. *Alfonsina: época, dolor y obra de la poetisa Alfonsina Storni.* Buenos Aires: Ediciones Centurión, 1948.

———. *Lugones.* Buenos Aires: Aguilar Argentina, 1973.

———. "Leopoldo Lugones." *Revista Nacional de Cultura* (Caracas) 14–15 (1939–1940): 89–96.

Carilla, Emilio. *Estudios de literatura argentina (Siglo XIX).* Tucumán: Universidad Nacional de Tucumán, Facultad de Filosofía y Letras, 1961.

———. *Una etapa decisiva de Darío: Rubén Darío en la Argentina.* Madrid: Editorial Gredos, 1967.

———. *El romanticismo en la América hispánica.* Madrid: Gredos, 1958.

Carter, Boyd G. *Las revistas literarias de Hispanoamérica.* México: Ediciones de Andrea, 1959.

Cascarrabias, Severo. "La propiedad literaria." *Buenos Aires* 2 (23 June 1894): 358–359.

Castellani, Leonardo. *Lugones.* Buenos Aires: Ediciones Theoría, 1964.

Chapman, G. Arnold. *The Spanish American Reception of United States Fiction, 1920–1940.* Berkeley and Los Angeles: University of California Press, 1966.

Collazos, Oscar. *Los vanguardismos en la América latina.* Barcelona: Ediciones Península, 1977.

Corvalán, Octavio Electro. *La madurez de Leopoldo Lugones.* Dissertation, Yale University, 1963. Ann Arbor, Mich.: University Microfilms, Inc., 1971.

———. *El postmodernismo.* New York: Las Américas, 1961.

Coyné, André. *César Vallejo.* Buenos Aires: Ediciones Nueva Visión, 1968.

Cúneo, Dardo. *Leopoldo Lugones.* Buenos Aires: Editorial Jorge Álvarez, 1968.

Darío, Rubén. *Escritos dispersos de Rubén Darío.* Ed. Pedro Luis Barcia. La Plata: Universidad Nacional de la Plata, Facultad de Humanidades y Ciencias de la Educación, 1968.

———. *Escritos inéditos: recogidos de periódicos de Buenos Aires y anotados.* Ed. E. K. Mapes. New York: Instituto de las Españas, 1938.

———. "El modernismo." *Obras completas.* Ed. M. Sanmiguel Raimúndez. 5 vols. Madrid: A. Aguado, 1950–1955. Vol. 3: 300–307.

———. *Poesías completas,* 11th ed. Ed. Alfonso Méndez Plancarte y Antonio Oliver Belmos. Madrid: Aguilar, 1968.

Debicki, Andrew P. *Poetas hispanoamericanos contemporáneos.* Madrid: Gredos, 1976.

Díaz-Plaja, Guillermo. *Modernismo frente a noventa y ocho: una introducción a la literatura española del siglo XX.* Madrid: Espasa Calpe, 1951.

Doll, Ramón. *Lugones: el apolítico y otros ensayos.* Buenos Aires: Editorial Peña Lillo, 1966.

Dromundo, Baltasar. *Vida y pasión de Ramón López Velarde.* México: Editorial Guarania, 1954.

Echagüe, Juan Pablo. *Seis figuras del Plata.* Buenos Aires: Losada, 1938.

Englekirk, John. *Edgar Allan Poe in Hispanic Literature.* New York: Russell and Russell, 1972.

Etchenique, Nira. *Alfonsina Storni.* Buenos Aires: Editorial La Mandrágora, 1958.

Faurie, Marie-Josèphe. *Le Modernisme hispano-américain et ses sources françaises.* Paris: Centre de Recherches de l'Institute Hispanique, 1966.

Ferguson, Raquel Halty. *Laforgue y Lugones: dos poetas de la luna.* London: Tamesis, 1981.

Fernández, Juan Rómulo. *Historia del periodismo argentino.* Buenos Aires: Librería Perlado, 1943.

Fernández Moreno, César. *Situación de Alfonsina Storni.* Sante Fe, Argentina: Castellvi, 1959.

Fernández Retamar, Roberto. Prólogo. *César Vallejo: obra poética completa.* Havana: Casa de las Américas, 1965. Vii–xx.

Ferrari, Américo. *El universo poético de César Vallejo.* Caracas: Monte Avila, 1972.

Flores, Angel, ed. *Aproximaciones a César Vallejo.* 2 vols. New York: Las Américas, 1971.

Franco, Jean. *César Vallejo: The Dialectics of Poetry and Silence.* Cambridge, Eng.: Cambridge University Press, 1976.

————. "Criticism and Literature within the Context of a Dependent Culture." *Occasional Papers* 15. New York: Ibero-American Language and Area Center, New York University.

Fuente, Carmen de la. *López Velarde: su mundo intelectual y afectivo.* México: Federación Editorial Mexicana, 1971.

Gálvez de Tovar. *Ramón López Velarde en tres tiempos.* México: Editorial Porrúa, 1971.

Ghiano, Juan Carlos. *Lugones escritor: notas para un análisis estilístico.* Buenos Aires: Editorial Raigal, 1955.

————. *Temas y aptitudes (Lugones, Güiraldes, Quiroga, Arlt, Marechal, Bernárdez, Borges, Molina).* Buenos Aires: Ollantay, 1949.

Gicovati, Bernardo. *Iniciación de poesía modernista.* San Juan: Ediciones Asomante, 1962.

————. *Julio Herrera y Reissig and the Symbolists.* Berkeley and Los Angeles: University of California Press, 1950.

Gimferrer, Pere. *Antología de la poesía modernista.* Barcelona: Ediciones Península, 1981.

Giusti, Roberto F. "Leopoldo Lugones (A propósito de *Lunario sentimental*)," *Nosotros* 3 (July–August 1909): 290–306.

————. "Lugones helenista." *Nosotros* 10 (May 1916): 180–183.

González, Alfonso Sola. "Las 'Odas Seculares' de Leopoldo Lugones." *Revista Iberoamericana* 61 (January–June 1966): 23–50.

González, Aníbal. *La crónica modernista hispanomericana.* Madrid: José Porrúa Turranzas, 1983.

————. "La escritura modernista y la filología." *Cuadernos Americanos* (Mexico) 40 (1981): 90–106.

González-Echevarría, Roberto. "Martí y su 'Amor de ciudad grande':

notas hacia una poética de *Versos libres.*" *Imagen* (Caracas) (1979): 8–13. Reprint in *Isla a su vuelo fugitiva.* Madrid: José Porrúa Turanzas, 1983. 27–42.

———. "Modernidad, modernismo y nueva narrativa: *El recurso del método.*" *Revista Interamericana de Bibliografía* 30 (1980): 157–163.

González Lanuza, Eduardo. *Los martinfierristas.* Buenos Aires: Ediciones Culturales Argentinas, 1961.

Groussac, Paul. "Boletín bibliográfico—*Los raros* de Rubén Darío." *La Biblioteca* 1 (1896): 274–480.

———. "Introducción," *La Biblioteca* 1 (1896): 5.

Gullón, Ricardo, ed. *Direcciones del modernismo.* Madrid: Gredos, 1963.

———. *El modernismo visto por los modernistas.* Barcelona: Guadarrama, 1980.

Hahn, Oscar. "Herrera y Reissig o el indiscreto encanto de lo cursi." *Texto Crítico* 5 (1979): 261–266.

Halperín Donghi, Tulio. *Historia contemporánea de América Latina.* Madrid: Alianza, 1970.

Henríquez-Ureña, Max. *Breve historia del modernismo.* México: Fondo de Cultura Económica, 1954.

———. *El retorno de los galeones y otros ensayos,* 2d ed. México: Ediciones Galaxia, 1963.

Hernández, Juan José. "El signo prohibido de Leopoldo Lugones." *Tiempo Argentino* Suplemento "Cultura" (15 Jan. 1984): 1–3.

Herrera y Reissig, Julio. *Páginas escogidas.* Barcelona: Casa Editorial Maucci, 1914.

———. *Poesías.* México: Editorial Porrúa, 1977.

———. *Poesías completas.* Buenos Aires: Editorial Losada, 1942.

———. *Poesías completas y páginas en prosa.* Ed. Roberto Bula Píriz. Madrid: Aguilar, 1961.

———. *Prosas: crítica, cuentos, comentarios.* Intro. Vicente Salaverri. Montevideo: Máximo García, 1918.

Huidobro, Vicente. *Altazor.* Madrid: Visor, 1973.

Irazusta, Julio. *Genio y figura de Leopoldo Lugones.* Buenos Aires: EUDEBA, 1968.

Iturburu, Córdova. *La revolución martinfierrista.* Buenos Aires: Ediciones Culturales Argentinas, 1962.

Jaimes Freyre, Ricardo. *Castalia bárbara y otros poemas.* México: Cultura, 1920.

Jitrik, Noé. *Las contradicciones del modernismo.* México: El Colegio de México, 1978.

————. *Leopoldo Lugones: mito nacional.* Buenos Aires: Ediciones Palestra, 1960.

————. *Producción literaria y producción social.* Buenos Aires: Editorial Sudamericana, 1975.

Jrade, Cathy L. *Rubén Darío and the Romantic Search for Unity: The Modernist Recourse to Esoteric Tradition.* Austin: University of Texas Press, 1983.

Jrade, Cathy L. "Tópicos románticos como contexto del modernismo." *Cuadernos Americanos* (México) 39 (1980): 114–122.

Lafleur, Héctor René, Sergio D. Provenzano, and Fernando P. Alonso. *Las revistas literarias argentinas (1893–1967).* Buenos Aires: Centro Editor, 1968.

Lermón, Miguel. *Contribución a la bibliografía de Leopoldo Lugones.* Buenos Aires: Ediciones Maru, 1969.

Leviller, Roberto. "Herrera y Reissig y Lugones." *Hommage a Ernest Martineche.* Paris: Edition D'Artry, 1939. 262–270.

Lezama Lima, José. "Exámenes." *Analecta del reloj.* Vol. 2 of *Obras completas.* México: Aguilar, 1977. 214–227.

————. *La expresión americana.* Havana: Instituto Nacional de la Cultura, 1957.

Litvak, Lily. *Erotismo fin de siglo.* Barcelona: Antoni Bosch, 1979.

————, ed. *El modernismo: el escritor y la crítica.* Madrid: Taurus, 1975.

López de Lara, Guillermo. *Hablando de López Velarde.* México: Ediciones Ateneo, 1973.

López Velarde, Ramón. *Obras.* Ed. José Luis Martínez. México: Fondo de Cultura Económica, 1971.

————. *Poesías completas y el minutero.* México: Editorial Porrúa, 1971.

Loprete, Carlos Alberto. *La literatura modernista en la Argentina.* Buenos Aires: Editorial Poseidon, 1955.

Lugones, Leopoldo. *Las primeras letras de Leopoldo Lugones.* Buenos Aires: Ediciones Centurión, 1963.

————. *Obras en prosa.* Madrid: Aguilar, 1962.

————. *Obras poéticas completas.* Madrid: Aguilar, 1959.

Lugones, Leopoldo, hijo. *Mi padre: biografía de Leopoldo Lugones.* Buenos Aires: Ediciones Centurión, 1949.

Magis, Carlos Horacio. *La poesía de Leopoldo Lugones.* México: Ediciones Ateneo, 1960.

Martí, José. *Ismaelillo, La edad de oro, Versos sencillos.* México: Editorial Porrúa, 1973.

Martínez-Estrada, Ezequiel. *Leopoldo Lugones: retrato sin tocar.* Buenos Aires: Emecé, 1968.

Mas y Pí, Juan. *Leopoldo Lugones y su obra: estudio crítico.* Buenos Aires: Ed. Renacimiento, 1911.

Mastronardi, Carlos. *Formas de la realidad nacional,* 2d ed. Buenos Aires: Editorial Sur, 1964.

Mejía Sánchez, Ernesto. *Estudios sobre Rubén Darío.* México: Fondo de Cultura Económica, 1968.

Mirza, Rogelio. *Herrera y Reissig: antología, estudio crítico, y notas.* Montevideo: Arca, 1975.

Monguió, Luis. *César Vallejo 1892–1938: vida y obra-bibliografía-antología.* New York: Hispanic Institute in the United States, 1952.

———. "En torno a 'El reino interior' de Rubén Darío." *Revista Hispánica Moderna* 34 (1969): 721–728.

———. *La poesía postmodernista peruana.* Berkeley and Los Angeles: University of California Press, 1954.

———. *"Sobre la caracterización del modernismo." Revista Iberoamericana* 7 (1943): 69–79.

Monner Sans, José María. *Julián del Casal y el modernismo hispanoamericano.* México: Colegio de México, 1952.

Moreau, Pierina Lidia. *Leopoldo Lugones y el simbolismo.* Buenos Aires: Ediciones La Reja, 1972.

Morejón, Nancy. "Desilusión para Rubén Darío." *Nueva poesía cubana,* ed. José Agustín Goytisolo. Barcelona: Ediciones Península, 1972.

Morello-Frosch, Marta. "Metáfora cósmica y ciudadana en el 'Himno a la luna' de Leopoldo Lugones." *Revista Iberoamericana* 30 (1964): 153–162.

Murena, H. A. "Ser y no ser de la cultura latinoamericana." *Expresión del pensamiento contemporáneo.* Buenos Aires: Sur, 1965.

Nalé Roxlo, Conrado, and Mabel Mármol. *Genio y figura de Alfonsina Storni.* Buenos Aires: Editorial Universitaria de Buenos Aires, 1964.

Navarro, Carlos. "La visión del mundo en el *Lunario sentimental.*" *Revista Iberoamericana* 30 (1964): 133–152.

Neruda, Pablo. *Para nacer he nacido.* Barcelona: Editorial Bruguera, 1981.

Nervo, Amado, "Leopoldo Lugones." *Obras completas.* Ed. Francisco González Guerrero and Alfonso Méndez Plancarte. 2 vols. Madrid: Aguilar, 1955–1956.

Nosotros (Número extraordinario dedicado a Leopoldo Lugones), 2d series, 2. (1938).

Obligado, Carlos. *La cueva del fósil, diálogos increíbles sobre la vida literaria argentina.* Buenos Aires: "La Facultad," 1938.

————. "La vida y la obra de Lugones." In *Obras poéticas completas* de Leopoldo Lugones. Madrid: Aguilar, 1959. 13–47.

Olivieri, Magda. "Herrera y Reissig: el modernismo." *Capítulo Oriental* (fascículo no. 13). Montevideo: Centro Editor, 1968. 193–208.

Omil, Alba. *Leopoldo Lugones: poesía y prosa.* Buenos Aires: Minor Nova, 1968.

Onís, Federico de: "Sobre el concepto del modernismo." *La Torre* 1 (1953): 95–103.

Ortega, Julio. *Figuración de la persona.* Barcelona: Edhasa, 1971.

Pacheco, José E., ed. *Antología del modernismo (1884–1921).* 2 vols. México: Universidad Nacional Autónoma de México, 1970.

Pagés Larraya, Antonio. "Leopoldo Lugones." *La Nación* (22 June 1966).

Payró, Roberto J. "El mercado de libros." *La Revista Nacional* 2 (1895): 341–342.

Paz, Octavio. *Cuadrivio.* México: Joaquín Mortiz, 1969.

————. *Los hijos del limo.* Barcelona: Seix Barral, 1981.

Pérez Petit, Víctor. "El pleito Lugones—Herrera y Reissig." *Nosotros* 2 (1938): 227–44.

Perus, Françoise. *Literatura y sociedad en América Latina: el modernismo.* México: Siglo Veintiuno Editores, 1976.

Phillips, Allen W. "La metáfora en la obra de Julio Herrera y Reissig." *Revista Iberoamericana* 16 (1950): 31–48.

————. "Notas sobre una afinidad poética: Jules Laforgue y el Lugones del *Lunario sentimental.*" *Estudios y notas sobre literatura hispanoamericana.* México: Editorial Cultura, 1965. 53–72.

————. *Ramón López Velarde: el poeta y el prosista.* México: Instituto Nacional de Bellas Artes, 1962.

————. "Rubén Darío y sus juicios sobre el modernismo." *Revista Iberoamericana* 24 (1959): 41–64.

Phillips, Rachel. *Alfonsina Storni: From Poetess to Poet.* London: Tamesis, 1975.

Picón Garfield, Evelyn, and Ivan A. Schulman. *Las entrañas del vacío: ensayos sobre la modernidad hispanoamericana.* México: Ediciones Cuadernos Americanos, 1984.

Pío del Coro, Gaspar. *El mundo fantástico de Leopoldo Lugones.* Córdoba: Universidad Nacional de Córdoba, 1971.

Prieto, Adolfo, ed. *El periódico "Martín Fierro."* Buenos Aires: Editorial Galerna, 1968.

Pultera, Raul. *Lugones: elementos cardinales destinados a determinar una biografía.* Buenos Aires: n.p., 1956.

Rama, Angel. *Los poetas modernistas en el mercado económico.* Montevideo: Facultad de Humanidades y Ciencias, Universidad de la República, 1968.

————. *Rubén Darío y el modernismo (circunstancia socioeconómica de un arte americano)*. Caracas: Ediciones de la Biblioteca de la Universidad Central de Venezuela, 1970.

Revista de América. Reprint, Carbondale, Ill.: Latin American Institute, Southern Illinois University, 1970.

Rodríguez Monegal, Emir. "La Generación del 900." *Número* 2 (1950): 37–61.

Roggiano, Alfredo. "Bibliografía de y sobre Leopoldo Lugones." *Revista Iberoamericana* 53 (1962): 155–213.

————. "Documentos: poemas de Leopoldo Lugones en la *Revista Moderna* de México." *Revista Iberoamericana* 35 (1967): 125–130.

————. "Una lectura de la disidencia: *Las montañas del oro*, de Leopoldo Lugones." *Homenaje a Andrés Iduarte*. Ed. Jaime Alazraki, Roland Grass, and Russell O. Salmon. New York: The American Hispanist, 1976. 321–329.

Sabat Ercasty, Carlos, and Manuel de Castro, eds. *Antología lírica de Julio Herrera y Reissig*. Santiago: Ercilla, 1942.

Sánchez, Luis Alberto. *Escritores representativos de América*. Madrid: Gredos, 1957.

Scari, Roberto Mario. "El idealismo del joven Lugones." *Cuadernos Americanos* (México) 37 (1978): 237–248.

————. "Enumeración caótica y poetización de lo feo en el *Lunario sentimental* de Leopoldo Lugones." *XVII Congreso del Instituto Internacional de Literatura Iberoamericana: el barroco en América; literatura hispanoamericana; crítica histórico-literaria hispanoamericana*. 3 vols. Madrid: Ediciones Cultura Hispánica, 1978. 2: 773–781.

————. *La formación literaria de Lugones*. Dissertation, University of California, Berkeley, 1963. Ann Arbor: University Microfilms, Inc., 1963.

Schulman, Ivan A. *Génesis del modernismo: Martí, Nájera, Silva, Casal*. México: El Colegio de México, Washington University Press, 1966.

————. "Reflexiones en torno a la definición del modernismo." *Cuadernos Americanos* (México) 25 (1966): 211–240.

Seluja, Antonio, M. Oliveri, and D. Pérez Pintos. *Homenaje a Julio Herrera y Reissig*. Montevideo: Concejo Departamental de Montevideo, 1963.

Seluja Cecín, Antonio. "El montevideano Jules Laforgue: su vida y obra." *Revista Nacional*, 8 (1963): 481–639.

Silva Castro, Raúl. *El modernismo y otros ensayos literarios*. Santiago: Editorial Nascimento, 1965.

Sobejano, Gonzalo. *Nietzsche en España*. Madrid: Gredos, 1967.

Storni, Alfonsina. *Poesías*. Vol. 1 of *Obras completas*. Buenos Aires: Sociedad Editora Latinoamericana, 1971.

———. *Obra poética completa*. Buenos Aires: Ediciones Meridion, 1961.

Sucre, Guillermo. *La máscara, la transparencia*. Caracas: Monte Avila, 1975.

Tello, Belisario. *El poeta solariego: la síntesis poético-política de Leopoldo Lugones*. Buenos Aires: Ediciones Theoría, 1971.

Torre, Guillermo de. Prólogo. *Poesías completas de Julio Herrera y Reissig*. Ed. Guillermo de Torre. Buenos Aires: Editorial Losada, 1958. 7–35.

———. *Tres conceptos de la literatura hispanoamericana*. Buenos Aires: Editorial Losada, 1963.

Torres Rioseco, Arturo. *Precursores del modernismo: Casal, Gutiérrez-Nájera, Martí, Silva*. Madrid: Calpe, 1925.

Ulla, Noemí, ed. *La revista "Nosotros."* Buenos Aires: Editorial Galerna, 1969.

Uriarte, Gregorio. "La obra intelectual de Leopoldo Lugones." *Nosotros* 30 (1918): 530–563.

Valenzuela, E. *"Lunario sentimental." Revista Moderna de México* 12 (1909): 191–192.

———. *"Lunario sentimental:* libro reciente de L. L." *Revista Moderna de México* 13 (1910): 259–261.

Vallejo, César. *Obra poética completa*. Vol. 3. Lima: Francisco Moncloa Editores, 1968.

———. *Obras completas de César Vallejo*. 3 vols. Lima: Mosca Azul Editores, 1974.

Vidal Peña, Leónidas. *El drama intelectual de Lugones*. Buenos Aires: "La Facultad," 1938.

Vilariño, Idea. "Julio Herrera y Reissig: seis años de poesía." *Número*. 2 (1950): 118–161.

Visca, Arturo Sergio, ed. "El país de los jueves extraordinario." (Suplemento Extraordinario en homenaje a Julio Herrera y Reissig) *El País* (Montevideo), June 5, 12, 18, 1975.

———. *"La Torre de las esfinges* como tarea." *Número* 2 (1950): 601–609.

Yurkiévich, Saúl. *Celebración del modernismo*. Barcelona: Tusquets Editor, 1976.

———. *Fundadores de la nueva poesía latinoamericana: Vallejo, Huidobro, Borges, Neruda, Paz*. Barcelona: Barral Editores, 1971.

———. *Valoración de Vallejo*. Resistencia, Argentina: Universidad Nacional del Nordeste, 1958.

Zum Felde, Alberto. Prólogo. *Obras poéticas de Julio Herrera y Reissig.* Montevideo: Artigas, 1967.

GENERAL WORKS

Abrams, M. H. *The Mirror and the Lamp: Romantic Theory and the Critical Tradition.* New York: Oxford University Press, 1953.

Allen, Virginia Mae. *The Femme Fatale: A Study of the Early Development of the Concept in Mid-Nineteenth Century Poetry and Painting.* Ann Arbor: University Microfilms, Inc., 1979.

Auerbach, Nina. *Woman and the Demon: The Life of a Victorian Myth.* Cambridge, Mass.: Harvard University Press, 1982.

Bakhtine, Mikhail. *Esthétique et théorie du roman.* Trans. Daria Olivier. Paris: Editions Gallimard, 1978.

Balakian, Anna. *Literary Origins of Surrealism: A New Mysticism in French Poetry.* New York: New York University Press, 1965.

Barthes, Roland. *Image, Music, Text.* Trans. Stephen Heath. New York: Hill and Wang, 1977.

———. *Writing Degree Zero and Elements of Semiology.* Trans. Annette Lavers and Colin Smith. Boston: Beacon Press, 1967.

———. *The Pleasure of the Text.* Trans. Richard Miller. New York: Hill and Wang, 1975.

———. *S/Z.* Paris: Éditions du Sueil, 1970.

———. *Sade, Fourier, Loyola.* Trans. Richard Miller. New York: Hill and Wang, 1976.

Bataille, Georges. *L'Érotisme.* Paris: Les Éditions du Minuit, 1957.

———. *Les larmes d'Eros.* Paris: Jean Jacques Pauvert, 1961.

Baudelaire, Charles. *Oeuvres complètes.* Paris: Editions Gallimard, 1961.

Baudrillard, Jean. *De la séduction.* Paris: Éditions Galilée, 1979.

———. *For a Critique of the Political Economy of the Sign.* Trans. Charles Levin. St. Louis, Mo.: Telos Press, 1981.

Benayou, Robert. *Erotique du surréalisme.* Paris: Jean Jacques Pauvert, 1961.

Benjamin, Walter. *Illuminations.* Trans. Harry Zohn. New York: Schocken Books, 1973.

Berger, John. *Ways of Seeing.* London: British Broadcasting Corporation and Penguin Books, 1978.

Berman, Marshall. *All that Is Solid Melts into Air: The Experience of Modernity.* New York: Simon and Schuster, 1982.

Bloom, Harold. *The Anxiety of Influence.* New York: Oxford University Press, 1973.

————, ed. *Romanticism and Consciousness: Essays in Criticism.* New York: W. W. Norton and Co., 1970.

Bourdieu, Pierre. *Ce que parler veut dire: L'économie des échanges linguistiques.* Paris: Fayard, 1982.

————. *Esquisse d'une théorie de la pratique.* Geneva: Librairie Droz, 1972.

————. *Outline of a Theory of Practice.* Trans. Richard Nice. Cambridge, Eng.: Cambridge University Press, 1977.

Brooke-Rose, Christine. *A Grammar of Metaphor.* London: Secker and Warburg, 1958.

Bruns, Gerald L. *Modern Poetry and the Idea of Language.* New Haven: Yale University Press, 1974.

Burger, Peter. *Theory of the Avant-Garde.* Trans. Michael Shaw. Minneapolis: University of Minnesota Press, 1984.

Caminade, Pierre. *Image et métaphore: Un problème de poétique contemporain.* Paris: Bordas, 1970.

Carroll, David. *The Subject in Question: The Languages of Theory and the Strategies of Fiction.* Chicago: University of Chicago Press, 1982.

Culler, Jonathan. *Structuralist Poetics: Structuralism, Linguistics and the Study of Literature.* London: Routledge and Kegan Paul, 1975.

Deleuze, Gilles. *Logique du sens.* Paris: Editions de Minuit, 1969.

————. *Masochism: An Interpretation of Coldness and Cruelty.* New York: George Braziller, 1971.

DeMan, Paul. *Blindness and Insight: Essays in the Rhetoric of Contemporary Criticism.* New York: Oxford University Press, 1971.

————. "The Rhetoric of Temporality." *Interpretation: Theory and Practice.* Ed. Charles Singleton. Baltimore: Johns Hopkins University Press, 1969. 173–209.

Derrida, Jacques. "La mythologie blanche." *Marges de la Philosophie.* Paris: Minuit, 1973.

————. *Of Grammatology.* Trans. Gayatri Spivak. Baltimore: Johns Hopkins University Press, 1976.

Ducrot, Oswaldo, and T. Todorov. *Dictionnaire encyclopédique des sciences du langage.* Paris: Editions du Seuil, 1972.

Durry, Marie Jeanne. *Jules Laforgue: Une étude,* 5th ed. Paris: Seghers, 1971.

Eagleton, Terry. *Criticism and Ideology: A Study in Marxist Literary Theory.* London: New Left Books, 1976.

Eco, Umberto. "Sémiologie des messages visuels." *Communications* 15 (1970).

————. *A Theory of Semiotics.* Bloomington, Ind.: Indiana University Press, 1976.

Eideldinger, Marc. *L'Evolution dynamique de l'image dans la poésie française du romantisme a nos jours.* Neuchatel: André Seiler et Fils, 1943.

Ferrater Mora, José. "De la ironía a la admiración." *Cuestiones disputadas: ensayos de filosofía.* Madrid: Revista de Occidente, 1955. 27–103.

Foucault, Michel. *The History of Sexuality.* Trans. Robert Hurley. New York: Vintage Books, 1980.

———. *Les mots et les choses.* Paris: Editions Gallimard, 1966.

Frank, Joseph. "Spatial Form in Modern Literature." *The Widening Gyre.* New Brunswick, N.J.: Rutgers University Press, 1963.

Freccero, John. "The Fig Tree and the Laurel: Petrarch's Poetics." *Diacritics* 5 (1975): 34–40.

———. "Medusa: The Letter and the Spirit." *Yearbook of Italian Studies.* Montreal: Italian Cultural Institute, 1972. 1–18.

Friedrich, Hugo. *The Structure of Modern Poetry.* Trans. Joachim Neugroschel. Evanston, Ill.: Northwestern University Press, 1974.

Frye, Northrop. "The Drunken Boat: The Revolutionary Element in Romanticism." *Romanticism Reconsidered.* Ed. N. Frye. New York: Columbia University Press, 1963.

Gauthier, Xavière. *Surréalisme et Sexualité.* Paris: Gallimard, 1971.

Genette, Gérard. *Figures II.* Paris: Editions du Seuil, 1969.

Gourmont, Remy de. *Le chemin de velours.* Paris: Mercure de France, 1911.

Greimas, A. J. *Essais de Sémiotique Poétique.* Paris: Larousse, 1972.

———. *Sémantique structurale: Recherche de méthode.* Paris: Larousse, 1966.

Guichard, Leon. *Jules Laforgue et ses poésies.* Paris: Presses Universitaires de France, 1950.

Harari, Josué V., ed. *Textual Strategies: Perspectives in Post-Structuralist Criticism.* Ithaca, N.Y.: Cornell University Press, 1979.

Hartman, Geoffrey, and David Thorburn, eds. *Romanticism: Vistas, Instances, Continuities.* Ithaca, N.Y.: Cornell University Press, 1973.

Herrmann, Claudine. *Les voleuses de langue.* Paris: Des femmes, 1976.

Hugo, Victor. *Oeuvres poétiques.* Ed. Pierre Ablouy. 3 vols. Paris: Gallimard, 1967.

Jakobson, Roman. "Qu'est-ce que la poésie?" *Questions de poétique.* Paris: Editions du Seuil, 1973. 113–126.

Jameson, Frederic. *Marxism and Form.* Princeton, N.J.: Princeton University Press, 1971.

Jones, Howard Mumford. *Revolution and Romanticism.* Cambridge, Mass.: Bellknap Press and Harvard University Press, 1974.

Kasson, John F. *Civilizing the Machine: Technology and Republican Values in America 1776–1900.* New York: Grossman, 1976.

Kristeva, Julia. "From One Identity to the Other," and "How Does One Speak to Literature?" *Desire in Language: A Semiotic Approach to Literature and Art.* Ed. Leon S. Roudiez. Trans. Thomas Gore et al. New York: Columbia University Press, 1980. 92–123, 124–147.

———. *Polylogues.* Paris: Editions du Seuil, 1977.

———. *La révolution du langage poétique.* Paris: Editions du Seuil, 1974.

Laforgue, Jules. *Deniers vers.* Ed. Michael Collie and J. M. L'Heureux. Toronto: University of Toronto Press, 1965.

———. *Poésies complètes.* Paris: Editions Gallimard, 1970.

Lefort, Claude. *Les formes de l'histoire: Essais d'anthropologie politique.* Paris: Gallimard, 1978.

Lotman, Yuri. *Analysis of the Poetic Text.* Ed. and Trans. D. Barton Johnson. Ann Arbor, Mich.: Ardis, 1976.

———. *Semiótica de la cultura.* Madrid: Ediciones Cátedra, 1979.

———. *The Structure of the Artistic Text.* Trans. Ronald Vroon. Michigan Slavic Contributions 7. Ann Arbor, Mich.: University of Michigan Press, 1977.

Mallarmé, Stéphane. *Variations sur un Sujet: Oeuvres complètes.* Paris: Editions Gallimard, 1945.

Marx, Leo. *The Machine in the Garden.* New York: Oxford University Press, 1976.

Mitchell, W. J. T. "Spatial Form in Literature: Toward a General Theory." *The Language of Images.* Ed. W. J. T. Mitchell. Chicago: University of Chicago Press, 1980. 271–299.

Nerval, Gérard de. *Oeuvres.* Ed. Jean Richer and Albert Beguin. 2 vols. Paris: Librairie Gallimard, 1952.

Poe, Edgar Allan. "The Poetic Principle." *The Complete Poetry and Selected Criticism of Edgar Allan Poe.* Ed.Allen Tate. New York: New American Library, 1968.

Poggioli, Renato. *The Theory of the Avant-Garde.* Trans. Gerald Fitzgerald. Cambridge, Mass.: Bellknap Press of Harvard University Press, 1968.

Poulet, Georges. *Les métamorphoses du cercle.* Paris: Librairie Plon, 1961.

Praz, Mario. *The Romantic Agony.* 2d ed. Trans. Angus Davidson. London: Oxford University Press, 1978.

Ramsey, Warren, ed. *Jules Laforgue: Essays on a Poet's Life and Work.* Carbondale: Southern Illinois University Press, 1963.

———. *Jules Laforgue and the Ironic Inheritance.* New York: Oxford University Press, 1953.

Raymond, Marcel. *From Baudelaire to Surrealism.* Trans. "G. M." New York: Wittenborn, Schultz, Inc., 1950.

Riffaterre, Michel. "Describing Poetic Structures: Two Approaches to Baudelaire's 'Les Chats.' " *Yale French Studies* 48 (1973): 200–242.

Ruwet, Nicolas. "Synechdoches et metonymie." *Poétique* 23 (1975): 371–388.

Sarduy, Severo. *Barroco.* Buenos Aires: Sudamericana, 1974.

———. *Escrito sobre un cuerpo.* Buenos Aires: Sudamericana, 1969.

Sonnenfeld, Albert. "The Yellow Laugh of Tristan Corbière." *Yale French Studies* 23 (1959): 39–46.

Tynianov, J. "De l'évolution littéraire." *Théorie de la littérature.* Ed. and trans. Tzvetan Todorov. Paris: Editions du Seuil, 1965.

Vickers, Nancy J. "Diana Described: Scattered Woman and Scattered Rhyme." *Critical Inquiry.* Special Issue, *Writing and Sexual Difference,* 2 (1981): 265–79.

Wellek, René. "The Concept of Romanticism in Literary History." *Concepts of Criticism.* New Haven: Yale University Press, 1971. 128–198.

Index

Designer:	U.C. Press Staff
Compositor:	Huron Valley Graphics
Text:	11/13 Baskerville
Display:	Baskerville
Printer:	Braun-Brumfield
Binder:	Braun-Brumfield

90-551

PQ
7082
.P7
K57
1989

Gramley Library
Salem College
Winston-Salem, NC 27108